Praise for Mitch Daniels

"Governor Daniels has emerged as one of our nation's leading voices for reform and common sense in government."

—Speaker of the House John Boehner

"The onetime Reagan White House political director and Bush White House budget chief is not your run-of-the-mill intellectual. His style is to be down-home, but his record of accomplishment is dazzling."

—David S. Broder, *The Washington Post*

"He's one of the brightest governors in America."

—New Jersey Governor Chris Christie

"[Daniels is] the rare politician telling it like it is. . . . I would pay cash money to watch him debate Obama on these issues, and I suspect the Republic would be much the better for it."

—Joe Klein, *Time*

"Mitch is the only one who sees the stark perils and will offer real detailed proposals. . . . He would be the anti-Obama."

—Former Florida Governor Jeb Bush

"A principled but practical conservative who respects the intelligence of voters and would rather get something done than score political points."

—Steven Pearlstein, *The Washington Post*

"He does not tweet. . . . But he is good at one thing in particular: governing."

—*The Economist*

"[Daniels is] the most credible Republican spokesperson on economic recovery, the man whose results as Indiana governor would compare most favorably to the man in office. Now that he's not running, the Republican field lacks a credible Obama antithesis."

—Marc Ambinder, *The Atlantic*

"Daniels is and long has been enviably popular in his home state, largely thanks to what can only be called his prudent conservatism. He is a conservative, no two ways about it; but he has not shackled himself to ideology. . . . Instead, he has espoused sensible and politically workable solutions to Indiana's woes, neither demonizing all government nor idolizing all private enterprise."

—*Esquire*

"[Daniels] had made clear that the national debt would have been issues no. 1, 2, and 3 for him. His sense of urgency is warranted, and he had the record as governor to back up his message. . . . he might have succeeded in pushing President Obama toward more seriousness on deficit reduction than the president has shown thus far and sparked a valuable, honest debate about the proper size and role of government."

—editorial, *The Washington Post*

"[Daniels] would be a great president. Are there [other] people who right now know these issues, have the principles, have the courage of their convictions, and are willing and able to defend them? Nobody comes to my mind."

—U.S. Representative Paul Ryan

"No other prospective candidate had a record of accomplishment as impressive as his. More important, I think Mitch Daniels has personal qualities that Americans yearn for in public leaders even as our political culture impedes them."

—Mark Slater, Real ClearPolitics

"This governor is a man of policy conviction and commitment, not politics. The country is overrun with politicians who are not reliable people. This is a man who rises above politics with a real commitment to sound public policy. He has an outstanding track record. You can count on him— he's reliable. He gets the work done. It's a rare thing to find among those who hold public office."

—Former House majority leader and Tea Party leader Dick Armey

"Daniels has called the federal deficit "the new Red Menace, this time consisting of ink." Nice metaphor. But unlike some big talkers about deficits, Daniels can match his rhetoric with his record."

—Vincent Carroll, *Denver Post*

"I am very pleased he did not get into the race. . . . He would have been a force to be contended with at the national scene and would have provided the Republican Party with a very smart candidate who knows the issues and has an uncanny ability to take complicated problems and have the electorate understand and then support his position. He would have assuredly done this with a myriad of far more complicated subjects at the national level."

—Former Indiana House Democratic majority leader Russ Stillwell

"The most presidential man in America."

—Jacob Perry, The Pundit League

Mitch Daniels was elected governor of Indiana in 2004 and reelected in 2008. He was previously the director of the Office of Management and Budget (a cabinet-level position) under President George W. Bush and a senior aide to President Ronald Reagan. He also spent many years in the private sector as a senior executive at Eli Lilly and Company and as the CEO of one of the nation's most influential research centers, the Hudson Institute. He and his wife, Cheri, have four daughters and live in Indianapolis.

MITCH DANIELS

KEEPING THE REPUBLIC

Saving America by Trusting Americans

SENTINEL

For Cheri and the girls

Like everything else

SENTINEL
Published by the Penguin Group
Penguin Group (USA) Inc., 375 Hudson Street, New York, New York 10014, U.S.A. • Penguin Group (Canada), 90 Eglinton Avenue East, Suite 700 Toronto, Ontario, Canada M4P 2Y3 (a division of Pearson Penguin Canada Inc.) • Penguin Books Ltd, 80 Strand, London WC2R 0RL, England • Penguin Ireland, 25 St. Stephen's Green, Dublin 2, Ireland (a division of Penguin Books Ltd) • Penguin Books Australia Ltd, 250 Camberwell Road, Camberwell, Victoria 3124, Australia (a division of Pearson Australia Group Pty Ltd) • Penguin Books India Pvt Ltd, 11 Community Centre, Panchsheel Park, New Delhi—110 017, India • Penguin Group (NZ), 67 Apollo Drive, Rosedale, Auckland 0632, New Zealand (a division of Pearson New Zealand Ltd) • Penguin Books (South Africa) (Pty) Ltd, 24 Sturdee Avenue, Rosebank, Johannesburg 2196, South Africa

Penguin Books Ltd, Registered Offices: 80 Strand, London WC2R 0RL, England

First published in the United States of America by Sentinel, a member of Penguin Group (USA) Inc. 2011
This paperback edition with a new epilogue published 2012

10 9 8 7 6 5 4 3 2

Photograph credits
Insert page 1 (bottom), 2 (bottom): The White House
Other photographs courtesy of the Office of the Governor

THE LIBRARY OF CONGRESS HAS CATALOGED THE HARDCOVER EDITION AS FOLLOWS:
Daniels, Mitchell Elias, 1949–
Keeping the republic : saving America by trusting Americans / Mitch Daniels.
p. cm.
Includes bibliographical references and index.
ISBN 978-1-59523-080-5 (hc.)
ISBN 978-1-59523-096-6 (pbk.)
1. United States—Politics and government—2009– 2. Political culture—United States. I. Title.
E907.D36 2011
973.932—dc23
2011023331

Printed in the United States of America
Designed by Carla Bolte
Graphs rendered by Daniel Lagin

CONTENTS

FOREWORD

Although American politics has never been particularly decorous, we live in notably noisy times. If the lungs were the seat of wisdom, we would have a surplus of Aristotles. Instead, we have a boiling ocean of empty vehemence—high-decibel harangues with low information content. That is the bad news.

The good news is that in cacophonous times, the attention of thoughtful people is drawn to someone who talks softly, thinks clearly, and respects the intelligence of the public. The author of the book you are holding is such a person. By now, many people around the nation have noticed Mitch Daniels. His intellect, candor, and wit—attributes that earned him election and resounding reelection as Indiana's governor— suffuse this volume of reflections on our current discontents.

It takes a worried man to write a worried book, and Daniels has done so. But his worries are not the thin gruel of evanescent headlines. Rather, they are grounded in a profound understanding of the pathologies that necessarily flow from the promiscuous expansion of government, such as the "shock and awe statism" of the Obama administration.

I once wrote, rudely but accurately, that during my friend Daniel Patrick Moynihan's years in the Senate he wrote more books than some of his colleagues read. Mitch Daniels is a reader as well as a gifted writer. When he, together with some other leading conservative thinkers, was asked to name the books that made important contributions to his intellectual development, his six choices, listed in the following order, were instructive:

- *The Road to Serfdom* by Friedrich Hayek (1944), because of its depiction of what Daniels calls "the inexorable tendencies in statism to self-perpetuation of bureaucracies."
- *Free to Choose: A Personal Statement* by Milton Friedman (1980), because of its argument establishing what Daniels calls the "moral underpinnings of free economics, if one starts from the premise that the highest value is the autonomy and dignity and freedom of the individual," a value "best . . . promoted by property rights, by free economic voluntary exchange."
- *What It Means to Be a Libertarian* by Charles Murray (1997), because of its demonstration that the welfare state sometimes, in Daniels's words, "produces the very misery that it was supposed to eliminate."
- *The Rise and Decline of Nations* by Mancur Olson (1982), because it explains how free societies become "encrusted"—Daniels's word—with interest groups, including big businesses, that become forces that buttress a stultifying status quo. These truly reactionary interests impede economic dynamism, thereby blocking avenues of upward mobility for the least fortunate. As Daniels understands, these interests "may travel under different banners or masquerade as something else but these are the folks who are more often than not trying to freeze in place arrangements that worked well for the 'ins.'"
- *The Future and Its Enemies* by Virginia Postrel (1998), because of its useful nomenclature, stressing the distinction not between right and left, but between those who favor stasism and those who promote dynamism. "I think," Daniels says, "in general, the Olson-like structures that we have to guard against in our country today tend to be those that favor the large interventionist state we built. I'm including here, by the way, the incumbent businesses that love the way in which it suppresses competition and puts up barriers to entry. . . . Look all around us right now—at this sudden explosion of subsidies. Look at who's going after them in the main—it's well-established companies, interests, or industries."
- *The Constitution of Liberty* by Friedrich Hayek (1960), because of its synthesis of the themes of the other five books. "I do believe," says Daniels, "that if your goal is to maximize individual freedom, to maximize

the upward mobility to the first and second rung of success, you cannot be for stand-still policies because inevitably they hold down growth, favor the ins versus the outs, the large versus the small, and the vested interests that inevitably grow up in a developed society like ours."

As Daniels's own book demonstrates, he has a penchant for speaking his well-stocked mind. While he was director of President George W. Bush's Office of Management and Budget, he was invited to speak to House Republicans at the Capitol. In an open meeting, he said the problem was that both parties' appropriators operated on this principle: "Don't just stand there, spend something." His service high in the executive branch of the federal government taught him that there are, indeed, institutional imperatives that have helped to drive the federal government, and with it the national economy, into severe difficulties. His governmental service has strengthened his conviction that something akin to "bariatric surgery" is necessary to cure "morbidly obese" government. It is necessary because, he says, such government is impeding economic dynamism and social fluidity: "Upward mobility from the bottom is the crux of the American promise, and the stagnation of the middle class *is* in fact becoming a problem, on any fair reading of the facts."

Obviously, Daniels does not think the facts about our current situation allow us to think that it now is, or soon will be, morning in America—the bright dawn of an unchallenging day. He does not, however, think it is dusk—a darkening era of inevitable decline. We have enormous problems, but they were not created by irresistible, impersonal forces. Rather, they are the result of improvident choices and mistaken policies. That means they are problems that can be solved by our *deciding* to solve them.

It takes political leadership to persuade a democracy to make difficult decisions—to alter what once seemed to be a pleasant, comfortable course of action. Daniels knows that we have made promises to ourselves that we cannot afford to keep. He knows that we have enlarged the public sector to the detriment of the vigor and creativity of the private sector. He also knows this: "Change of the dimension we need requires a coalition of a dimension no one has recently assembled."

As governor, Daniels produced changes that made Indiana thrive in difficult times. It went from a huge structural deficit to a reserve fund almost twice as large as the deficit had been. This is why, for the first time in its history, Indiana has a triple-A credit rating from the three independent rating agencies. From education to infrastructure, his Indiana accomplishments have given him something rare in contemporary politics: the charisma of competence.

His successes in office have reinforced his durable midwestern cheerfulness, which is rooted in his confidence in the common sense of the American public. He believes Americans will choose well when their elected representatives frame the choices honestly. I think his book does so.

I believe in the power of the written word, and in the ability of books to alter the trajectory of events. The philosophy of governance explained in this volume—call it the Daniels Doctrine, or conservatism for grownups—might do just that.

—George F. Will

Introduction

Despite a long involvement with public life, I have read very few books by public officials, past or present. Judging by the ones I have read, many are written to justify the authors' actions or, worse, to settle personal scores. Others aim to embellish the authors' role or proximity to major events, and still others are thinly veiled exercises in self-advertisement.

The typical politician's book tends to be all about "the author," and narcissism always puts me off. Someone once called one of Churchill's books "autobiography disguised as a history of the universe." But at least *244* Churchill had a fabulous life full of genuine and diverse accomplishments. As far as I can tell, I haven't cheated myself much by skipping the last couple thousand titles by senators, presidents, or former thises and thats.

So if you're looking for a book full of self-revelation and tales of a tortured childhood, try the next shelf. What follows is most determinedly not about me because, frankly, I'm not that interesting. I've led a boringly typical postwar American life, which is to say I'm among the luckiest people who ever walked the earth.

Plus, I dislike the self-absorption that has characterized my generation. We Baby Boomers have always confused our numbers with our importance. Landon Jones, in his landmark book on the Baby Boomer generation, *Great Expectations*, called us "the kids the war had been fought for." We were frequently coddled and taught how special we were. We were destined to be the center of attention throughout our lives, not because we deserved to be but merely because there were so many of us. We thought we invented sex, discovered nature, and conquered racism single-handedly. Retailers catered to our changing tastes and designed their advertising campaigns around us.

And as a generation of disproportionate size, our equally disproportionate number of reckless decisions brought our country to a fiscal crisis. The men and women who licked the Great Depression and won World War II have been dubbed the "Greatest Generation." But as I remarked in a 2009 commencement speech at Butler University, no one will ever hang such a moniker on the Baby Boomers. "As a group, we have been self-centered, self-absorbed, self-indulgent and all too often just plain selfish," I said. "[W]e voted ourselves increasing levels of Social Security pensions and Medicare health benefits, but never summoned the political maturity to put those programs on anything resembling a sound actuarial foundation." To underscore the importance of reversing these decisions and putting the country on sounder footing, I told the graduating class that my generation's "parents scrimped and saved to provide us better living standards than theirs. We borrowed and splurged. . . . It's been a blast. Good luck cleaning up after us." When my contemporaries on the faculty scowled and the student body rose in a standing ovation, I knew I had gotten my point across.

So I wouldn't embarrass myself or try to pick your pocket by writing a book about myself. All the words here are my own, so that much is personal, and I sometimes illustrate a point with a fact or anecdote drawn from my personal experience as governor of Indiana. But as proud as I am of what we Hoosiers have accomplished, I learned long ago that telling people about your home state is like showing people your home movies: the visitors trapped on the couch are only pretending to be interested.

One more thing you won't find much of in these pages is labels. In seven years of elective politics I have never used the *c*-word (*conservative*) to define what my administration proposed to do, or the *l*-word (*liberal*) to disparage someone else's ideas. For one thing, these terms have been bent out of their original meaning. A "liberal," for most of history, was a person who defended freedom against the power of government, not, as today, someone who seeks to subjugate individual liberty to state control. What's more, most of the citizens I encounter don't see the world through doctrinaire eyes. As I travel through Indiana, I almost never stay in hotels.

Rather, I find a family with a spare bedroom or a free pull-out couch willing to put me up for the night. I enjoy the unhurried and unvarnished conversations around the kitchen table, and I've found that the people I meet don't typically identify with one particular political ideology. Instead, they are looking for workable solutions to pressing problems affecting their families and communities.

But, most important, labels often divide Americans into warring camps. This obscures the common threats we face and makes it more difficult to solve national problems. The nation doesn't need yet another purple political polemic, at least not from me.

So, personal anecdotes, details about Indiana, and discussions of political ideology are included here only where they are necessary to underscore my larger point: for the first time in my life, I am desperately alarmed about the condition and direction of the American republic. What recently seemed a secure, ever more prosperous, internationally dominant nation is now endangered in a way it never has been before. In the dark days of the cold war, Soviet nuclear confrontation posed a grave danger. During the Civil War the country fractured and fought itself. And during the Revolution and immediately afterward, the infant nation was at risk of disintegrating. But today the danger stems from a central element of our free system. As a people, we have discovered the ability to vote ourselves largesse from the federal treasury in such vast sums that we are destroying our own chances at prosperity. The level of government spending we are engaging in may soon leave us with a defunct, bankrupt, destitute economy. If we don't find a way to restore the goose to good health, we will soon run out of golden eggs.

The danger here is far greater than simple material well-being. The power of free institutions has always rested on their ability to produce prosperity, which in turn empowers free peoples to engage in personal and creative pursuits in every field ranging from business to charity to the arts. Our prosperity has enabled our society to become not only the wealthiest in the world, but also the fairest, most creative, and most generous the world has ever known. It has also been able to fund a military capacity unmatched anywhere, which has reinforced our position of global leadership. We are not only a free people; we are a strong country.

This broad success has spurred other peoples to seek free institutions of their own.

At the end of the cold war, the natural superiority of free systems seemed so assured that the highly respected Francis Fukuyama famously published a book titled *The End of History and the Last Man*, which argued that the age-old struggle between freedom and oppression was largely over. Freedom won, and the world would never look back.

Unfortunately, that proved to be too optimistic. Today, our system of governance is being challenged by China and other authoritarian cultures that are generating far faster economic growth than anything we seem capable of. Tyrants have long wanted to have their cake and eat it, too—to plunder economies that would somehow thrive despite political and economic oppression. But the success of the United States seemed to prove that reaching the highest levels of prosperity was possible only through the use of free economic and political institutions; that to be rich, a people first needed to be free. That belief led leaders of other nations to admire and seek to emulate our system despite a natural inclination toward control.

Now the fundamental belief in free systems is being called into question. Our recent financial collapse has accelerated phenomena that have been growing for decades, but that were masked by the almost unbroken prosperity of the quarter century between the Reagan Recovery in 1983 and the 2008 meltdown. Burgeoning government at every level, from federal to township, has been financed at an alarming rate by borrowed money. A miserably underperforming public school system is now taking its inevitable toll on our society and producing a workforce woefully unprepared to compete with those of other countries and woefully ignorant of the duties and requirements of citizenship in a free society.

History teaches us that all national greatness is temporary. Every great civilization—from the Roman Empire to the British Empire—has eventually collapsed. Americans have grown complacent in their position of dominance, but the term "the American Century" suggests how relatively brief this period of dominance has been. An ancient Roman would not have been impressed by a less-than-one-hundred-year run on top.

Decline and fall are only occasionally foreseen by those en route to those destinations, and still less often forestalled by forceful and timely action. Denial of reality is a powerful human impulse, as is the tendency to mistake the status quo for the natural and inevitable order of things.

Today's American suffers from a diminished sense of his own national history and, too often, a profound ignorance of the history of other nations and civilizations. He probably has even less awareness than a Victorian Brit, a sixteenth-century Spaniard, or even a fifth-century Roman that the world is always subject to a fundamental shakeup. What's more, he has likely not given any thought to the fact that our way of governing ourselves remains an anomalous and unproven experiment in the eyes of history. Sages throughout time have doubted that, to paraphrase Lincoln, a government conceived in liberty can long endure.

Our Founding Fathers knew how long the odds were against their experiment. They worried to their dying days that their work would be undone by the excesses to which democracies might be prone, or by an atrophy of the character traits—self-discipline, self-reliance, a "don't tread on me" insistence on individual liberty—that gave birth to our independence and freedom in the first place. Subsequent generations, especially Lincoln's, feared a dying out of the "mystic chords of memory," the historical knowledge and appreciation of the precious uniqueness of America.

Now evidence abounds that we have reached the point that centuries of skeptics predicted. The overpromising of politicians, catering to the immediate wants of their constituents, has stacked up obligations far beyond our government's ability to afford them. A growing near-majority of citizens is now dependent on government for a substantial percentage of their livelihood. Increasingly, the burdens of a growing public sector are paid for by a dwindling percentage of the population. It is now reaching the point where society's ability to generate new wealth is being threatened and the non-payers have nothing to lose by demanding still more from their richer neighbors.

Meanwhile, large majorities of Americans are clueless, or even badly mistaken, about their own history and the history of past fallen empires. Encouraged on every side to think of themselves as victims of an unfair system and their country as nothing special, they can quite logically react to economic adversity not with a bootstraps resolve but with self-pity and a search for villains. The republican virtues that the Founders saw as indispensable to liberty's preservation appear to be in short supply just when we need them most.

Consequently, we have amassed a ruinous amount of national debt, current and committed, mathematically beyond the capacity of any economy to pay. This is a survival-level threat to the America we have known. Left unaddressed much longer, it will permanently hobble the prosperity engine that has made us the world's great power and exemplar. It will undermine the uniquely American promise of upward mobility for all and compromise our government's ability to fulfill its most important responsibility: national security and the physical safety of Americans.

If this picture seems hyperbolic, or if America's subsiding (or plummeting) into a position of parity or secondary world importance is acceptable to you, then see the cashier for a refund for this book. But if you accept that democracy is always fragile and despotism always in the wings, and that our drift into debt and dependency, accelerated by the recent surge of statism, is dragging us into the great dismal swamp of economic stagnation and personal subservience, read on.

If you do grasp our dilemma, and it bothers you, then here's an important preview: The handwringing does stop. I devoutly believe there is a route to renewal, a way to reconstruct both our economy and an ethic of citizenship that will preserve both prosperity and liberty. There are strong grounds for believing that Americans will summon the resolve necessary to pull this off. I've said I'm not about to write an autobiography; I'm not into writing obituaries, either.

Back when American students learned history, every student knew how Benjamin Franklin responded when asked, after finishing his work at the Constitutional Convention, what sort of government the country was to have: "A republic, if you can keep it." Decisions of the next few years will answer Mr. Franklin's implied question.

CHAPTER 1

The Skeptics

To my knowledge, no one has pinpointed either the originator or the birth date of the word *democracy*. But it seems likely that, within days of the first Greek's coinage of the term, the scoffing began, and a long, unbroken line of cynics arose to disparage and dismiss the silly notion that average people, with all their failings and selfish urges, could actually govern themselves for long. Down the ages, in only slightly varying analyses, these Skeptics have confidently predicted that any attempt to invest political authority in the people was doomed and would prove temporary.

The Greeks themselves produced the first skeptics, most memorably Plato, who believed that "Democracy leads to anarchy, which is mob rule" and "Dictatorship naturally arises out of democracy, and the most aggravated form of tyranny out of the most extreme liberty." Thus began the line of thought that holds that most human beings are not capable of disciplining their appetites, postponing gratification for the sake of the long term, or deciding for the common good, and therefore cannot be trusted with the ultimate political control of society.

The logical conclusion from this assessment is that a nation can be well governed only by an elite class, which is wiser, more farsighted, and more benevolent than the citizenry in general. As Plato put it, "Unless the philosophers rule as kings . . . while the many natures . . . are by necessity excluded, there is no rest from ills for the cities."

Plato had reason to be dubious. The earliest forms of what is often called Greek democracy would never meet a modern definition of the term. Sparta in the seventh century B.C. is often credited as the birthplace, but the franchise in its assembly, the *apella*, was limited to about 2 percent of the population, and even its members had difficulty exerting any real influence over matters of state. Lycurgus was a Spartan king whom ancient historians place in the seventh century and credit with creating a constitution. He is once said to have replied to an adviser who had asked him to establish a truer democracy, "Begin, my friend, by setting it up in your own family." (Those of us men whose families consist of five females and one male are still waiting to be granted such suffrage!)

Later, Solon brought the rule of written law to Athens, and with it a broader range of freedom and political participation. It lasted only as long as Solon did. His successor, Persistratus, promptly set up a dictatorship, albeit a relatively benign one. Setting a precedent that would often be emulated in the future, he was careful to pay lip service to the popular will even while subjugating it. As Will Durant recorded in *The Life of Greece* (the second installment in his eleven-volume primer on Western history, *The Story of Civilization*), "He knew how to adorn and support dictatorship with democratic concessions and forms." Unfortunately, similar lip service to democracy is in particularly active use today.

In halting steps, democratic principles advanced. Cleisthenes is credited with bringing the first true democracy to Athens around 507 B.C. But the strange new practice struggled to take root: the city-state of Syracuse instituted it in 495, but by 485 a dictatorship had displaced it. The Athenian archon (chief magistrate) Pericles was perhaps the greatest proponent of democracy in the ancient world, having instituted a number of democratic reforms in the late fourth century. But even his supporter Thucydides conceded that Pericles was often a demagogue, instituting laws that placed additional restrictions on who could be declared a citizen.

The Romans gave some space to popular sovereignty, though it was limited, and all affairs of state were overseen by the aristocratic Senate and, in most periods, emperors and tyrants. By 49 B.C., corruption, including the widespread bribery of Assembly members, was rampant. "Potential dictators maneuvered for position, the capital filled with the odor of a dying democracy," Durant wrote in *Caesar and Christ*, the third volume of the *Civilization* series. Julius Caesar led his legions across the Rubicon, and leadership by princes returned. In 27 B.C., Caesar's nephew Augustus installed himself as the first Roman emperor after years of military campaigns to consolidate his own power, establishing the Roman Empire.

After that, experiments in even limited political participation by common people disappeared for centuries. Although some medieval philosophers, most notably Thomas Aquinas, developed a political philosophy partially based on classical conceptions of democracy, a large-scale rediscovery of the history and philosophy of antiquity would not come until the Renaissance, in the fourteenth century. This revived study of the ancient humanities in turn spurred a fresh exploration of democracy, and by the eighteenth century, the ideas of the Enlightenment began to permeate society. The Skeptics appeared immediately. Voltaire opined, "Democracy seems suitable only to a very small country, . . . Small though it may be, it will make many mistakes, because it will be composed of men." He was echoed more bluntly by innumerable others, such as the French philosopher Joseph de Maistre: "It is impossible to consider a human society, a people without a sovereignty, as it is for a hive and a swarm of bees without a queen."

Rousseau, sometimes thought to be godfather to the French Revolution, was anything but a democrat: "In the strict sense of the term, a true democracy never existed, and never will exist. It is against natural order that a great number should govern and that the few should be governed." Montesquieu was an ardent advocate of democracy but pessimistically predicted that free societies would be victimized by their own success, as the very virtues that produced them—thrift, self-reliance, self-improvement— would eventually become atrophied as a result of affluence.

The arrival of the American Republic was heard "round the world," but it convinced few of the prominent thinkers of the time that self-government would actually work. The Skeptics viewed the French Revolution and its prompt collapse into Bonapartist monarchy as an affirmation of their arguments, and America as nothing more than the exception that proved the rule. Even the flowering of the United States, and its emergence from its Civil War stronger than it was before, failed to persuade the Skeptics. In the second half of the nineteenth century, Nietzsche wrote contemptuously that democracy was not a mark of human progress but a step backward: "[T]he democratic movement is . . . a form of the decay of political organization." Popular sovereignty will not elevate men to new heights of dignity and self-reliance, he argued. "The democratizing of Europe will tend to the production of a type [of man] prepared for slavery in the most subtle sense of the term: the strong man will become stronger and richer than he has perhaps ever been . . . the democratizing of Europe is an involuntary arrangement for the rearing of tyrants."

It wasn't just from the supposedly more authoritarian culture of Germany that the Skeptics emerged. In Britain, H. G. Wells wrote a book whose title tells all: *Anticipation: An Experiment in Prophecy, the Passing of Democracy.* He summed up his view as follows: "I know of no case for the elective democratic government of modern states that cannot be knocked to pieces in five minutes."

The skepticism was not limited to academics and philosophers. Oscar Wilde declared, "Democracy means simply the bludgeoning of the people by the people for the people." America's own H. L. Mencken said, "Democracy is the theory that the common people know what they want and deserve to get it good and hard." Reading these wisecracks amid the soaring debts and economic travails that self-indulgent spending has created in present-day America is enough to make the most committed friend of freedom wince.

It is worth noting, however, that none of this contempt for the "great experiment" would have surprised our Founders in the slightest. They were fully conscious of freedom's past failures, of the arguments of the Skeptics, and of the ever-present temptation to dictatorship that exists within societies. They knew exactly what they were up against, and they worried about it before, during, and after they gave birth to the American project. In the first of the Federalist Papers, Alexander Hamilton wrote, "It has been frequently remarked that it seems to have been reserved to the people of this country, by their conduct and example, to decide the important question, whether societies of men are really capable or not of establishing good government from reflection and choice, or whether they are forever destined to depend for their political constitutions on accident and force."

Hamilton, whose co-authorship of the Papers was not revealed until he disclosed it in a postmortem testament prepared just before his fatal duel with Aaron Burr, posed perhaps the central dilemma: "Has it not ... invariably been found that momentary passions, and immediate interest, have a more active and imperious control over human conduct than general or remote considerations of policy, utility, or justice?" When we examine the impossible fiscal corner into which "momentary passions" and "immediate interest" have painted us, we can almost hear Hamilton, Madison, and the other greats of that founding generation saying, "Weren't you listening? Didn't we try to tell you? Couldn't you see this coming?"

Skimming the Skeptics, one quickly grasps that they are not really pontificating on political theory, or at least not on the alternative forms and arrangements by which nations can be governed. They are expressing their views on human nature. They simply looked into the instincts and behaviors of the people of their day and found them unsuited to self-government. The Platos, Nietzches, Wellses, and their ilk concluded that the adverb *hopelessly* should be included in that sentence. Even America's Founders and admirers saw the problem (*Federalist* 6 reminds us that "men are ambitious, vindictive, and rapacious"), but they realized that tyrannies themselves were run by men. And they thought that the intrinsic characteristics of humans were surmountable, given two preconditions.

The first was a set of constitutional provisions that moderated the people's more selfish impulses and short-term temptations. So, for instance, the Founders bequeathed us a system designed to enable factions to counter and offset one another's attempted excesses. They devised a bicameral legislature, with a House of Representatives designed to reflect the current will of the people and a Senate geared for longer terms and presumably longer-term reflection.

The Founders understood, however, that what truly determines whether a democracy can survive is not the character of government's structures but the character of the people who are to be governed through those structures. And they knew that the characteristics requisite to sustaining a government by the people do not come naturally but must be learned, fostered, and practiced. Writing near the end of his life, that great advocate of the common man Thomas Jefferson said, "The qualifications for self-government are not innate. They are the result of habit and long training."

Even in the triumphant days of the late 1700s, as American democracy overcame the world's most powerful monarchy and took successful shape in George Washington's presidency and his voluntary relinquishment of office after his second term, the Founders worried incessantly that human nature would reassert itself. John Adams fretted that the "Republican virtues" would inevitably erode away, probably in no more than two generations. The most likely sources of this atrophy would be a loss of the historical memory that reminds us of the cost and responsibilities of liberty and the indolence that liberty's very success, in bringing affluence to the multitude, would deliver.

Visiting the United States a half century into its experiment, Alexis de Tocqueville came away impressed but highly cautionary. "Republican government is fragile by nature," he warned. "It relies only on a certain sentiment of order, virtue, and moderation on the part of the governed. The immoderate desires of parties ... constantly threaten the existence of republics." If he made a return visit today, to an America in which spending for the moment has been, to say the least, "immoderate," in which both private and public debt have ballooned beyond any responsible level, de Tocqueville's only surprise might be that it took this long for us to get in this fully foreseeable fix.

It seems only yesterday that one of the most incisive minds of the day could write about history ending in a permanent victory for free institutions. The sharp social interest in economic gain made possible through modern science, Francis Fukuyama wrote in *The End of History and the Last Man*, would be "driven by unlimited desire and guided by reason." For countries to embrace the old model of success through conquest rather than individual liberty, he wrote, "in the modern world would mean a break with this powerful and dynamic economic world, and an attempt to rupture the logic of technological development."

It is no wonder, then, that the seeming incapacity of the world's leading free nation to discipline its own finances, or maintain the economic vitality that made it the world leader, has spawned a new host of Skeptics, many of them right here in the cradle of liberty.

Surveying the incapacity of our current political system to change either large or even small federal programs, Robert Samuelson laments, "The system can no longer make choices, especially unpleasant choices, for the good of the nation as a whole.... The trouble is that, despite superficial support for 'deficit reduction' or 'tax reform,' few Americans would surrender their own benefits, subsidies and tax breaks—a precondition for success." Samuelson describes the situation as "suicidal government." The Skeptics of earlier days would have seen it not as suicide but as the expected, geriatric failing of an aging democracy near the end of its natural life.

Bestselling savants such as Thomas Friedman write wistfully of the superior ability of authoritarian regimes such as China's to act quickly and plan for the long term. On television's *Meet the Press* in May 2010, Friedman blurted out, "I have fantasized—don't get me wrong—but what if we could just be China for a day? I mean, just, just, just one day. You know, I mean, where we could actually, you know, authorize the right solutions."[2]

The tone of some modern Skeptics has turned fatalistic, and harsh. Richard Longworth spoke for the defeatists when he wrote, "Basically, America has thrown in the towel. We owned the 20th Century, but we've conceded the 21st Century to China."

Like Friedman but more explicitly, Longworth thinks the answer is to be more like the Chinese: "China's regime is a top-down leadership, promoting a guided prosperity. It decrees that something will be done, and then does it.... [N]ot only our economy but our political system is being judged here."

In other words, when we Americans let everyone in on the decisions, we just can't cut it in today's world. The only way to compete is to let a few smart people—Plato's philosopher kings—have the power to do what is best for the rest of us. As we have seen, these ideas have a long, if not proud lineage.

Reams have been written about our "dysfunctional" and "gridlocked" political system, with fingers pointing to a variety of failures in that system—from the pernicious lobbyists to our political fund-raising rules to the noncompetitive districts created by gerrymandering. All of these structural issues are real and contribute to our predicament.

But the most critical, and chilling, of the modern Skeptics are those who locate the fatal failure of our current political system in the American people themselves. Everywhere it is alleged, by people of the left and right alike, that we are just no longer up to the job of governing ourselves.

From the left, home to those whose philosophy naturally favors rule by enlightened elites, this conclusion is unsurprising. It is how they justify the need for the state, run of course by the well-educated and well-intentioned (namely, them), to take charge of all our affairs.

Despair comes from the center, too. On a cable talk show in December 2010, I listened as former Colorado governor Richard Lamm, a moderate and thoughtful Democrat, sounded this defeatist note: "I guess that America is now sufficiently overindulged that a majority of voters are never going to vote to do the kind of things that are necessary to reform entitlements, balance the budget, do those other things that I think we know are necessary."

Increasingly, and even more alarmingly, one finds the supposedly strongest advocates of freedom, those on what we call the right, lamenting the degraded character of their fellow Americans. They despondently point out the high and rising percentages of Americans who depend in part or even entirely on government for their income; the ignorance by most citizens of even the most basic of facts of our history or principles of our Constitution; the decline of the cultural commitment to self-discipline and personal responsibility; and so on.

The criticism is most sobering when it comes from outside. Edmund Morris, the brilliant Kenyan-born British biographer of Theodore Roosevelt and Ronald Reagan, could be thought of as a current de Tocqueville, a visiting observer sympathetic to our principles but clear-eyed about their health status. On a November 2010 television show, Morris was asked about the condition of the U.S. nation and its politics. He replied by describing the American people as "lazy, obese, complacent, and increasingly perplexed as to why we are losing our place in the world to people who are more dynamic than us and more disciplined.[13] Ouch. 244

Hard as they are to hear, comments like these are essential for us to digest at this moment in our history. If they prove true, and there is ample evidence to support them, the American prospect is exactly the one that the Skeptics, in all their variety, so smugly told us to expect.

I'm not buying it. I say this with full awareness of the data backing up the prophets of democracy's decline. Much of it will be openly discussed in the chapters that follow.

But I have some data of my own. It comes from the years I have spent as the employee of six and a half million of those allegedly degenerate Americans we so often read about. It comes from direct experience in restoring public finances damaged by years of overindulgence; from asking free citizens to accept at least modest measures to live within our collective means, to think about the future more than the present, to build for that future so we might leave our children a stronger and more prosperous state.

It comes from years of firsthand, intimate exposure to the entire cross-section of people in a state that is, as much as any state I know, reasonably representative of America as a whole. It comes from eight years of constant travel, to the smallest towns and the densest inner cities; from more than a hundred overnight stays in the homes of my fellow Hoosiers; from thousands of personal conversations in their businesses, stores, schools, barns, and coffee shops.

Of course, we Americans, like every human who has ever lived, have our obvious weaknesses. But without denying any of our shortcomings, I choose to believe we can and will fight our way out of today's dangerous corner of debt and economic stagnation. We will summon the fortitude to face down our challenges and bring back into view that brighter future that Americans, uniquely among the world's peoples, have always assumed awaited them. In so doing, we will refute the Skeptics and prove that, yes, government of and by the people can "long endure," and is in fact the model to which people everywhere should aspire.

I admit there is a strong element of faith involved. But faith is at the core of every great endeavor. Early currency printed by the infant American Republic bore the words *Exitus in dubio est*. "The outcome is in doubt." Resolving to put this doubt to rest once again is the task of our age, and as noble an assignment as any generation could wish for itself.

CHAPTER 2

The Red Menace

14 NOTES
P. 244-5

Imagine the following scenario:

Monday 6:00 A.M.—Americans awake to breathless cable television reports that a Chinese official, chairman of an agency most have never heard of, has just issued the following statement: "For years, the Chinese people have lent money to the United States by buying Treasury securities with the anticipation that doing so would allow America to solve its economic problems. These loans amount to an exchange in which we sent the United States goods made by Chinese workers and received not real money but a mere promise to be repaid. We are now holding over $5 trillion of these promises.

"This will no longer continue. We see no evidence that the United States will take the steps necessary to grow its economy or limit its spending so it can afford to repay the loans we have extended. Instead, we conclude that the United States will sidestep its obligations by lowering the value of the dollar and thereby cheating those who have lent it money in good faith by reducing the relative size of its debts. We regret to announce that China has withdrawn from the U.S. Treasury market until current leadership and policies are replaced."

Monday 9:30 A.M.—The dollar drops 10 percent, and futures markets suggest the drops have only begun. The New York stock market opens in free fall.

Monday 12:00 P.M.—Alarmed by reports of a market crash and predictions of a sharp rise in the prices of commodities including oil, millions of Americans take the prudent step of topping off their gas tanks. In a matter of hours the nation's gasoline reserves disappear, long lines begin to form, and pump prices begin to skyrocket.

Monday afternoon—Not wishing to be left behind by the Chinese, other nations' central banks begin to sell off U.S. Treasuries. As buyers become more scarce, prices plummet and interest rates begin rising in all categories.

Monday evening—In a nationwide address, the U.S. president declares his confidence in the dollar and Treasuries. He is joined by the chairman of the Federal Reserve, who announces that public Treasury auctions will be suspended and the Fed will purchase all Treasury securities until further notice. He goes on to state the Fed's intention to buy stocks in whatever amount is needed to hold the Dow Jones Index at the day's closing level.

Tuesday morning—When European and U.S. markets open, the dollar drops 25 percent and there is a massive sell-off of U.S. stocks. Meanwhile, anguish grows among business analysts as U.S. banks, which had been able to borrow money from the Fed at artificially low rates and then make an easy profit by lending it to consumers at much higher interest rates, are quickly seeing their capital wiped out.

Tuesday 12:00 P.M.—Panicked Americans, watching their investments evaporate and desperate to salvage their savings from banks rumored to be imperiled, throng to the nearest branches, which quickly run out of cash to pay them. Assurances from the Federal Deposit Insurance Corporation that its guarantee limit will be lifted and all deposits backstopped do nothing to stem the demands.

Wednesday—The spreading collapse of the banking system begins to affect commercial credit and the finance of trade. As shipments slow or stop, shortages of consumer goods, including food in some locales, begin to be reported. Television-induced panic buying turns a minor, isolated phenomenon into a major, widespread one.

Thursday—Declaring "the dollar is dead" as a world currency, OPEC ministers hold an urgent conference call to decide whether the renminbi or gold should become the new medium of exchange for oil. The price of gold rockets to $5,000 per ounce. The New York Federal Reserve asks for a cordon of troops around its building, home of the world's single largest gold stores.

Friday—The first speeches are delivered in Congress branding the Chinese decision to stop lending the United States money an "act of war" and demanding retaliatory action. Meanwhile, Chinese naval maneuvers are interpreted by some as a sign of impending action against Taiwan, on the theory that a bankrupt and distracted United States will not live up to its commitment to defend the island.

Saturday—The first state governors declare martial law and deploy National Guard units to protect government buildings and retail districts against looters and angry protesters . . .

It's All Too Real

This scenario may sound like something out of a horror movie, but it's actually very possible. For three quarters of the twentieth century, the world lived under the threat of the brutal, totalitarian, expansionist shadow of communism. This dogma, while it lasted, confidently forecast its own inevitable triumph and eventual domination over all other systems of government, especially those naïvely constructed on principles of human freedom.

For almost half that century, it fell to the United States to lead the resistance to this most recent incarnation of the oldest and most common form of governance: the tyranny of the few. Americans were called by presidents of both parties to "pay any price, bear any burden" to preserve freedom for themselves and others, and over and over they accepted the call. In 1989, the so-called Red Menace collapsed in its own contradictions and has disappeared in all but name, outside the reliquaries of university humanities departments.

In the new century, America faces a threat that, if somewhat less physical in character, is at least as dangerous to our freedom and future as the Soviet Union ever was. I refer, of course, to the debt, current and coming, that our federal government has accumulated. Now we confront a second Red Menace, this time in the form of the red ink that could destroy the promise of America and, with it, our position as an influence for good around the world.

Thankfully, in the eighteen months since I first thought of writing a book, the need for this chapter has steadily shrunk. The public's awareness of the size, sources, and implications of the debt levels our federal government has run up has grown dramatically. A spontaneous, authentic grass-roots movement dedicated to promoting fiscal responsibility and calling itself the Tea Party has sprung into existence, and alarm about the issue was a central factor in the sweeping repudiation suffered by President Obama and his allies in the 2010 midterm elections. Specific rhetorical terms I began using back then—"child abuse" to describe the debt's burden on the young, "grown-up conversation" to suggest the more mature kinds of fiscal decisions we would have to make—have entered common usage and are approaching cliché status. But even those sharing this heightened awareness and concern do not always grasp completely the dimension of the danger we face. The risk is even higher than lost jobs, income, or hope for a better future and higher living standards. Our position of world leadership could be eclipsed, and with it the power of our free political system as a model for other countries. It's not out of the question that the American republic could undergo a full economic and social collapse, with consequences beyond our ability to imagine.

That is the premise of all that follows in this book: that the American project in personal freedom is at risk from a threat that is not more terrible than the cold war Soviet nuclear menace, but is far more likely to befall us. Those who do not agree with this threat assessment cannot be expected to concur in the suggestions and conclusions that follow. But before rejecting this premise, please note that there is nothing ideological about it. The problem is mathematical, not philosophical.

History teaches us that nations are likely to fall through financial failure instead of—or sometimes as a precursor to—military conquest. As our most persuasive expert on the topic, Harvard historian Niall Ferguson, has written, "Imperial falls are associated with fiscal crises: sharp imbalances between revenues and expenditures, and the mounting cost of servicing a mountain of public debt. . . . Think of Spain in the 17th century, which came to see nearly two-thirds of its ordinary revenue go to interest on the juros, the loans by which the Habsburg monarchy had financed itself. ⓞ 244

Or, Ferguson goes on, "think of France in the 18th century: between 1751 and 1788, the eve of Revolution, interest and amortisation payments rose from just over a quarter of tax revenue to 62 per cent. Finally, consider Britain in the 20th century. Its real problems came after 1945, when a substantial proportion of its now immense debt burden was in foreign hands.[2] 244

Undoubtedly, most of those living in those doomed empires never saw the collapse coming. Denial is among the most human of impulses, and the most deadly. Just as the watchword of every economic bubble is "This time is different," the prevailing conviction in the late stages of every fallen empire is "It can't happen here."

Surveying the debris of those once-proud empires, many pessimistically foresee a period of long, slow decline for the United States. In a healthy beginning of wisdom, we have begun to speak far more often about the "bills we are leaving to our children," and there is no doubt we have been piling up tremendously large bills for future generations to pay off. But we might not have the time for reform that those predecessor nations had. In today's world of instant communication, when trillions of dollars (and euros, and yen) change hands daily at the speed of light, financial collapse need not be gradual. A loss of confidence in an indebted counterparty can bring about a ruinous run, a "flash crash," in a heartbeat. Just ask Lehman Brothers.

David Brooks has summed up how this could happen: "It will come with amazing swiftness. The bond markets are with you until the second they are against you. When the psychology shifts and the fiscal crisis happens, the shock will be grievous: national humiliation, diminished power in the world, drastic cuts, and spreading pain."[3] 244

Today's most authoritative scholar on debt and its consequences, Kenneth Rogoff of Harvard University, asks, "Will 23rd-century historians look back on today's fiscal follies with the same mixture of bemusement and disdain with which we now view the financial affairs of 18th-century French kings?" He also proclaimed that "They will surely be incredulous to see pensions and health insurance financed via Ponzi schemes as transparently unsustainable as the 1700s South Sea bubble.[4] 244

Even if disaster were not immediate, a variety of historians have speculated that we are already perilously near a "tipping point" past which national economic decline would be irreversible. Some have ventured to identify a quantitative point of no return, when federal debt reaches 90 percent or 100 percent of GDP. If we continue on our current trajectory, we're set to reach this point in a few decades (see Figure 1). Plus, the weight of interest owed on debt this large imposes an irreversible drag on growth and incomes. That drag could be as much as 2 percent of GDP. Some of the best work in this area in recent years has been done by Rogoff with Carmen M. Reinhart of the University of Maryland. In a recent paper that looked at forty-four countries over the course of two hundred years, they conclude that countries with debt levels below 30 percent of their GDP have averaged growth rates of a robust 3.7 percent, while those with debt exceeding 90 percent of their GDP grow on average at an anemic rate of 1.7 percent.⑤ This suggests that the United States is putting 244 itself in a position where in the coming decades it will not be able to grow fast enough to remain competitive in the global economy, keep up with increases in population, and acquire enough wealth to pay off the debt it is amassing. In other words, the United States could soon lose its preeminent position in the world while capital shifts to other countries.

Figure 1 | **Our National Debt**

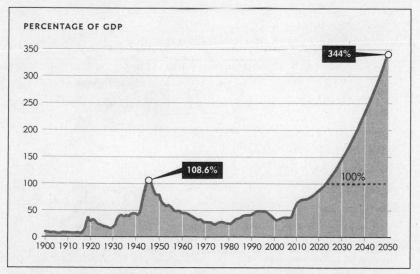

Source: Heritage Foundation Calculations based on data from the U.S. Department of the Treasury, Institute for the Measurement of Worth, Congressional Budget Office, and White House Office of Management and Budget.

If this occurs, Mark Steyn will likely not be too far off the mark in writing in *The New Criterion* in January 2011 that the "United States is facing nothing so amiable and genteel as a Continental-style 'decline,' but something more like sliding off a cliff.⁶He went on to note that within the next ten years, the United States will spend more on interest for its debt than it does for its military, while in "the next five years the [Chinese] People's Liberation Army will be entirely funded by U.S. taxpayers." In any case, it's hard to argue with Steyn when he points out that "Decline starts with the money. It always does." And even as federal spending continues to grow, the average income of the American worker, who will ultimately shoulder the burden of our spending spree, has essentially flatlined. See Figure 2 for a sense of how wide this gap is.

Whether one prefers big government or limited government, a social welfare state or a market economy state, has nothing to do with the brute fact that no enterprise—not a family, a small business, or a modern nation-state—can survive, let alone thrive, while carrying the incredible debt burdens we are about to confront. This is not a matter of opinion based on a preference for limited government. It's a brutally objective fact of life. I often say to Hoosiers who ask about this subject, "Let's have

Figure 2 | Federal Spending vs. Median Income

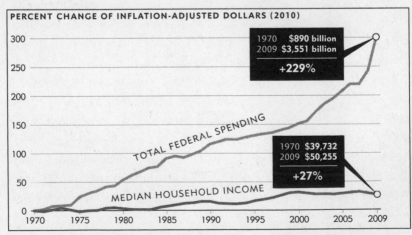

Source: Heritage Foundation Calculations based on data from the U.S. Census Bureau and White House Office of Management and Budget.

the philosophical debate tomorrow. For today, can we agree that the arithmetic here does not work?"

The retirement arrangements that our politics has made for older Americans amount to a form of child abuse because they heap tons of debt on our children. Social Security and Medicare are destined to cost vastly more than can possibly be funded and still leave room for rising future living standards. It is unlikely that any system so constructed will even exist when today's young people reach retirement age.

With each successive estimate, insolvency draws nearer: In May of 2011, the Medicare and Social Security Trustees issued their most recent report projecting bankruptcy for Medicare by 2024 and for Social Security by 2036. And given the report's completely unrealistic assumptions of huge cuts in medical provider payments, odds are that the days of reckoning are even closer.

Time is very short to deal with the problem. Precious years were squandered while our politicians denied there was a problem, and in fact used every opportunity to make things worse. In 2010 there was no measurable inflation and therefore the annual cost of living adjustment, or COLA (the formula that has for years overcompensated for inflation) for once did not call for an increase in Social Security payments. Preposterously, President Obama promptly called for a $250 special handout to every Social Security recipient regardless of income or wealth. Fortunately, his proposal didn't make it through Congress. But it did resurface in the president's 2011 budget. For the American political class, pandering is a reflex action, a nearly unbreakable habit.

Let's review the depth of the hole we have dug. The outright federal debt owed to "the public" is around $9.65 trillion. At 62 percent of the national economy, that's a peacetime record. And, of course, it's only the beginning. We owe another $4.65 trillion to the Social Security and Medicare "trust" funds. (Quotation marks are necessary when using this term, because there is absolutely nothing of value held in trust, nothing to trust.) So the taxpayer is on the hook for this money just as directly as if it had been lent by the Chinese.

For seventy years, Americans were misled to believe that they had been putting aside money for their own retirement, that there were actual assets being held somewhere that would provide for them in their Golden Years. This misrepresentation has been aptly named "the noble lie" for its use of falsehood to effect a supposedly moral purpose. As is now slowly becoming understood, there never was anything in the trust funds, just a growing mountain of obligations. Retirees weren't providing for themselves during their working years, they were simply paying for current retirees. And what was left over—the program's "surplus"—was spent by the federal government.

The system worked for years because there were far more workers than retirees. But as Baby Boomers work their way through the system and Americans live longer, the number of workers per retiree has fallen dramatically. We are now fast approaching a point where there will not be enough workers per Social Security recipient to keep the system solvent. In 1940 there were forty-two workers for every retiree receiving benefits. In 1950 the ratio was sixteen to one. Today, we are nearing a system that relies on three workers for every one person drawing a Social Security check.[8] 245

The most nakedly political of Social Security's design flaws is that every American collects from it, no matter how wealthy they are or how little they need retirement help. There never was any reason of policy or compassion for this absurdity, only the cold calculation that putting everyone in the system would protect it politically over the years. By the 1970s, in fact, noting that the program benefitted rich people more than poor people, compared to their payments into it, Milton Friedman raised the issue with the then Social Security commissioner Wilbur Cohen, who confessed, "You are right. However, a program for poor people will be a poor program.[9] With justification, it has been written that "The design of the Social Security system still embodies the most successful strategy of structural political manipulation in the history of American politics."

The IOUs in the fund today are tiny compared with what is coming. The promised future benefits grotesquely outstrip the future taxes we are scheduled to pay by some $5.4 trillion for Social Security and as much as $46.0 trillion for Medicare. This whole setup is enough to give Mr. Ponzi a bad name—or a legitimate job. If old Carlo were around today, he'd have

Figure 3 | **Current and Projected Entitlement Spending
as Percentage of GDP**

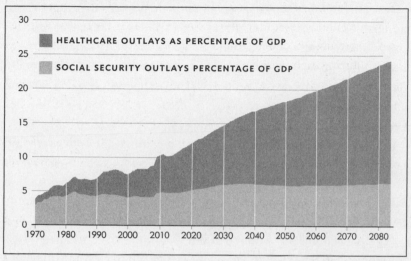

Source: SilverLake.

made an ideal Social Security commissioner. Figure 3 should give you a
good indication of what I'm talking about.

All this has been well understood by national leaders for a very long
time. But it hasn't prevented people in both parties from perpetuating
misleading myths. One such myth has been "There is no problem; these
programs run surpluses." And another, "A taxpayer is just getting back
what he paid in." Incredibly, our political leaders have often only added
to the coming nightmare.

Meanwhile, it's now clear that the subsidized expansion of coverage
in the Obama health care legislation, directly contrary to the claims at
the time of its passage, will add a couple trillion dollars to the next generation's bill. On top of that, the legislation created a brand-new entitlement, the Community Living Assistance Services and Supports (CLASS)
Act, this time for long-term care insurance. Whatever kind of act this is,
it isn't classy. Long-term care insurance is almost by definition a program
that pays for the most expensive health care costs most Americans will
incur. The entitlement program prohibits charging higher premiums for

sicker applicants and is therefore certain to implode. Every analysis, by bodies ranging from the Congressional Budget Office to the Medicare actuary to the American Academy of Actuaries, agrees that CLASS is an untenable mess that will inevitably need trillions in taxpayer bailouts to stay in existence. Even Kathleen Sebelius, secretary (and czarina) of health and human services, admitted that the program was "totally unsustainable." And it was created well after the recession had exposed and exacerbated the Red Menace to terrifying levels. The authors of Obamacare just plowed ahead anyway.

In 2010, President Obama appointed a commission to recommend possible actions against the debt threat. Ably led by a prominent Democrat, Erskine Bowles, and a respected Republican, former senator Alan Simpson, the group produced an admirable effort that, if enacted, would have taken the United States a long way toward solvency.

The president ignored their recommendations. His 2011 budget submission adopted none of them. Instead, it called for additional debt of more than $1 trillion per year for the next decade. His proposed budget made no proposal at all about the disastrous unfunded entitlement liabilities. On the biggest danger to our nation, the biggest problem we face as a people, the president went AWOL.

He should have stayed there. His silence would have been better than what he did next. In early April 2011 the White House suddenly announced that the president would make a "major address" about our fiscal problems, and on April 13, 2011, he did.

Just when the nation needs to unite around change that heads off a debt crisis and rebuilds our economy, the president lashed out divisively at any who disagreed with his Big Government philosophy. In the speech, he criticized Republican plans to cut spending as a vision "that is deeply pessimistic" about America and that would lead to slashing investments in education and infrastructure, and would rip health insurance away from fifty million Americans—all of which was false. Just when we need to start building public understanding of the true nature of our safety net programs and the impossible arithmetic of their current configuration, he repeated all the "noble lies"—at this point, there is nothing the least bit noble about them—and told Americans that we could do just fine by taxing other people (the "wealthy") and freezing the big ticket items in place.

Medicaid? No change. Social Security? No problem. Medicare? No change—just keep squeezing doctors and hospitals and drug companies (his gullible allies from the Obamacare debate). The speech was roundly denounced as having failed to move the process of fiscal recovery forward; but it was much worse than that.

By reiterating the mathematically untrue version of the difficulties we face, the president not only missed an opportunity to advance our understanding as citizens, he set it back. It was the most disappointing display of demagoguery and dereliction we have seen in a long while.

What can we blame for this sort of behavior? When the plain arithmetic says that we already have bills we will never be able to afford, that the top national priority should be reducing them, what term captures the action of piling new debt onto old? Arrogance? Willful blindness?

Uncle Sam has not been the only drunken sailor in port. State and local governments have gotten in on the act, too. State after state binged on spending during the bubble years of the past decade, then wound up in desperate deficit condition when the revenue gusher suddenly stopped. Outrageously generous pension commitments were ladled on top of big pay and benefit increases for government workers as well as new spending programs aimed at pleasing one constituency or another. If anything, these future liabilities, like those of the federal government's entitlement programs, are even more dangerous than the unbalanced budgets of today, because they bind future decisions of state and local governments. Pension obligations alone could swamp state budgets. Andrew Biggs of the American Enterprise Institute has calculated that collectively states today face a deficit for their unfunded pension liabilities that tops $3 trillion[10] 245

The view from Indiana of all this financial wreckage has been a bit unique. We have been, one could say, countercyclical in our fiscal trajectory. When our crew came to office in 2005, most states were riding high, but Indiana was broke. Still, as I'll discuss later in the book, we were able to reverse the slide and thus put Hoosiers in the odd position of passing dozens of other states in opposite fiscal directions. As we became steadily more solvent, those other states went broke. As we paid down debts, they piled them up, sometimes in the least responsible way, borrowing money to pay current expenses. As our credit rating was upgraded, theirs went down. By mid-2010, credit default swaps—the lender's insurance that became famous during the financial collapse—became more expensive on the debt of U.S. states such as Illinois and California than on that of bankrupt nations such as Ireland and Portugal. But we watched in puzzlement as state after state sank deeper into indebtedness and struggled to make even the most minor prospective changes to their impossibly lucrative pension plans.

We could ignore state debt if it were absolutely clear that a series of state defaults would not lead the national authorities to step in and backstop or, as we now say, "bail out" the debtors. Once again, perhaps even more loudly than in 2008–9, we would be told we faced "systemic risk" in which the failures of states to make good on their debts would lead to an avalanche of failure among those who had lent to them, and then to those who had financed those lenders, and so on to Armageddon.

Those of us in more responsible states would have cause to protest if that day came. For the sucker's mistake of having kept our books balanced and providing reasonably for pension promises, we would be forced to join in welfare payments to sister states that had done neither.

Whether or not one counts state and local borrowings, our country will soon rank among the most indebted in the world and, in fact, in world history. Measured against gross domestic product, and therefore against the size of the economy that has to generate repayments, by 2020 we will be among the top ("bottom" would be more descriptive) debtors in the world, in a league with Portugal, Spain, Ireland, and Greece. Debt/GDP, which was actually brought down from 49 percent in 1994 to 41 percent when the recession began in 2008, has swiftly rocketed to 62 percent today and is on track to hit 90 percent of GDP at the end of this decade.

Governments and their top officials are not held to anything like the same standards of disclosure, accounting, and financial responsibility that their business counterparts are. It's a good thing, because if they were, we'd need a lot more prison space. In a tongue-in-cheek but seriously purposed exercise, the editors of *Grant's Interest Rate Observer*, a leading periodical of the fixed-rate financial world, have taken to producing an occasional "prospectus" of the United States of America, a facsimile of the disclosures that any business borrower has to release before accessing credit markets.

In a list of fourteen risk factors, *Grant's* March 2010 prospectus included the thought that "U.S. states and municipalities are experiencing severe economic distress and may require intervention from the federal government." But its most important "disclosures," scary even in the dry terminology of bond analysis, are that "The U.S. economy is heavily indebted at all levels," "A rise in interest rates could adversely affect Government finances," "Mandatory outlays for retirement insurance and health care are expected to increase substantially in future years," and "Foreign official institutions [meaning government-run central banks, not merely private financial firms] hold a significant amount of U.S. government debt."

These and other risks could combine to produce the worst of consequences, one that has, throughout history, signaled the impending demise of a once-powerful nation: "The dollar may not continue to enjoy reserve currency status and may decline in the future.... Foreigners may lose confidence in U.S. economic policies or financial stability."

Coupled with other statements about "ineffective internal controls over financial reporting" and "improper payments by the federal government" on the order of $100 billion per year, the report concludes that the federal government is a borrower that a prudent investor should think more than twice about entrusting with a loan. A few months after the *Grant's* bulletin, the bond rating service Standard & Poor's announced that for the first time, the United States' AAA credit rating was at risk of a downgrade. A year later, in April 2011, another danger sign appeared when, concerned about America's ability to close its deficits, the organization warned of a one-in-three chance of a downgrade over the following two years. This admission quickly caused the Dow to tumble one hundred points. It felt odd to read these announcements in Indiana, where, inconceivably, our credit rating had surpassed that of the greatest country on earth.

Even in the measured language of Fed-speak, the dangers announce themselves loudly. Testifying before Congress in early 2011, Fed chairman Ben Bernanke said, "[I]f government debt and deficits were actually to grow at the pace envisioned [by the president's budget], the economic and financial effects would be severe. Sustained high rates of government borrowing would both drain funds away from private investment and increase our debt to foreigners, with adverse long-run effects on U.S. output, incomes, and standards of living." Allow me to translate: we either deal with this problem soon, or we're hosed. And as with any debt, there comes interest. To get a sense of the interest we're accruing on our ballooning national debt and our increasing dependence on foreign creditors, take a look at Figures 4 and 5.

The fact that other major economies such as Japan and the United Kingdom are similarly encumbered is no consolation; instead, that fact reveals that the world is closer than previously thought to a credit collapse even larger than the one we so recently went through.

But Japan and some of these other nations have one advantage that we increasingly don't: They owe most of the money to themselves. By contrast, the shocking run-up in U.S. national debt has been paralleled by

Figure 4 | **Projected Net Interest on National Debt**

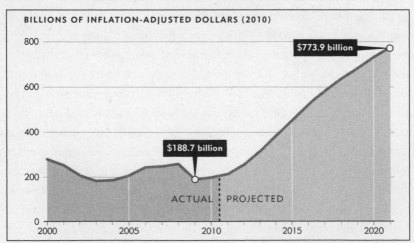

Source: Heritage Foundation Calculations based on data from the White House Office of Management and Budget and Congressional Budget Office.

Figure 5 | **Percentage of National Debt Held by Foreign Creditors**

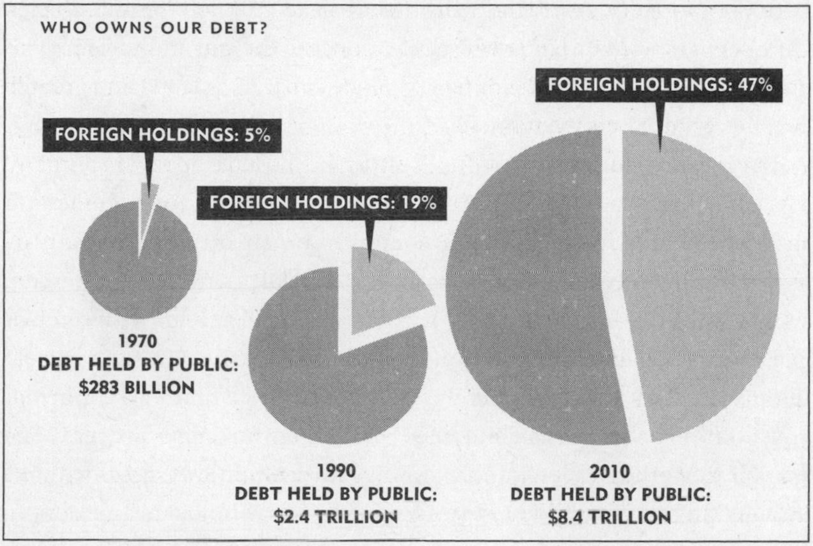

WHO OWNS OUR DEBT?

FOREIGN HOLDINGS: 5%

FOREIGN HOLDINGS: 19%

FOREIGN HOLDINGS: 47%

1970
DEBT HELD BY PUBLIC:
$283 BILLION

1990
DEBT HELD BY PUBLIC:
$2.4 TRILLION

2010
DEBT HELD BY PUBLIC:
$8.4 TRILLION

Source: U.S. Department of Treasury.

a similar leap in the share owed to foreigners, which climbed from 30 percent in 2001 to 46 percent in 2009.

This means that a permanently weaker economy is only the first-order effect Americans will feel from continued drift. Our run as leaders for good in the world will come to an end. It's pretty much an iron rule of history that no one follows a pauper.

At present, we enjoy an unrivaled military status. Our technology is unmatched, our forces regrettably battle-tested, and our spending levels higher than those of the rest of the world's nations put together.

But how long can that last, in a situation of massive and mounting debts? Think about it this way: we are now borrowing the entire defense budget (we've been spending about $700 billion a year on defense while running a deficit of about $1.4 trillion), much of it from the very countries, most notably China, against whom our forces might one day have to be deployed. Fiscal failure will inevitably lead to defense decline.

We like to assert that our world leadership derives from the power of our ideas and from our example. The yearning for freedom and personal autonomy is universal, we say, so the land of its birth will always be admired and respected. As others emulate our system, the world will be better for us all. Democracies will be more peaceful than the autocracies they replace; free citizens will not support wars and militarism. The spread of free market policies will produce expanding trade and greater prosperity for all participants.

But it is far from clear that our Western ideals have appeal in as many quarters as we like to imagine. In Islamic eyes, even as quasi-democratic movements take shape in Muslim countries, we are often viewed as godless, materialistic, and libertine. Robert D. Kaplan, in his book *Monsoon*, writes that progress in Oman "is indeed varied and at odds with some of the ideals of the liberal West.[11] He goes on to write that "In some societies, particularly in the Middle East, democracy is a matter of informal consultation between ruler and ruled, rather than an official process." His point is that other nations are seeking to gain economic progress without also making strides in individual freedom. And he holds up an example of how democracy can undermine prosperity: "Bangladesh illustrates how the kind of government a state has is less important than the degree to which that state is governed—that is, a democracy that cannot control its own people may be worse for human rights than a dictatorship that can."[12]

In the emergent countries of Asia, order, discipline, and an emphasis on the collective good have always been prized over individualism and the chaos that comes with democracy and free markets. Henry Kissinger has written, "Confucianism is essentially hierarchical and elitist . . . Unlike democratic theory . . . Confucianism maintains that truth is objective and can only be discerned by assiduous study and education of which only a rare few are thought to be capable.[13]

Ronald Reagan used to say that an economist is "someone who sees something work in practice and wonders if it would work in theory." To the extent that the American example has been adopted, or that other nations have seen fit to take direction from us, it is because of the way our system has worked in practice, creating extraordinary material wealth of a kind never before imagined. If that falters, and if other approaches to governance seem to be producing more dynamic economic results, there is little reason to believe that our international influence will not diminish in a linear fashion with our declining economic performance.

Indeed, the logic works in the other direction. Viewing the contrast between their own vigorous expansion versus our struggles, Asian nations can only conclude that their traditional cultural and governance principles are being vindicated. Samuel Huntington, writing in 1993, well before the full rise of China was apparent, spotted the "Asian affirmation," and cited figures such as Singapore's Lee Kuan Yew who contrasted "the virtues of Asian, basically Confucian, culture—order, discipline, family responsibility, hard work, collectivism, abstemiousness—to the self-indulgence, sloth, individualism, crime, inferior education, disrespect for authority, and 'mental ossification' responsible for the decline of the West. To compete with the East, it was argued, the United States 'needs to question its fundamental assumptions about its social and political arrangements and, in the process, learn a thing or two from East Asian societies.'"

China has already shown on multiple fronts that American views are of no particular interest to it. This is apparent by almost daily headlines· "China Rejects U.S. Complaints on Its Currency" (*New York Times*), "China Rebuffs U.S. Trade Criticism" (Reuters), "China Rejects U.S. Pressure on Iran Trade Ties" (*International Business Times*)." By late 2010 the disregard was even being displayed in the genteel world of face-to-face diplomacy, as President Obama's calls for more fiscal stimulus actions were dismissed out of hand at a G-20 summit. In early 2011 his directive that Saudi Arabia not intervene in Bahrain was ignored without the courtesy of a reply.

On a November 2010 business trip I took to China and Japan, it seemed each day's papers brought fresh signs that Asia was intent on cutting its own path. The Asian *Wall Street Journal* wrote "has there ever been a major economic summit where a U.S. President and his Treasury Secretary were as thoroughly rebuffed as they were at last week's G-20 meeting in Seoul?" A column by the *Washington Post*'s David Ignatius that appeared in Japan's *Daily Yomiuri*, began with a recitation of "recent disrespect for America: China downgraded its debt rating for American debt. . . . South Korea refused U.S. pressure for a new trade deal; European and Asian nations joined in protesting the Federal Reserve Board's plans to print more money to stimulate growth." ⑭ 245

By now there are bookshelves full of documentation, by authors far more learned than I, that the problem we face is as huge as I've said and as certain as a mathematical proof. If the reader requires any further evidence, if his simple common sense does not tell him that the land of promise we modern Americans have taken for granted is mortally threatened, then I'd be powerless to persuade him.

My goal is a different one, anyway: that is, to challenge the idea that a government of and by the people is incapable of dealing with such a crisis once it has gone this far; to explore the ways in which we can come back from the precipice and renew national preeminence without yielding our freedom or our right to self-governance; and to refute the notion that we have to rethink our "fundamental assumptions about [our] social and political arrangements."

In their warnings to Americans, both *Grant's* and S&P zeroed in on the greatest risk factor of all: the lack of any assurance that the political system of the country is up to the job, that it would address its dangers in time. In a Reuters account, S&P said that the "gigantic deficit and the debt burden" were a "challenge for the government" and that "We don't think these political decisions on tackling the public finances can be put off forever."

Grant's, consistent with its "duty" of honest disclosure, went further: "Elected officials may not take necessary steps to ensure long-term debt sustainability. . . . Sustained decreases in Government expenditures as a percentage of GDP will likely require curbs in either defense, Social Security, or Medicare and Medicaid outlays." In what the editors clearly saw as a dry understatement, they concluded, "Deficit reduction has proven to be difficult historically because of the nature of the U.S. political system."

We have arrived at the moment that the Skeptics so cynically predicted. Our politicians, currying short-term popularity, and counting on the people's ignorance, selfishness, or lack of long-term perspective, have committed us to bills we cannot possibly pay. And while outsiders such as our Asian competitors may assume that our affluence and liberty have made us weak in character, too soft to impose discipline or even modest changes on ourselves, or to insist that our government do so, I believe there is still hope for us. The challenge we face is difficult, but it is not impossible.

One thing is sure, if we as citizens are not up to it, our politicians will never be. My money's on us, but it's fair to acknowledge that the jury is still out. Once again, *exitus in dubio est.*

CHAPTER 3

The Great Inversion

Sometimes by brute force of arms, sometimes by claims of divine right, despots through the ages have dominated the lives of those within their reach. People have schemed and groveled to become part of their courts, as the best route to riches for themselves. Tyrants have gone by various titles, their tyranny has taken different forms, but in all cases government has been at the top of society, with the lives of others subordinated to its demands.

The United States started from the opposite presumption. Our Founders proclaimed to a startled world that individuals are endowed by their Creator with inalienable rights, meaning that no government can strip them away. Governments, they said, are called into existence, and are legitimate only to the extent that they protect and nurture these rights. In this society, power lies in the hands of the people, at whose discretion governments can be changed or overthrown if necessary.

That's why the shot at Concord in April 1775 was heard around the world. Countless shots had been exchanged among humans throughout history, mostly at the order of tyrants, occasionally in rebellion against them. But never had shots so emphatically announced that the days of the tyrant's domination were through. Henceforth, the people were the boss.

Seen this way, politics and governmental service are what members of a free country undertake to make sure that liberty, the paramount value, survives. The freedom of property, to own the fruits of one's labor or ingenuity; the freedom of assembly, and to form private associations of any and all kinds—these freedoms are the heart of society, and a government is only as good as the protection and encouragement it gives to them.

The early Americans venerated the ethic of Cincinnatus, an aristocratic Roman who in the fifth century B.C. left his farm during a crisis to serve as dictator of Rome only to resign his position and return home after he had done his job. George Washington's greatest acts of leadership involved a similar disinterest in power. Instead of seeking high office, he resigned his military commission after the Revolution and returned to *his* farm. Later, he declined to seek a third term as president, preferring instead once again to return to Mount Vernon. This sent a message to his fellow Americans and the world that there would be no monarchy, no permanent or hereditary government in the United States.

For many years after Washington, it was politically unacceptable for presidential and other political aspirants even to campaign openly. To do so was to suggest an unseemly personal ambition. Public office was about serving the people, not one's own interest, and one should not thrust one's self forward but should await the people's call. Washington's two-term precedent lasted for a century and a half, and was quickly amended into our Constitution after its only violation, by Franklin Roosevelt.

We have had long-time or even lifelong politicians, but in general, over the sweep of our history, political careers have been short. In the first century of our republic, a typical election saw more than 40 percent of the seats in the House change hands by an incumbent either voluntarily retiring or being defeated in his bid for reelection. Today, turnover in Congress is a fraction of that. Many states—including my own until the 1970s—limited governors to one term. Virginia still bars governors from serving two consecutive terms. Where statutes did not limit the amount of time a politician could serve in office, vigorous competition often did. Incumbents have been routinely turned out of office in our history. In 1800 our second president, John Adams, became the first to lose reelection. He also saw his party lose control of Congress that year. Fame, celebrity, or past achievements have often been no protection. Davy Crockett was defeated for reelection to his seat in Congress in 1834 after clashing with President Andrew Jackson. After his defeat, he uttered words about his Tennessee constituents that other defeated incumbents might appreciate: "I'm going to Texas, and they can go to hell."

For much of our history, nonelected public officials have also had short tenures. The so-called spoils system that took root in the administration of Andrew Jackson pushed out workers hired by a past administration and replaced them with people who owed their jobs to the new president. As a consequence, those in office were not always the most honest or competent. But then again, the stakes were low. For most of our two and a quarter centuries, government was small in comparison with the rest of society. (Federal spending typically equaled less than 5 percent of GDP, with exceptions for periods of war, until FDR's New Deal in the 1930s. Since the conclusion of World War II, federal spending has hovered closer to 20 percent of GDP, sometimes more and sometimes less.) It mattered more to national success that the railroads and banks, rather than the Interior Department, were run well.

Given these circumstances, government employees were underpaid and vulnerable to mistreatment. A change of administration generally meant a wholesale firing of workers, regardless of performance. In Indiana the old patronage system lasted longer than almost anywhere, well into the 1980s. As a young City Hall intern in 1970, I recall watching the cigar box being passed around in local government offices so employees could maintain their membership in the "2 Percent Club" by "voluntarily" donating 2 percent of their meager pay to whichever party was in power, thereby maintaining their jobs.

The Progressive Era of a century ago was in part a reaction to this overly politicized system. Reformers in both parties pushed for change. Over time, government employees in the federal departments and most states were granted what amounted to tenure in their jobs and were paid through a step-and-grade system that handed out raises regardless of performance. In large part, job security was thought to be an offset to the low pay most public employees received.

In exchange for tenure in their jobs, public employees were not subject to the same labor-management relationships common in the private sector. Calvin Coolidge, who as governor of Massachusetts in 1919 broke a Boston police strike and then refused to allow the striking officers to be rehired, explained why he drew such a hard line: "There is no right to strike against the public safety by anybody, anywhere, anytime." Labor giant George Meany also saw the public sector as different from the private sector, remarking in the 1950s, "It is impossible to bargain collectively with the government." Franklin Roosevelt once sounded a similar note: "The process of collective bargaining, as usually understood, cannot be transplanted into the public service." Government workers were there to serve the public, not themselves.

In 1962, President John F. Kennedy launched a new era when he issued Executive Order 10988 authorizing collective bargaining across the federal government. Within a couple of decades, public-sector union membership soared. In 1962 just under 14 percent of all government workers, local, state, and federal, were members of a union. Today, that figure tops 36 percent. That change brought with it a huge shift in the relative economic status between government employees and their ostensible employers: other taxpayers.

Now the traditional concept of public service has been stood on its head. With almost no one noticing, government workers rose from underpaid public servants to the position of a privileged elite. They are paid higher salaries and given vastly more generous fringe benefits than the average taxpayer. They are guaranteed sometimes bizarrely lavish pensions when they "retire," which they are usually able to do after about twenty years. Often these retirees will turn around and start a second career in the public sector, for which they will earn a second pension (a process cheerfully referred to as "double dipping"). And they almost never, ever lose a job for lousy performance or any other reason.

Ronald Reagan once joked, "A taxpayer is someone who goes to work for the federal government without having to take the civil service exam." The jest is less funny now that, including benefits, the average public employee in the federal government earns on average $123,049 a year— twice that of the typical worker in the private sector whose income taxes on their annual salary (averaging $61,051) provide that government worker's paycheck) 𝟤𝟦𝟧

State and local employees are moving similarly ahead of those they serve. In Indiana the average public school teacher outearns the average private-sector worker by 22 percent; when benefits are counted, the gap widens significantly. This, of course, is for a 186-day work year, compared to the private-sector norm of 240 days; those school employees who choose to work during their two and a half months off in the summer can expand the earnings differential still further.

In New Jersey, state workers have long enjoyed lavish benefits that far outstrip what's available at for-profit companies. Garden State employees didn't pay a dime toward their health insurance until 2007, and teachers enjoyed free care until Governor Chris Christie came into office. In total, the state has promised health benefits to more than six hundred thousand current and retired government workers. And here's the kicker: the state hasn't set aside any money to pay for these benefits. New Jersey has been on a pay-as-you-go system, so unless reform comes soon, taxpayers will be expected to foot a nearly $69 billion tab in the coming decades to cover already promised benefits, the largest of any state.[2]   245

In California some public servants long ago figured out how to get the taxpaying public to serve them. Bruce Malkenhorst, Sr., is probably the most "successful" at this. In March 2011, the *Washington Post* noted that he is collecting a government pension that tops $43,000 a month, or nearly $520,000 a year. His benefits are so enriching because he is actually collecting six pensions from various jobs he held for the city of Vernon. In total, there are nearly fifteen thousand retirees collecting more than $100,000 a year in pensions from the California Public Employees' Retirement System (CalPERS).[3]   245

The nation passed a meaningful tipping point in 2009, when for the first time the number of union members working for government surpassed the number of union members working in the entire private sector. The movement begun by people such as Samuel Gompers and Eugene V. Debs to protect the coal miner, the steelworker, and the sweatshop seamstress now belongs to white-collar types who live off taxes paid by coal miners, steelworkers, and their modern counterparts in the productive economy.

Often the unions have captured huge numbers of new dues payers without the nuisance of secret balloting, or balloting of any kind. Collaborating politicians simply sign over the workers' rights by agreeing to recognize the unions, and the contract they sign takes care of the risk that workers might not want to go along with paying compulsory dues. The state simply withdraws the dues from workers' pay and gives it to the union. This is a whole lot more effective than the old-fashioned approach of gaining workers' approval by winning an organizing election.

A more brazen organizing technique occurred in Michigan in 2006. It swept into a union unsuspecting mom-and-pop day care operators who served parents receiving state subsidies. The day care operators learned what happened when they received letters informing them that the state had signed a contract with a new company, the Michigan Home Based Child Care Council, to whom the operators would now be subcontractors. The new company was a fiction, a shell company created by the state to give unions an employer to organize against. The move succeeded in sweeping thirty-four thousand workers into a union organized through a mail-in election that many of the workers later said they knew nothing about but that coincidentally drew heavy union turnout and support. Patrick J. Wright followed the issue closely as the director of the Mackinac Center Legal Foundation. He wrote an op-ed for the *Wall Street Journal* with Michael D. Jahr of the Mackinac Center for Public Policy pointing out that the blueprint for this type of unionization drive was hatched in California, where it was quickly squelched but nonetheless spread to nearly two dozen other states.[4] 245

With unionism comes political power, and with that power, still more of an upending of the original relationship between the people and those who work for them. In a now-familiar cycle of corruption, dues are forcibly withheld from the pay of public employees and funneled into union coffers. After the cost of the unions' bureaucracies are covered, much of the rest is poured into political activity.

Through the raw power of coercive dues, government unions amass staggering amounts of money, which they use to elect shills for their demands for ever higher pay, benefits, and pensions, and to intimidate their opponents. On the eve of the 2010 elections, federal disclosures revealed that the biggest spending interest group in the country was the American Federation of State, County, and Municipal Employees (AFSCME), which had laid out $87.5 million to support various political campaigns. The union's top political operative, Larry Scanlon, proclaimed, "We're the big dog.[5] 245

But not by much. In fourth and fifth place, at $44 million and $40 million respectively, came the Service Employees International Union (SEIU) and the National Education Association (NEA), bringing the total of these three government unions to more than $170 million. Said Mr. Scanlon, "We're spending big. And our members are damn happy it's big— it's their money." Not really. It was extracted from members' pay with or without their permission, and before that extracted from taxpayers' pockets, without anyone asking if they approved of its use for political activity.

A dwindling but noisy lobby continues to agitate for public financing of political campaigns, on the theory that using tax dollars will somehow make politics "cleaner." It seems to have escaped the notice of these advocates that we already have public financing of campaigns, at least of a partial and one-sided type. As we've seen, dollars are collected from taxpayers and paid to government employees. Then, whether the employee likes it or not, a portion of these dollars are transferred to the union in the form of compulsory dues. From there tens of millions of these dollars are used to fund campaigns of the compliant. Of course, instead of reducing special interest influence, this "public financing" magnifies it, and benefits only one set of interests. Politicians who get into the ring with the union monster seemingly always come away losers, usually by knockout. Even Governor Arnold Schwarzenegger found out who the real Terminators are, at a time when he was still personally popular in California. In 2005 he proposed a series of ballot initiatives to trim the power of government unions. The unions spent $100 million or so on TV ads and other political activity and crushed the effort. Neither the reforms nor Schwarzenegger as a reformist governor were heard from again.

My team saw firsthand the nakedness of government union power politics during my reelection year in 2008, when two Democratic aspirants faced off in a primary. The SEIU, which had essentially zero members in our state, public or private, gave large amounts of money to one, while the United Auto Workers (UAW) and AFSCME, which did represent Indiana state employees, backed the other.

After the SEIU-supported candidate won the primary, the union gave her $850,000 in a single check. This was the largest donation given to a single political candidate in Indiana history, and the SEIU promised it would do "whatever it takes" to help the candidate win the general election. Despite their status as core Democratic auxiliary groups, the UAW and AFSCME hung back for months, finally chipping in a fraction of what they had customarily given to Democratic gubernatorial candidates.

It was clear what had happened. The SEIU expected that after the election, the new Democratic governor would allow it to unionize state employees and collect dues payments. Despite the immensity of their contribution, SEIU stood to reap a large and immediate return. Total dues harvested from Indiana state workers, at just under 2 percent of wage income, would have amounted to several million dollars per year, with zero cost to collect it, as the state would simply subtract it from worker paychecks. There aren't many investments that pay off that well or that quickly.

Of course, we spoiled the party by winning the election. But placing big bets like this is savvy strategy for the unions, which have to elect only one compliant governor out of five or ten to enjoy a gigantic payoff. It beats the squash out of having to get the workers' support and permission.

This deal was possible in the first place only because I had struck down the collective bargaining agreement in place when our insurgency broke the Democratic grip on the state's governor's office in 2004. When I reflect on how critical the decision to end collective bargaining for public employees was to a series of government reforms it made possible, I frown recalling how close I came to ducking it.

We ran for office on a highly specific set of some seventy reforms that ranged from revamping economic policy to closing ethical loopholes that invited corruption to cutting spending and restoring the state to solvency. I was eager to launch into this program on the first day. The final words of my inaugural, before a jubilant and hopeful crowd of ten thousand at our Fairgrounds Coliseum, were "Now, if you'll excuse me, I have to go to work," and I headed downtown to begin.

By then I had decided to strike down Governor Evan Bayh's 1989 executive order handing over our state employees and their dues to the unions. I ordinarily don't dither over decisions, but I hesitated over that one. I had visions of our first weeks being dominated by "Daniels Hates

Workers" placards and angry protests that would make it more difficult for me to enact sober-minded reforms. Could I defer the decision until after the four-month legislative session, giving us a better shot to effect our reform plans? Could I split the difference by freeing the workers in some departments but not all? I confess that I looked for a way around taking the full, bold stroke.

But many conversations with people familiar with the innards of state government convinced me that we could never undertake the transformation we had in mind with the 160 pages of contracts that were then in place. The agreements were so specific and dense that, under their stipulations, we could barely move a photocopier without union permission. As for paying the best workers more, moving the worst workers out, reorganizing departments, or outsourcing services to private companies, that was simply impossible.

So, after ceremonially delivering a stack of proposed bills to the legislature, signing executive orders implementing ethics reforms and other campaign pledges, and visiting our environmental management agency with some pro-jobs guidance, I turned to the matter of the unions.

At about 2:00 P.M. on my second day in office, I signed Executive Order 05-14, ending Indiana's sixteen-year era of compulsory government unionism. As a courtesy, I walked to the nearby state office building and personally told the UAW and AFSCME leadership of the decision. I returned to my office, pulled the figurative covers over my head, and waited for the worst. And then ...

Nothing happened. No protests, no placards, no planted media stories of fear and resentment among the workers. The only result of the action was that our appointees, most of them fresh-faced idealists with no previous public experience, were free to go to work transforming agency after broken agency.

Oh, there was one reaction. Within a few months, 90 percent of state workers stopped paying union dues. Once free to do so, they made the rational decision to award themselves a 2 percent pay raise.

In 2011, when new Wisconsin governor Scott Walker attempted the same change we had effected, he touched off exactly the type of riot I had worried about back in 2005. No special interest, once it has achieved a position of advantage through political power, gives it up without a struggle. In Wisconsin, New Jersey, and other states, we have seen the ferocity with which today's richest and most powerful special interest, government itself, defends its privileges.

But as Walker's efforts evidenced, our actions put Indiana at the cutting edge of what later turned into a national movement. Starting in 2010 with the heroic efforts of New Jersey governor Chris Christie, and then in a number of states as new administrations in Wisconsin, Ohio, and elsewhere confronted their own bankruptcy challenges, government collective bargaining has come under critical scrutiny. Most of the attention has been on the costs of runaway union control, high pay, and lavish pensions.

In Indiana our actions were only secondarily about finances. It is true that the freedom to restructure departments, consolidate functions, and so on saved Hoosier taxpayers tons of money. But the principal motive, and equally important gains, came in the transformation of state services. There simply was no way we could have revolutionized our Bureau of Motor Vehicles (more on this later), our state parks, our prison system, or so many other services if we had been hogtied by the old union agreement.

One of the most important changes this new freedom allowed involved the protection of children, one of the few literally life-and-death duties state government has, and one that Indiana was failing miserably at when my administration entered office. By almost every measure, Indiana had one of the worst child welfare systems in the country. Rates of child fatality and abuse in the system were shockingly high, and the average caseworker was overwhelmed with twice as many cases as the national average. There was tremendously high turnover among caseworkers, and incoming workers were rarely trained properly. At the same time, we had one of the poorest records anywhere of collecting child support for single parents. Only one of every two dollars in support ordered by a court was ever delivered to a single mom (or, occasionally, dad) in Indiana.

First alerted to the problems by a compelling series of articles in the *Indianapolis Star*, I pledged as a candidate to reform child protective services. On my first day in office, I took steps to do that by severing child protective services from the large, ineffective, and fraud-ridden social services conglomerate in which it had been buried. I recruited a long-serving juvenile judge, one of the nation's most respected experts on the protection of children, to run a new Department of Child Services. I charged him with two jobs: to vastly improve our child welfare system and to increase the number of single parents receiving the child support they were entitled to.

Six years later our child welfare system was winning national awards from private evaluators, such as the Annie E. Casey Foundation, and from the same federal Department of Health and Human Services that was preparing to penalize the state for maintaining an atrocious system before we took office. Today, 60 percent of single parents who are owed child support in the state receive it. That's a significant improvement—although it is not nearly enough, so I continually press for more progress.

Fixing the department required making thousands of organizational, process, and personnel changes. Hundreds of workers either were reassigned or, in some cases, dismissed for poor performance. The agency of 2011 looks totally different, and operates in a totally different way from its predecessor. If every one of these steps had required union consultation or signoff, as the old agreement provided, we would still be trying to take some of the earliest actions.

The vulnerable children of Indiana could not wait on a ponderous process built to safeguard union prerogatives and keep union dues flowing by slowing and impeding change. Ending public-sector collective bargaining, and sending it back to the private sector—where champions of organized labor such as Samuel Gompers, Fiorello La Guardia, FDR, and George Meany all agreed it belongs—is at least as much about delivering government that works as it is about preventing raids on the public treasury.

In 2011 we extended the liberation of state workers by passing a bill that will require legislative permission before they are ever again pressed into union membership. No governor will be able simply to sign over employees, and part of their wages, as repayment for political support. Now Indiana is unlikely to go the way of other states that have abused their taxpayers and mortgaged their futures through unconscionable public employee wages, benefits, and pensions. But Indiana is the exception. Across the country, state after state remains trapped in a situation in which public "servants" enjoy a standard of living, and a privileged status, well beyond that of those they supposedly serve.

Who's in Charge Here?

As troubling as it is, the explosion of government unionism and the emergence of government employees as the new privileged class are just a reflection of a more fundamental question Americans face: Who's in charge here? Should we exchange our traditional view of public service for a new conception, one in which we accept that the complexities and unfairness of life require that we cede to public authorities many of our historic powers of decision making? Instead of the public sector existing to protect and promote private action and private institutions, should the norm be that government makes all the big calls?

Americans who always thought that "public service" meant that the government works for them must now wonder if they had it wrong. People who have salaries, benefits, and protections against layoffs that far exceed anything in the private sector are now issuing orders to them and making all kinds of choices for them: where and when they can build, what equipment they can add to their businesses, where their children can go to school, what kind of health insurance they must carry, what kind of credit card they may use, and so on.

The new supremacy of the public sector was underscored by the Obama administration's "stimulus" package. Supposedly intended to get America working again, the money the administration spent did almost nothing to boost productive employment, but instead showered resources on preserving government jobs. Infrastructure spending, thought at the outset to be the focus of the program, wound up being a small fraction of the money spent. Interesting ideas, such as Dr. Martin Feldstein's proposal to devote much of the money to rebuilding depleted defense inventories, which might have funneled funds into private companies—were ignored.

Amazingly, as private employment plummeted in the recession, government jobs grew. Since January 2009, nearly 2 million jobs in the private sector have disappeared. Meanwhile, at the same time, the federal payroll has hit an all-time high. The surge in government employment can easily be seen in the suburbs surrounding Washington, D.C., which are awash not just in government jobs but in jobs for government contractors, too. As cities around the country struggled, Washington became a boom town. In the federal setting, job security is almost absolute, as infinitesimal percentages of workers there are dismissed in any given year. Moreover, it is almost impossible for a government employee not to receive a pay increase. A March 2011 study by the *Federal Times* examined official Office of Personnel Management data and reported that only 1 of every 1,698 U.S. government employees was denied a raise for performance reasons in 2009.

The unfairness of such a system to taxpayers is matched by its unfairness to the countless hardworking federal employees, and they know it. As the *Federal Times* reported, "Surveys of federal workers consistently show sizable dissatisfaction at how poor performers are held accountable. In the government's 2010 work-force survey, less than 31 percent of respondents felt their work unit took steps to deal with a poor performer . . . almost 42 percent said the opposite was true. Indiana's bell curve performance pay system has declined to raise pay for the 5 to 10 percent least diligent and effective workers, while delivering unprecedentedly high increases to the best of the best.

In state governments, the recent recession finally did bring some layoffs, but that was only after an enormous expansion of government payrolls in the preceding years. Total government employment in most states remains well above the level of a decade ago. So, it is clear, the government unions' political muscle has paid off handsomely by insulating its members nicely against the economic storm to which their neighbors were so cruelly exposed.

Watching the continued expansion of government, and its privileged, preferred status even in severe economic times, Americans must now wonder who's working for whom? That question also has its roots in the Progressive era of a century ago.

Beneath the surface of the Progressives' civil service reforms was a premise that went beyond protecting vulnerable employees against the vagaries of politics. It was the assumption of the superiority of elites, the ability of "experts" to supervise and direct the affairs of Americans better than the people and their chosen representatives could manage them for themselves.

This antidemocratic impulse has contended with the tradition of free institutions for the last century, with surges forward in the 1930s under Roosevelt and the 1960s through the Great Society expansions. It was countered most forcefully in the 1980s, during what some remember as the Reagan Revolution but which today's Big Government advocates smugly refer to as the "Reagan Interruption."

Beginning with the New Deal, federal departments have proliferated like termites. The presidential cabinet has doubled from eleven during FDR's day to today's fifteen cabinet secretaries and another seven individuals who hold cabinet rank, such as the president's chief of staff. The Departments of Energy and Education were invented in the 1970s; 245 the Department of Homeland Security in the aftermath of the 2001 terrorist attacks. The Environmental Protection Agency was created in 1970 and its administrator subsequently given cabinet rank. If this keeps up, pretty soon someone will have to knock out a wall and enlarge the West Wing Cabinet Room.

But that's only a part of the phenomenon. A host of sub-cabinet agencies, with names such as the Bureau of Land Management, the Center for Medicare and Medicaid Services, and the Federal Energy Regulatory Commission have sprung up as well. Depending on its focus, each has tremendous power to shape land use, health care, or energy policy in ways that directly impact Americans. Through their administrative rule making authority, sub-cabinet agencies have the ability to effectively make law via the arcane processes of the Administrative Procedure Act. (Today there are 82,589 pages in the Federal Register; the first copy, printed in 1936, contained 16.)

Here is the experts' ultimate playground: the chance to make new rules for the private sector, with no effective oversight by Congress. (Congress did pass the Congressional Review Act—as part of the Small Business Regulatory Enforcement Fairness Act—in 1996, which in theory enables it to overrule agency edicts. But in its entire history the act has been used only once.) Agency decisions are also virtually immune from judicial scrutiny based on their substance. The law basically permits the courts to step in only where an agency has failed to dot its procedural *i*'s by being "arbitrary or capricious."

You might say, but when the federal bossiness gets excessive, can't the people elect a new administration committed to restraining or rolling back the interventions? Not so fast. Large numbers, often majorities, in Congress have battled to keep the bureaucracies free from meaningful supervision. Once an agency is licensed by Congress to act in a given area, courts have generally given it free rein. So, increasingly, the bastions of our new bosses have been fortified against even the control of the president, to whom the agencies in theory report.

In the 1980s the Reagan administration tried to rein in lawmaking by the unelected by forming a new Office of Information and Regulatory Affairs (OIRA) within the Office of Management and Budget. OIRA was given the charge to review and reject, or order changes in, rule makings that failed to demonstrate greater benefits than costs. When I was asked to head the OMB in 2001, the chance to direct OIRA was one reason I accepted the job.

Since President Reagan's 1981 order requiring a tabulation of new regulations, some 114,000 (not a misprint) have been issued. Well over a thousand of them have been found to cost consumers at least $100 million each, and the total regulatory bill, a hidden tax, is now estimated at somewhere between $5,000 and $7,000 per year for every household in the country. Yet very few of these decrees have ever been subjected to any real analysis to see if they produce benefits justifying this burden.

What could make more simple sense than to ensure that a given action's benefits outweigh its costs? Who else but the people's elected leadership should make final calls about new laws that often will cost private citizens billions of dollars?

Under the expert direction of Dr. John Graham, whom I recruited from the Harvard Department of Public Health, OIRA in the early "zeroes" (someone's slang for the decade 2001–10) made a concerted effort to bring reason to regulation. Dr. Graham laid down some highly sensible principles for lawmaking by the unelected. For example, not only did a new rule have to demonstrate a favorable benefit-to-cost ratio, but it also had to contain sunset provisions that provided for reevaluation after a certain number of years. Dr. Graham also stipulated that, before creating a new rule, an agency should search for an existing one that may only need to be repealed or modernized.

Reasonable as these notions are, and moderate as Dr. Graham was in his approach to his job, his tenure was marked by the same contentiousness that has afflicted everyone attempting to rein in the runaway regulatory machine. But at least Dr. Graham was able to win Senate confirmation. Several previous nominees were blocked from even taking up their duties, by legislators who believed that any restraint on "expert" government power was unacceptable.

So the regulatory juggernaut has proceeded in almost undiminished fashion, even in those presidencies that sought to slow it down. When a presidency arrived that believed more strongly than any of its predecessors in government by experts, the stage was set for open season on liberty.

Fiat Government

The year 2009 brought a new administration to Washington, born of recession, weariness with unpopular wars, the romance of history in the candidacy of a minority for president, and the simple tendency of voters to rotate leadership between the parties. What did not play a role was any popular demand for a larger, more intrusive federal government. But that's what we got.

The door opened by the crisis was too good to waste, to paraphrase a close confidante of the president, so Barack Obama and his congressional allies embarked on a blitzkrieg assault on free markets and free institutions unlike anything FDR ever dreamed of. A campaign of shock and awe statism attempted, with almost unbroken success, to overwhelm the defenders of freedom before any meaningful opposition could be mustered.

Entire industries such as housing were effectively nationalized. In the fall of 2008, both Fannie Mae and Freddie Mac, government-sponsored enterprises, were taken over by the feds and placed in "conservatorship." John Lanchester, in his book *I.O.U.*, pegged the takeover as "the largest nationalization in the history of the world." And it was just the start. With Fannie and Freddie in federal hands and Obama in the White House, Congress passed a $275 billion housing bailout (on top of a $787 billion stimulus package) in February 2009. The following month, the administration launched a public-private $1 trillion "toxic" asset program, which enlisted the U.S. Treasury and the Federal Deposit Insurance Corporation in an effort to remove bad loans from bank balance sheets. By midyear 2010, the federal government, through Ginnie Mae (another GSE) as well as Fannie and Freddie, was guaranteeing nearly 97 percent of all new mortgages being written.

The U.S. government also took direct ownership of private corporations. In "bailing out" huge financial companies such as AIG, the insurance giant, and several of the largest banks, the government took large equity positions. The private student loan industry, which had been a fast-growing segment of the student loan market and a vital resource for students facing rising tuition rates, was effectively legislated out of existence in favor of a government monopoly. And, in the biggest conquest of all, the health care sector, which constitutes some 18 percent of the entire economy, was turned into a federally regulated utility by the president's health care "reform."

One of the most egregious examples of government expansion into the private sector involved the failing auto industry. Chrysler and GM, represented by the administration's UAW supporters, received massive infusions of cash, but continued shrinking and losing market share to about the degree they probably would have in a conventional bankruptcy. The administration not only took stock in Chrysler and GM for itself, but it also handed huge amounts of ownership to its union cronies. The UAW's retiree health plan received 55 percent of Chrysler's stock as an outright gift, worth some $4.5 billion. When no one else wanted the company, the administration handed control (and 20 percent ownership, with the ability to increase that ownership by hitting certain benchmarks) to

Fiat of Italy, an ironic move to benefit a union that regularly bashes "globalization."(*)

In this episode—we might call it "Fiat government"—we saw not merely the use of political power to reward allies, but also a new willingness to stop at nothing, not even the rule of law, to dictate private-sector outcomes. In its determination to bail out its buddies, the administration bulldozed centuries of unambiguous, black letter law safeguarding the rights of secured creditors. In order to hand over so much value to the union, and to evade creditors' right to demand a formal reorganization process, the government simply announced its intention to disregard all those old-fashioned rules and, in effect, confiscate the property of creditors whose claims on Chrysler's assets should have come first and to give that property to union and other allies.

At first, shocked investors protested loudly. Well, not all of them. The bigger investors, which had received money through the federal government's Troubled Asset Relief Program (TARP), quickly agreed to take a large haircut on their investments. But a smaller group calling itself the Committee of Chrysler Non-Tarp Lenders dug in its heels and insisted that a bankruptcy judge, not the administration, make decisions about the company's future. The administration responded by attacking the resisters. Obama called them "speculators" and said, "I don't stand with those who held out when everybody else is making sacrifices."

Intimidating phone calls were also placed from the White House to money managers, who one by one submitted. The White House "car czar," Steven Rattner, who led this campaign, tried one such call to me, diplomatically suggesting that the politically smart course for a governor with Chrysler facilities in his state was to go along with the deal. (He later paid $6 million to settle charges that he engaged in an alleged "pay-to-play" scheme to win business from a New York pension fund.)

After private investors capitulated under this pressure, Indiana remained the sole holdout. Among the losers in, as we Hoosiers termed it, the "Chrysler cramdown" were two pension funds that serve our

---

* In June 2011, Fiat completed its acquisition of majority control of Chrysler at a total cost of $1.85 billion.

retired teachers and state workers. Those pension funds had invested $19 million in Chrysler and, under the administration's plan, were going to be fleeced of about $6 million they would otherwise have gotten in a traditional bankruptcy. Coincidentally, I was sitting at a table of highly impressive people, all more erudite than I, discussing the very topic of the Obama blitzkrieg—as I recall, I had just tossed out the phrase "shock and awe statism"—when the time for decision came. I received a phone call from Indiana's treasurer, Richard Mourdock, who said the deadline for filing a lawsuit to stop the cramdown was just hours away.

Despite the complete clarity of the law saying that secured creditors such as our pension funds came first in the event of insolvency, our attorneys could provide no assurance of success. What court would have the temerity to block the federal government at the last minute, amid loud if unprovable assertions that a standard bankruptcy process would lead to terrible business losses rippling through the entire automotive supply chain and beyond?

We had little reason to believe we would succeed. We also knew that filing such a lawsuit would draw attacks from not only political adversaries but also well-intentioned citizens who could see Chrysler's distress but not the illegality, unfairness, or long-term danger to commerce of the administration's actions. My main concern was the loss to our pensioners, but the last point was important, too. What would happen to credit markets if lenders who previously thought their investments were safe even if something went wrong now had to consider the chance that politicians might step in and give their principal to some politically favored party, leaving them with the table scraps?

Mourdock and I, as trustees of the pension plans, decided that submission was just not an acceptable course. We authorized the lawsuit and, with the help of cut rates from attorneys incensed about the principles being violated, pursued it even after the courts allowed the cramdown to go through.

Indiana's retirees never got their $6 million back, but our resistance was not totally fruitless. A fascinating bit of legal history was made months later, when, almost surreptitiously, the U.S. Supreme Court, on December 14, 2009, announced that the Chrysler case would be accorded no precedential value. The rights of secured creditors were secure once more.

In the lower court that first declared it would not be bound by the Chrysler case, the judge likened Indiana's efforts to "the little man in Tiananmen Square when the tanks rolled in." The tyranny here was more benign, but the government's disdain for law was pronounced nonetheless. Without question American creditors were entitled to protections their government dictatorially stripped away. So the question remains: Who works for whom?

President Alinsky

The Obama administration's answer to that question can be found in its actions. It is no accident that the sum total of its policies have padded the government and protected it at the expense of the private sector. The compulsively hostile attitude members of the administration hold toward business and individual liberty reveals their fundamental theory of government: "You work for us, or at our sufferance, and don't you ever forget it." Not only are their constant public deprecations of business and the Americans who comprise it, their rhetorical and substantive attacks, unfair and insulting, but they threaten to stunt our abilities to make decisions for ourselves and for our economy for years to come.

Despite showy photo ops and tête-à-têtes with business leaders, the president and his colleagues have from the outset ridiculed whole industries, specific companies, and individuals. Health insurers, pharmaceutical manufacturers, oil companies and other energy producers, and of course Wall Street financial firms have all had their day in the barrel. When the U.S. Chamber of Commerce began to argue against various presidential policies, the president personally led his minions in public attacks on the organization itself and its president, Tom Donohue.

To some extent we can view this as a product of the president's tactical training in the Saul Alinsky school of radicalism. Alinsky, the author of the book *Rules for Radicals*, was openly hateful about the free enterprise system and those involved in it, and he is famous for preaching the doctrine of personal attack. His acolytes, including President Obama, who proudly acknowledges being one, were taught that demonization of an opponent is the basis of victory, and that any capitalist is fair game.

Especially revealing is the pejorative manner in which those who believe that the public works for the government use *p*-words such as *private*, *privatization*, and *profit*. In an almost reflexive fashion, our would-be overseers treat as illegitimate the private economic activity on which the nation's success depends. We can see it in politics. Nancy Pelosi let slip her disdain for private enterprise during the health care debate in 2009 when she said on PBS's *NewsHour* [12] that insurance companies were making "immoral profits" and therefore needed to come in for a drubbing of new taxes and mandates. Our efforts to privatize government services met a similar disdain in Indiana. In 2010, perhaps echoing Pelosi, state speaker of the house Pat Bauer called on the federal government to launch an investigation into WellPoint for having the brass to raise the cost of its health insurance in the state. Actually, he was a consistent critic, attacking us for outsourcing welfare services and bringing in private companies to help run our prisons, among other things. He said my administration was putting "profit before people."

That is, of course, perhaps the most shopworn political catchphrase of our times and is meant to imply that those who seek financial gain for themselves or their businesses are heartless wretches who remorselessly exploit others. It ignores one of the most basic facts of economic life: if no one makes a profit, no one has a job. Worse yet, it sneeringly deprecates the genuine altruism that motivates most business owners, the gratification they derive from seeing their innovations, their hard work, and the capital they attract create jobs and opportunities for . . . people.

Arthur C. Brooks, a social scientist and president of the American Enterprise Institute, has done fascinating work on what truly increases social happiness. It turns out that hard work and the belief that it is possible to climb up the economic ladder play a major role in determining an individual's happiness and are a basis for his motivation [13] In refuting John Edwards and other Democrats who have talked about "two Americas" and complain that rising income inequality leads to public distrust and conflict, Brooks concludes that if that were true, a deepening unhappiness over the past forty years would show up in social statistics. But the statistics show the number has remained essentially the same. However, "happiness does rise if people believe that their families have a chance of improving their standard of living," he wrote in the Manhattan Institute's *City Journal* in 2007. In a measure of happiness, "That belief is worth 12 percentage points in the likelihood of being 'very happy.'" What Brooks's work suggests is that efforts to equalize income are actually counterproductive at increasing social contentment or raising living standards to the extent that they curtail new opportunities and human freedom. In other words, creating a better life for oneself and for others is a primary motivator in our economy.

We are currently led by those who sincerely believe that free individuals, acting in concert as businesses or investors, cannot be trusted to produce satisfactory social outcomes. They must be viewed with suspicion lest they do injury to themselves or others. In this view of the world, life's highest calling is not to produce wealth that creates opportunities for us all, but rather to safeguard hapless and defenseless Americans from those who do.

Again and again, President Obama has revealed his disdain for those who choose lives of private enterprise. In 2009–10, as he advanced his extreme agenda of expanding federal domination over the private economy, he selected what seemed a scapegoat of the week. Entire industries, specific companies, and even individuals were singled out for condemnation. But in a State of the Union Address, he took this scorn for the for-profit world a step further by noting his admiration for those who eschew careers in the crass, ugly world of private enterprise and dedicate themselves instead to the morally superior world of government. In that speech, he proposed forgiving the student loans of college graduates who dedicated their lives to working in the nonprofit or government world. First Lady Michelle Obama spoke to a similar idea during a 2008 visit to Zanesville, Ohio, saying, "We left corporate America, which is a lot of what we're asking young people to do.... Don't go into corporate America. You know, become teachers. Work for the community. Be social workers. Be a nurse. Those are the careers that we need, and we're encouraging our young people to do that. [M]ake that choice, as we did, to move out of the money-making industry into the helping industry."

I doubt the First Couple ever contemplated how disparaging such remarks sound to the millions of young people who are aspiring to lives in the for-profit sector. I'm sure they never contemplated how economically foolish this advice is for the nation a president is supposed to lead. After all, where exactly is the money to pay all those teachers, social workers, and community activists supposed to come from?

Setting aside the moral hauteur of the president's outlook, his proposal is exactly backward from a practical standpoint. If we are going to start forgiving student loans, we should start with those held by graduates most likely to generate new inventions, businesses, and jobs, and the wealth that alone can pay for the next generation's college tuition. If our best young minds all enter government or the nonprofit world, soon there will be far less wealth available to support both government and nonprofits.

Ironically, no one needs the tax revenue a thriving private sector produces more than those who wish to spend additional trillions through government, but this reality never seems to occur to such people. The worst problem of the statist position, whether one feels attracted to it or not, is that in the real world it is totally self-defeating. The recessionary economy of the last couple of years led to a severe drop in contributions to the nonprofit sector. Another simple rule: no profits, no nonprofits. Those who have nothing left after paying their bills have nothing to donate to nonprofits. The president and his ilk seem not to have mastered a basic fact of life known to every Hoosier 4-H'er: when the cow dies, the milk stops.

Faced with a willful president and his overwhelmingly supportive congressional majorities, many pillars of the private sector initially succumbed to the 2009 blitzkrieg. Big-business groups such as the U.S. Chamber of Commerce and the Business Roundtable attended numerous photo-op sessions, withheld criticism of the early sectoral takeovers, and generally made nice with the new powers that be.

Some, such as the health insurance industry and, I'm sad to say, the pharmaceutical industry in which I once labored opted for what might be called preemptive surrender. That is actually the charitable way to look at their behavior, as beleaguered and outnumbered targets seeking to cut the best deal they could get. Think of their approach as appease-ment or, in Churchill's memorable phrase, as "feeding the alligator in hopes of being the last one eaten."

A sterner but probably more accurate description is that these indus-tries chose the course of collaboration, seeking to enhance their own pri-vate interest through collusion with a powerful government. In that sense, they were less like Neville Chamberlain than like the Vichyites or Quislings who actively collaborated with their conquerors in exchange for preferential treatment in the New Order.

It did them no good. In the Washington cliché, you are either "at the table or on the menu." These cooperative industries had their seats at the table pulled out from under them, and wound up as entrees anyway.

The recipients of bailouts fit this category. Chrysler and GM, who should have paid the price for years of marketing and labor-management misjudgments, are clear examples—as are a host of financial institutions that were bailed out by the government either directly or through AIG. Worst of all are those original, most obvious prototypes of business-government collusion, the GSEs Fannie Mae and Freddie Mac. For years the GSEs' profits were boosted by a federal government that pro-vided them low-cost funding while pushing private lenders into loaning money to homeowners who had little chance of paying it back. In many cases these borrowers simply lied on their loan applications. Lanchester, in *I.O.U.*, gets at how rife fraud was in the mortgage market by quoting the author of *Confessions of a Subprime Lender*, Richard Bitner: "70 percent of mortgage applications were erroneous or fraudulent, and that was before the worst of the excesses." Lanchester goes on to note that loans were given to "NINJAs" (those with no income, no jobs, and no assets). He also cites a survey dating to 2007 that found a full "60 percent of sub-prime applicants were lying about their income by more than 50 per-cent.[14] The GSEs' losses are being passed on to taxpayers. The St. Louis Federal Reserve has calculated that the losses from Fannie and Freddie will likely range between $135 billion and $259 billion through 2013.[15]

When it came to "health care reform," for insurers, collaboration meant supporting a bill that would require Americans to buy their prod-uct, even though (or because) this would lead to an industry consolidation and the demise of smaller competitors. The pharmaceutical industry, in return for what it imagines will be much higher volume sales to those newly covered by Medicaid or newly mandated (and taxpayer-subsidized) to buy coverage, not only supported the president's health care plan but agreed to $80 billion in new taxes and discounts over ten years.

Despite all the attacks and warnings about the menace posed by the private sector, by far the worst dangers to the public occur when business and government get in cahoots. Milton Friedman taught that the time to really worry about Big Business is when it combines with Big Government. We saw ample evidence of Dr. Friedman's wisdom in 2009. Belatedly, American business caught on to the future of punishment and subjugation that the Obama types have in mind for them, and began to fight back. Those trapped, at least for now, in the coming nightmare of the 2,700-page health care legislation will soon come to appreciate the wisdom of another economic thinker, Ronald Reagan, who once observed, "When you climb in bed with the federal government, you get a lot more than a good night's sleep."

Our Benevolent Betters

Let me be clear that my criticism of the left's impulse to make decisions on our behalf does not stem from an unwillingness to extend the great benefits of our society to as many people as possible. I would hope that advocates for pro-freedom and pro-government policies share the same goal of increasing opportunities and benefits to all Americans. Our public disagreements are about means, not ends. They are about who should decide as much as they are about what our public decisions should be.

The danger our statist friends represent stems from their unspoken assumption that a certain class of people, a class to which they belong, has the ability and duty to take the reins of society. In their eyes, our existing economic system permits too much power to private organizations, such as businesses, and leaves too many decisions to democratic processes where expert opinion may not be sufficiently appreciated, so it must yield to their leadership.

The reciprocal assumption, of course, is that the vast majority of Americans are too intimidated by our modern world, or too gullible at the hands of rapacious corporations, or just plain too dim-witted, to make these decisions for themselves. In this worldview, most people are victims, incapable of judging what kind of health care they need, how much mortgage or credit card debt they should carry, or where their child should go to school. Vulnerable as they are, they desperately need the tender ministrations of their Benevolent Betters.

It must occasionally intrude on our Betters' consciousness how neatly their altruistic determination to improve the lives of others coincides with their own self-interest. The ever more expansive governments they have built furnish not only today's above-market government salaries, but also myriad lucrative opportunities in the concentric rings of influence peddling and grant seeking that a massive government inevitably spawns. It is now quite common for people to spend entire careers and wind up very wealthy without ever working a day in a private enterprise or even in a profession related to the productive sector.

We once used the phrase "Doing good by doing well" to describe a business whose success spun off great opportunities and charitable donations for others. These days we are awash in those who "do well by doing good"—that is, they become rich by doing good, as they define it, for the benighted, powerless people around them. Our Betters never seem to notice that those they are out to help don't seem to be benefiting to nearly the extent that they are. In an extreme case laid out in detail by Gretchen Morgenson and Joshua Rosner in their book *Reckless Endangerment,* Democratic operative and former Fannie Mae chief executive James Johnson made off with millions while, in David Brooks's words, "supposedly helping the poor."

But more than money is at stake. The power grabs of recent years confront us with the question: What kind of nation will we be? A republic, the one Ben Franklin hoped we would keep, or a two-class society in which an anointed few make the key choices for the rest of us?

Still more fundamentally, the new statism forces us to the most basic of questions: What kind of *people* will we be? Autonomous creatures of dignity, resolved to make the big decisions of life for ourselves? Or objects of therapy, gratefully ceding these complicated choices to wiser folks who, they assure us, care deeply about our well-being?

It has been fashionable in recent years to lament an "Era of Greed," in which a wealthy minority supposedly damaged the public interest through their unbridled avarice. And though money has been the root of all evil for quite a while now, the 1990s and 2000s did see their share of wretched excess.

But greed comes in more than one form. The lust for control over others may, for some people, be a more compelling urge even than the quest for wealth. When people suffering from this addiction gain access to the vastly expanded powers now possessed by the state, a very different nation and a very different relationship between a once sovereign citizenry and its once subservient government eventuate.

This will to power has been on daily display during Obama's presidency, but never more plainly than when Health and Human Services Secretary Kathleen Sebelius, in a letter the *Wall Street Journal* aptly labeled "thuggish even by her standards," wrote to the nation's health insurers, "there will be zero tolerance for this type of misinformation.[16] The companies' sin? They dared to inform their customers that Obamacare would force them to raise their premiums.

Many relationships are mistakenly thought of as zero-sum when they are not. Economic growth is never a taking from some for the benefit of others, but, in President Kennedy's words, a tide that lifts all boats. But the seizure of power by government really is a zero-sum affair: the more decisions the state makes, the fewer decisions are left for the people to make, either as individuals or acting in concert as businesses or private associations. The more one sphere grows, the more the other shrinks. It is the shrunken citizen to whom we next turn our attention.

CHAPTER 4

The Shrunken Citizen

Elmer Kelton, perhaps our greatest Western novelist, is best remembered for his tales of the early Texas frontier. In my opinion his most compelling work is *The Time It Never Rained*, a saga of the devastating West Texas drought of the 1950s.

The book's protagonist, rancher Charlie Flagg, differs from and eventually angers his neighbors by his obstinate refusal to accept government assistance, even as the drought destroys everything he has worked a lifetime to build.

In one scene, his friend Page Mauldin expresses exasperation at Charlie's unwillingness to accept a government handout even though everyone else has their hands wide open. Charlie replies, "I'll spend my own money if I spend any at all."

When Page tries to reason with him, explaining that he might as well try and get some of his tax money back rather than let someone else run off with it, Charlie is nonplussed. "If you get to dependin' on the government, the day'll come when the damn federales will dictate everything you do. Some desk clerk in Washington will decide where you live and where you work and what color toilet paper you wipe yourself with. And you'll be scared to say anything because they might cut you off of the tit."

It would be hard to find a Charlie Flagg these days. Over the past several decades there has been a push in Washington to expand the scope of federal power and hand out government subsidies to as many Americans as possible. Some of these efforts have been curtailed over the years, most notably through welfare reform in the 1990s. But the push has continued and has expanded to include subsidies for working Americans through health care benefits, subsidies for buying a home, and refundable tax credits. The Obama administration even created, as part of its stimulus package, a tax credit called "Making Work Pay," which targeted lower-income Americans but benefited couples making as much as $190,000 a year. The result of this push has been a string of government deficits and, even though we may laugh at Charlie's suggestion that the government might dictate the color of toilet paper, an explosion in federal mandates that impact our daily lives. Indeed, recent years have seen superfluous legislation enacted that Charlie essentially predicted. Just imagine, for example, drought-stricken Charlie's reaction to the 2010 EPA rules that attempt to control the amount of dust farmers are permitted to create on their own land. Or his reaction to mandates that dictate how many gallons of water a toilet can flush or the type of light bulb one can buy.

If Charlie foresaw the shape of things to come, he wasn't the first. Both the Skeptics and the Founders predicted that democracy's demise would most likely come not from runaway debt, dangerous as that would be, but from an erosion of the character traits (they always said "virtues") that give rise to liberty in the first place. The founding generation worried from the outset that what Lincoln later termed the "mystic chords of memory" would fade away, that a free people would come to forget what freedom requires, or what life without it would be like.

Madison said, "To suppose that any government will secure liberty or happiness without any virtue in the people, is a chimerical idea." Franklin concurred, saying, "Only a virtuous people are capable of freedom. As nations become more corrupt and vicious, they have more need of masters." Patrick Henry was the most concise: "Bad men cannot make good citizens."

Many of today's Americans are tone-deaf to the "chords of memory." In fact, it may be more accurate to say that they've never even heard them. Stunning percentages of us know almost nothing of the nation's history, its principles, or of what is sacrificed when security and subservience become prized above personal independence.

No one has echoed the Founders more eloquently than our greatest modern president, Ronald Reagan. In his farewell address, he said, "If we forget what we did, we won't know who we are. I'm warning of an eradication of the American memory that could result, ultimately, in an erosion of the American spirit." As usual, no one has said it better.

Launching a new organization aimed at civics education, former Supreme Court justice Sandra Day O'Connor said, "Barely one-third of today's Americans can name the three branches of government, much less say what they do. . . . Less can say what the Declaration of Independence is, and it's right there in the title. I'm worried."

Judging from tests of our young people, the trend line is heading down, not up. On the National Assessment of Educational Progress (NAEP), the best national measure we have, less than a quarter of students are proficient in civics and American history. Sadly typical is the high school junior who in 1995 was surprised to learn that the school he attended, Grover Cleveland High School in Los Angeles, was named after a former U.S. president: "I always thought it was named after that city in Canada." And it's not as if things are getting better. In June 2011, the latest round of NAEP results revealed, yet again, that young Americans have inadequate understanding of their own history.

Further reinforcing this distressing decline, a recent *Newsweek* survey revealed that the vast majority of Americans do not know why we fought the cold war, can't name the incumbent vice president, and are unable to even define the Bill of Rights.

In recent years, Arizona has figured prominently in the national debate over illegal immigration. Among other concerns, many in that debate worry about the erosion of our national culture and patriotism that a huge, unassimilated ethnic group might pose. Ironically, when Arizona's own high school students were given ten basic questions from the U.S. citizenship exam given to legal immigrants, only 3.5 percent of students passed the test.[2]

Findings like these are not new. In 1994 longtime *Harper's* editor Lewis Lapham memorably described the NAEP scores of that year as "a coroner's report [that] returned a finding of mortal ignorance." Scores have declined since then.

The public education system bears most of the blame for this abysmal civic ignorance. This failure may well be its greatest disservice to our nation, outweighing even the more publicized disaster of students who cannot read, compute, or grasp rudimentary scientific concepts.

Entire volumes have been written on these shortcomings. SAT scores have dropped almost linearly since 1972. U.S. students trail badly in every international comparison, particularly in the critical subjects of math and science. Recent marginal improvements offer no real comfort. Indiana ranks generally in the middle among American states; as I pointed out to our General Assembly, "At the recent rate of improvement, it would take 21 years for us to catch Slovenia, and that's if Slovenia stands still." It is an iron law of the modern economy that a nation so poorly educated will fall behind in its standard of living. In 1983 the groundbreaking education study titled "A Nation at Risk" stunned the country with the stark assessments that "[T]he educational foundations of our society are presently being eroded by a rising tide of mediocrity that threatens our very future as a Nation and as a people. . . . If an unfriendly foreign power had attempted to impose on America the mediocre educational performance that exists today, we might well have viewed it as an act of war." Now, decades into the education reform movement, almost nothing has been accomplished, although at long last some structural change has begun.

It's easy to blame the failures of our public education system on bad teachers, overcrowded classrooms, and inadequate resources, but the root of the problem lies within the system's own bureaucracies, in particular, the government unions such as the National Education Association and the American Federation of Teachers. The adults who hijacked education for their own advantage did not intend for our young people to suffer as a consequence, but it was inevitable that they would suffer once the unions sought to protect incompetent teachers, principals, and superintendents against any accountability for producing well-prepared students.

The second disaster visited on our educational system was more intentional. A huge and equivalent danger comes from the content of schooling that does nothing to foster a sense of national mission, pride, or personal responsibility. The tragic civic ignorance we see today represents a purposeful reversal of the entire basis on which public education came into being in the first place.

Public education was invented with the goal of producing citizens endowed with the knowledge and character traits needed to govern themselves responsibly and without the corrective supervision of despots. It was created explicitly to promote knowledge of the founding principles, the heroic figures who forged and preserved our republic, and an overt patriotism for the nation.

Jefferson was an outspoken education advocate and recommended the study of history as a means of improving "moral and civic virtues"—there's that word again—all in the service of effective self-government. He warned, "If a nation expects to be ignorant and free . . . it expects what never was and never will be." In today's United States we have people who appear willing to bet that Jefferson was wrong.

Until the 1840s, education was privately provided, usually by religious denominations, and was therefore usually available only to the wealthy. Reformers such as Horace Mann argued for public provision of education specifically on the basis that it would produce better citizens. Public schools, as Pennsylvania's Walter Johnson put it, were essential in order "to give every member of American society a portion of knowledge adequate to the discharge of his duties as a man and a citizen of the Republic."

And yet, in 2010, the North Carolina State Department of Education recommended that eleventh-graders stop studying U.S. history before 1877.[3] Their idea of a high school history course would cover "international relations, the struggle for human rights, and understanding how changes in the physical environment have impacted American society," whatever any of that means. The recommendations went on to say, "Major emphasis will be given to political and social movements, and students will be asked to critique the outcomes of major political decisions." Mercifully, a public outcry is forcing those standards to be revised.

It would be bad enough if today's students were merely left unaware of the greatness and superiority of the free institutions America has brought to the world. In reality, they are more often taught the converse: that we are a deeply flawed nation, with few if any past heroes to look up to, and no cause to view ourselves as any better than any other country or culture. Scan any modern civics textbook for clear statements that free citizens have a responsibility to take care of themselves whenever possible and to demand the right to personal autonomy, and you will most likely find none. Another search for any intimation that a government by the people must of necessity be limited in its scope, having no power that is not expressly enumerated, will most likely turn up the same result.

What is easy to find is denigration of our institutions and our past. An especially atrocious example comes in the form of *A People's History of the United States*, a textbook drafted by an avowed Marxist, the late Howard Zinn. Since 1980 the book has sold more than a million copies and has found its way into numerous high school classrooms. It offers a decidedly slanted version of American history that downplays the triumphs of our Founders and free systems. In 2010 the release of FBI files detailed Zinn's extensive connections to radical leftists and communist organizations that dated back to investigations of him that started in 1949. Picking up on the released files, Daniel J. Flynn wrote an article for *City Journal* that noted a quote Zinn gave back in 1998. "I wanted my writing of history and my teaching of history to be part of social struggle," he told the *Revolutionary Worker*. "I wanted to be part of history and not just a recorder and teacher of history. So that kind of attitude towards history, and not just as a political act, has always informed my writing and my teaching.④ 246

A recent review of world history textbooks in widespread use found extensive treatment of the internment of Japanese Americans in World War II but virtually nothing about Japanese aggression, or about Japanese atrocities committed against prisoners of war and civilian populations.

At least in their official, organized form, the teaching profession seems quite comfortable with this rewritten history. The American Historical Association, which weighed in recently on a new history curriculum being drafted in Texas and can influence what ends up in new textbooks, never led a push to oust Zinn's text from classrooms. Likewise, the NEA has inserted itself into a wide variety of left-wing causes over the past decades, but hasn't come to the defense of teaching the virtues of America's free institutions. Indeed, the NEA, which recently spent more than $2 million on a ballot initiative aimed at raising corporate taxes in California, has donated money to the Sierra Club and to ACORN (the later disgraced and disbanded left-wing community activist group), and has been a stalwart opponent of education reforms aimed at raising the quality of education through testing, vouchers, and charter schools. It has even opposed education reforms, such as merit pay, that are supported by President Obama. In a free society, such organizations are well within their rights to wage political campaigns, but we shouldn't pretend that such campaigns are entirely motivated by what's best for the children and that they don't impact the individual rights the rest of us enjoy.

As American citizens, we have never encountered such a massively intrusive state as the federal government of today. We have never been so poorly equipped to detect its creeping (or, in the age of Obama, leaping) encroachments on our traditional liberties, because so few of us remember that we are supposed to possess such liberty in the first place. We are told time and again that the government knows what is best for us, and we are thus resigned and acquiescent in the face of losses to our freedom and personal dignity.

Consider the stoic acceptance of the unprecedented inconvenience and privacy intrusions of the post-9/11 bureaucracy known as the Transportation Security Administration (TSA). Starting with hour-long waiting lines to pass through metal detectors and other scanners, the TSA lumbered on mindlessly, as bureaucracies do, until it was practically molesting plainly innocent and harmless passengers who just wanted to catch a flight home for Thanksgiving.

Columnist Charles Krauthammer, with his customary incisiveness, pointed out, "[E]veryone knows the entire apparatus of the security line is a national homage to political correctness. . . . This has nothing to do with safety—95 per cent of these inspections, searches, shoe removals, and pat-downs are ridiculously unnecessary. The only reason we continue to do this is that people are too cowed to even question the absurd taboo against profiling—when the profile of the airline attacker is narrow, concrete, uniquely definable and universally known.[5] 246

The decline in our grasp of freedom's requirements has been paralleled by a sharp increase in the degree to which Americans are dependent on government, which is to say, subsidized at the expense of their neighbors. A Census report that looked at American households in 2008—before the more recent spike in unemployment—found a surprisingly increasing number of Americans now receive some form of public assistance. At the time, 28.4 million households, or one out of every four in the country, were receiving checks through welfare programs. This was up from 16 percent in 1984. Add in social insurance programs, such as Social Security, Medicare, and Medicaid, and the number of households with at least one person receiving government assistance was 45 percent⑥ ⋷ ४ ५

During the 2008–9 recession, and well beyond the point at which it technically ended, unprecedented amounts of unemployment compensation were distributed to those out of work. Presumably everyone can agree that a system of temporary assistance is the right thing in bad economic times, and unemployment insurance (UI) has been a fixture of our system for decades, seeing us through a host of previous recessions.

But the latest round was different. UI had historically been offered for twenty-six weeks, with an option in the law for extension to fifty-two weeks. Between 2008 and 2010, benefits were eventually lengthened to ninety-nine weeks, essentially two years. The question is begged: Where does it end? Are we in favor of permanent payments to those not working?

Employers and individual Hoosiers related to me on countless occasions that UI recipients were rejecting employment offers, telling me that "UI is a better deal." My concern is deeper than that. Companies that have laid off employees in the recession won't necessarily hire them back once the good times return. Many of them are undergoing a restructuring that may lead them to hire new workers in the future for different types of jobs than they hired for in the past. Similarly, American workers have to make hard decisions to seek retraining or otherwise restructure their lives in order to make themselves eligible for new jobs in the future. Extending unemployment benefits for years may be a compassionate thing to do in one sense, but in another sense it creates an entitlement mentality and an incentive for workers not to restructure their lives. These programs offer benefits but do not require workers to make themselves ready to take advantage of new opportunities down the road.

The hundreds of billions paid out in UI benefits were also charged to the very businesses we hoped would start hiring again. Having already been crippled by one of the worst economic downturns in recent history, these companies found it even more difficult to recover under this added pressure. As odd as it may seem, at some point the worthy and compassionate programs we have put in place become economically self-defeating. But the worst defeat suffered at the hands of this system is that of our citizens' personal responsibility and dignity.

American "Entitlement"

Maybe solving our debt problem starts with vocabulary. As the late Patrick Moynihan once said, he who controls the dictionary controls the debate. I have come to disagree with the word we use to describe Social Security, Medicare, Medicaid, and similar programs: *entitlements*.

When one stops to think about it, an American is entitled to life, liberty, and the pursuit of happiness, period. We are entitled to be safe in our homes, and to the freedom to live our own lives, and make of ourselves whatever our talents and hard work can produce. That's what we're entitled to from our government, and our Constitution.

Everything government does after that is a matter of choices we make as a caring and compassionate people. When we decide together that some of us will contribute some of our substance so that others may have good health care, or avoid destitution in their older years, those are good things we opt to do for one another, not something anyone is *entitled* to. These programs got their name because of their design, which says that anyone who meets a certain description can access them by definition. But those definitions are not in the Constitution; nor are they on the Supreme Court cornerstone. They were established as matters of choice by the American people through their elected representatives, and they are subject to change in the same way.

The comedian George Carlin once asked, "What's another good word for 'synonym'?" We need one in this situation. We should retire the misleading term *entitlement* in favor of *safety net* or *social welfare* or some other noun that avoids implying that any citizen of our nation, apart from the conscious generosity of his fellow Americans, automatically has a claim on one dime of his neighbor's property. The notion that he does is not only a prescription for national poverty, but also an affront to the freedom and the dignity of each one of us.

Neither Charlie Flagg nor his creator, Elmer Kelton, who wrote his book in 1973, could have conceived the extent of the dependence we now have on government. But they saw clearly the effect such dependence would have on the character of those receiving it. In the book, when another acquaintance of his tells Charlie that he should accept government handouts for the sake of everyone else, Charlie consoles him: "[T]hey won't cut off your aid. They're too busy buyin' your vote with it." In Charlie Flagg's view, when a person sells his vote for a government transfer, he throws in an unconscious gratuity: a little bit of his own dignity and self-reliance. He becomes a shrunken citizen.

A Dollar Less Free

There is a game I like to play whenever I visit high school classrooms. I ask if anyone has a dollar bill handy, and when some unsuspecting youngster produces one and hands it to me, I thank him, stick it in my pocket, and continue talking. As the giggles and tittering build, I pause theatrically as if to say, "What?!" and when I "realize" that young Brandon wants his dollar back, I make the following point:

"Please note," I say, "that Brandon is now a dollar less free than he was a minute ago. If he still had that dollar bill, *he* could decide what to do with it. Now I get to decide. And that's why we need to be so careful before we take away Brandon's money, or yours, through the coercive power of taxation. If we really value personal freedom the way we say we do, then we should never take a dollar away from a free citizen without a very good reason. And then we have a solemn duty to spend it as wisely and effectively as possible. Otherwise, we should never have taken it in the first place."

Of course I give Brandon his dollar back, but I also leave the class with a lesson that, I can tell, they have never heard before.

Unfortunately, when we talk about government, we're talking about trillions of dollars, not just one. Over the past four decades, federal spending per household has grown by more than 160 percent (see Figure 6), putting us deeper into the pockets of our Benevolent Betters.

In case our increasing dependence on cash from "government" isn't enough to convince us how much we need our Betters, regular reinforce-

Figure 6 | **Federal Spending per Household**

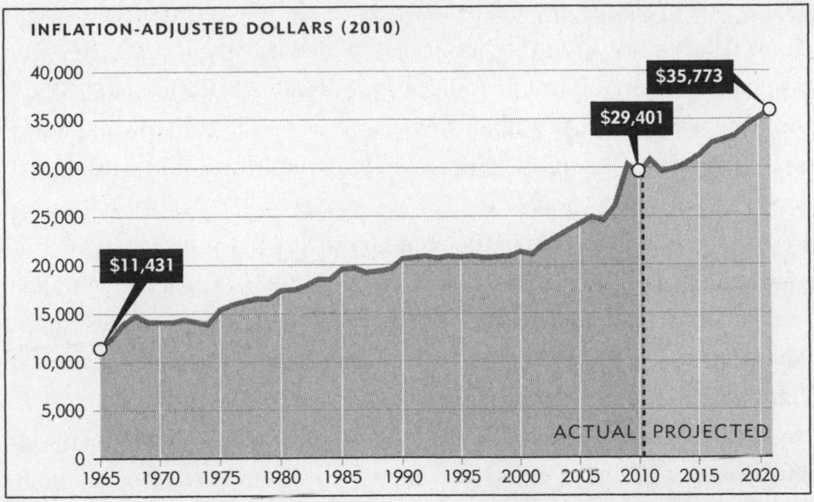

INFLATION-ADJUSTED DOLLARS (2010)

Source: Heritage Foundation Calculations based on data from the U.S. Census Bureau, White House Office of Management and Budget, and Congressional Budget Office.

ment of a sense of victimhood is there to help. Consider the way in which business, and business leaders, are depicted.

Among the many things today's young people are unlikely to learn either at school or in front of a television or movie screen is where wealth comes from. Even if they are lucky enough to be exposed to some sort of basic economics class, they probably won't be told that the creation of wealth is among life's highest and most important achievements. One can search K–12 textbooks at great length before finding any laudatory comments about those who built America's great businesses or the industries that opened the way for millions of impoverished citizens to build a better life for themselves. And the chances of hearing anything positive after a student gets to college are even more remote.

Determining bias is, of course, a subjective endeavor. However, there has been enough research done on the political slant on college campuses for us to conclude with confidence that many students are offered a one-sided view of the world when in college. Consider the results dug up by the Center for the Study of Popular Culture in 2003. In a study that looked at the political affiliation of faculty and administration members at 32 elite colleges, the center found that the ratio of Democrats to Republicans was decidedly lopsided. The overall ratio was more than 10 to 1 (1,397 Democrats to 134 Republicans), while at some schools the ratio was much wider. At Bowdoin College, for example, the ratio was 23 to 1. At Brown it was 30 to 1. At Williams, Oberlin, Haverford, and the Massachusetts Institute of Technology, not a single Republican could be identified among the faculty⑦ 246

Portrayals of business in the popular culture are ludicrously inaccurate and unfair. Michael Medved has chronicled bias against capitalism embedded within our TV shows and movies. In the two decades that followed the end of World War II, Medved reports in his book *Hollywood vs. America*, just 11 percent of Hollywood's villains were businessmen. By 1986, 67 percent of characters who committed felonies on-screen were businessmen. "Big business has become television's favorite villain," he 246 writes⑧And over the past two decades, the trend has only continued. Moviemakers become enormously wealthy by tediously denigrating the very free market system that allows them to thrive, but that irony never seems to deter them or even catch their attention.

As a result of these portrayals, Americans are left to believe that the private sector is a jungle of predators against whom the average citizen must be safeguarded by an ever-vigilant government. Villains are everywhere, and if things go badly for you, it must have been someone else's fault.

If you borrowed huge amounts of money to buy a house beyond your present means, someone deceived you. If you compounded the risk by refinancing the home, based on the wishful expectation that its value would shoot up in the future, it's only because you were misled. If you maxed out all your credit cards, you must have been tricked by a devious marketing ploy. In all cases, it's someone else's fault, and your caring federal government must intervene to get you off the hook.

Medved once spotted a telltale indicator of the Benevolent Better worldview in President Clinton's First Inaugural Address: "We must provide for our nation the way a family provides for its children." As Medved pointed out, "In other words, [Clinton] viewed his fellow citizens—or at least many of his fellow citizens—as helpless kids who couldn't support themselves." That is exactly right, and exactly the problem we face.

As we've come to say, when you are child and you are deceived into losing money, someone must come in and bail you out. And why not? After all, we did it for Chrysler, and AIG, and Bear Stearns, so why not for you? Of course, the answer is, there's only one boat, and we're all in it. Bailing from one side of a sinking vessel to the other is a futile exercise that simply delays the search for a real solution.

Victimhood and Its Enablers

The absurdity and destructiveness of the American legal system as it applies to civil wrongs, or torts, has been well catalogued for years. My concern here is with the way in which the tort system serves few interests other than the financial interest of the trial bar millionaires it spawns, while fostering a sense of victimhood.

In 2005 we saw in Texas what happens when wealthy lawyers persuade a large group of Americans to declare themselves victims and seek undeserved compensation. In that case, federal district court judge Janis Graham Jack uncovered a scheme that made national headlines. Apparently, in filing a class-action lawsuit aimed at winning money damages for individuals supposedly suffering from silicosis, a law firm had recycled many victims used in previous cases filed over ailments supposedly caused by exposure to asbestos. Upon close examination, it turned out that many of the "victims" in both cases had likely been fraudulently diagnosed. The aim of that scheme, of course, was to use the courts to extract money from innocent companies. After a remarkable hearing in Corpus Christi, Judge Jack issued a lengthy order with this conclusion: "these diagnoses were driven by neither health nor justice; they were manufactured for money. The record is not clear who originally devised this scheme, but it is clear that the lawyers, doctors and screening companies were willing participants.[9] 246

Most Americans remember the successful lawsuit against McDonald's for the "tort" of serving a customer the hot coffee she ordered. We as a people have been encouraged to treat every bad break in life as an opportunity to sue. As one foreign observer marveled, "You Americans are trying to outlaw the concept of bad luck." And if life doesn't deliver the right opportunity, you can always create your own bad luck. People in my hometown, for example, were caught by the news media encouraging their children to provoke confrontations with the police in the hope of producing grounds for a lawsuit.

People who are coached to shift the cost of their own bad luck, or their own mistakes, to their neighbors are actually being told, "You are incompetent." People who are supplied with increasing amounts of money, transferred from their neighbors in an open-ended fashion by the force of government, are being told, "You are not fit to provide for yourself and your family." Those who are described as helpless victims, at sea in an ocean of private-sector sharks, are being told, "You are incapable of looking out for yourself. You need us to protect you." Americans accepting these premises are not the kind of citizens Jefferson hoped to educate, or that Franklin had in mind when he hoped we could keep our republic. They sell themselves short whenever they submit to the idea that they are not the creatures of dignity and autonomy for whom, and on whom, a free society exists.

Every expansion of public power shrinks the citizen, automatically and axiomatically. Beyond all the arguments about spending, taxing, deficits, health care, regulation—and on and on—lies the largest decision of all: What kind of people do we want to be?

Abdication of the "People's Branch"

Even a civics-deprived product of today's typical public schools should know that we have three branches of government, and that the legislature (named after the Latin word for "law") owns the sole power to make the laws of the land. It is through the legislature, often referred to as "the people's branch," that free citizens acting through their representatives are supposed to set the rules of society. That's no longer the way it works. As detailed earlier, an astonishing amount of the laws created today are not made by elected, and therefore recallable, representatives, but by unelected bureaucrats and judges. Congress is not blameless in this situation. All too often its members have preferred to abdicate the details of their handiwork to agencies and move on to their next act of stylized benevolence.

The 2010 2,319-page financial regulation bill delegated to a variety of agencies the opportunity to write more than 240 separate sets of new rules. The Obama health care bill, a 2,000-page tome in its own right, lobbed to the Department of Health and Human Services several hundred more similar opportunities. In 2010, Americans tossed out of office dozens of those who voted for the underlying bill, but they had no means to remove from a much greater position of power Health and Human Services Secretary Kathleen Sebelius, who began her new career as the czarina of health care by sending threatening letters to the nation's insurers who had committed the sin of fully disclosing that the bill's mandates and coverage expansions were going to raise premiums and cause many customers to drop health insurance completely.

Sometimes our Betters simply arrogate new power for themselves without even bothering with the nuisance of securing legislative delegation. The Environmental Protection Agency (which probably should be renamed the Employment Prevention Agency) declared with no statutory basis at all that it had the power to regulate carbon dioxide, which is necessary to life on this planet, as a dangerous pollutant, on a par with mercury or lead. A compliant judiciary somehow found a way to defer.

Not only has Congress never empowered the EPA to limit CO_2, it has expressly refused to do so on multiple occasions, even when asked by President Obama during the highly compliant 111th Congress. No problem. The unelected EPA and the unelected federal judiciary collaborated to redefine CO_2 on their own, unleashing the agency to pursue the irrational, horrendously expensive, job-killing policy of carbon limitation despite the nonagreement of "the people's branch."

Skin in the Game

Resistance to the expansion of government is lowered further when a citizen senses no cost attached to it. Increasingly taxation is either indirect or invisible, so that fewer and fewer of us find reasons to question the way our dollars get spent. Indirect taxation includes the trillions we pay for the cost of federal regulations. Goods, services, and energy all cost far more than they would in the absence of these requirements. Sometimes we get our money's worth, sometimes not, but in neither case do we detect the dollars as they depart our pocketbooks. Many other mandated costs, and of course corporate taxes, are also passed on to consumers.

The taxes that are paid, and especially the individual income tax that is government's single largest revenue source, are increasingly imposed on a dwindling percentage of Americans. Most people would be surprised to learn that in 2009, 47 percent of Americans did not pay anything in federal income taxes. They either made too little or qualified for enough exemptions so as not to owe any tax liability. What's more, some 40 percent of Americans actually made money off the tax system through refundable tax credits and other provisions.

Both political parties—and this author—have been party to this enormous shift. When I worked in the Reagan White House I enthusiastically advocated the president's 1986 tax reform. One of our proudest talking points was the bill's promise to remove six million low-income Americans from the tax rolls altogether. Fifteen years later I was back in another White House making a similar claim on behalf of the Bush tax cuts of 2001.

Positive as these reforms were in many ways, cumulatively they have produced a distorted system and some perverse outcomes. First, fewer of us recognize and feel personally the burdens of even the largest and most expensive public sector the nation has ever seen. We're not invested. We have no skin in the game.

Second, the federal government and many states have become precariously dependent on a few high-income (and therefore highly mobile) individuals for very large shares of their revenue. In 2008, for example, the top 1 percent of earners paid more than 38 percent of federal income taxes. The top 10 percent of earners—those making about $114,000 a year or more—paid nearly 70 percent. Meanwhile, the bottom 50 percent of income earners paid just 2.7 percent.[10] The net result is that 24b today's federal government is overly reliant on taxes paid by a volatile and mobile group of individuals who have relatively large swings in their income and who have the luxury to withdraw either themselves or their capital from the marketplace during downturns.

California in recent years has demonstrated the pitfalls of building a tax system that is overly reliant on the wealthy. Writing in the *Wall Street Journal* in January 2011, Andrew G. Atkeson and William E. Simon, Jr., reported that in 2007 the state had nearly 36 million residents, but just 7,000 households—those with adjusted gross incomes above $5 million for the year—paid one-fifth of the state's income taxes. By the following year there were only 4,700 households making that kind of money. The result was that taxes paid by these households fell to about $7 billion from about $11 billion. That drop-off was half of all the revenue lost by the state. Nearly all of the rest of the revenue lost also came from "wealthy" households. Atkeson and Simon tell us that "The decline in tax receipts from those households earning more than $200,000 accounts for fully 93 percent of the decline in total tax revenues from 2007–08.[11] In other words, 246 as California plunged deep into deficit, more than ninety cents of every tax dollar lost in revenue can be attributed to the "wealthy" paying less because they either made less or fled the state. They now say in California, "When one of those people moves out, it's an event."

The result of such an imbalanced system is that government becomes ever more reliant on the growing prosperity of rich people, and therefore of income inequality, to pay for its expansion. Nothing could be more self-defeating than for the proponents of the social welfare state to attempt to limit the incomes of the wealthy. After all, the tax system they have constructed cannot produce the funds they long to spend unless the rich get even richer. I wonder if the deep irony of this conundrum ever dawns on our friends, the Betters.

When any change is suggested that would lower any tax rate, even in exchange for closed loopholes, the nation's left knees all jerk in unison, alleging that "the rich" will reap some undue benefit. Each time top rates have been reduced the fact that upper-income people wind up paying much more in taxes *and* a higher share of all taxes never seems to matter. The implication is that our current system already favors the wealthy.

If that's so, then so does every nation's on earth. Using data from the

OECD, both the Congressional Budget Office and the nonpartisan Tax Foundation found the United States to have the most progressive tax system of all twenty-four countries studied. Counting taxes of all kinds, a wealthy American is paying between 31 percent and 35 percent more than his proportionate share of income, whereas the one-fifth with the lowest incomes are paying only 20 percent of their proportionate share. The only way to extract more federal revenue from today's system is through an increase in income inequality. Is that really what our statist quo friends desire?

I learned a hard lesson in the dynamics of current federal taxation in my role as director of the Office of Management and Budget in 2001. The new Bush administration arrived in the third year of federal surpluses, the first since the federal government experienced a small surplus in 1969.[2] Much credit for this remarkable turn of events goes to the Clinton administration and a Republican Congress, which cooperated in restraining spending growth, and to President Reagan, who as Clare Booth Luce once said, "won the cold war without firing a shot" and produced a huge "peace dividend" of reduced defense spending.

But the surpluses more than anything could be traced to the combination of the dot-com bubble economy of the late 1990s and the lopsided tax system just described. To an extent that no one realized at the time, the huge surge in federal revenues that moved the nation into surplus came from a relatively few taxpayers whose income was highly correlated to the stock market's upward movement.

Income taxes on bonuses, stock options, and other incentive compensation were a large part of the surge. So were capital gains taxes paid on what turned out to be inflated stock values. Believing the new levels of revenue to be natural, all forecasts—those of OMB, the Congressional Budget Office, the Federal Reserve, and everyone else—assumed those levels as a base and projected upward from them depending on their chosen GDP growth assumptions. Reducing taxes as President Bush proposed was a straightforward call given these consensus projections; there was plenty of room to do that and keep paying off debt at the same time.

Proudly paying down debt as 2001 unfolded, we studied these forecasts and saw the potential to retire the whole federal debt within a few years.

The nation's most respected financial figure, Alan Greenspan, spoke of the need to leave at least some debt outstanding simply to preserve a liquid market for any occasional future public borrowing.

How wrong we all were.[13] The recession that had begun as President Clinton left office was a mild one by historical standards. It lasted only eight months, shorter than the average recession since the end of World War II, and was mild enough to spark a debate over whether the slowdown fit the technical definition of a recession. Revised economic data released by the Commerce Department's Bureau of Economic Analysis in 2004 indicate that the country might not have experienced three consecutive quarters of negative GDP growth in 2001.[14]

In any case, such a recession in the past would not have had a large impact on government revenues. But in the new tax system, a dropping stock market took a gigantic bite. Capital gains payments fell from $127 billion in 2000 to $49 billion in 2002. During this period, individual income taxes paid plummeted by 14 percent, the majority of the drop coming from the upper-income levels. The budget recovered within a couple years and, even bearing the enormous cost of the Iraq War and the new post-9/11 activities dealing with homeland security, brought deficits back down to a historically small 1.2 percent of GDP by 2007, before the next recession raised them again.

I take this digression only to underscore how detached from the costs of our national government most Americans have become. When the payroll taxes associated with Social Security and Medicare are counted, our overall tax burden is more widely shared than it appears. But half of those are listed on pay stubs as "employer" taxes, obscuring the fact that the worker's wages would have been higher by that amount if Uncle Sam hadn't claimed it first.

Full citizenship in a free society involves some measure of contribution to our necessary collective activities. And it is entirely just that those receiving more of society's income should contribute at least in proportion to their gains. But however we decide to apportion the bill for government, true democracy requires that we see the full size of the check we are paying.

In recent years, the most vigorous taxpayer uprisings have centered on state and local property taxes. When one thinks about it, it's no surprise. Property taxes are usually as visible as a tax can be. They are collected not in weekly dribbles but all at once, or maybe twice a year. The bill comes to the taxpayer directly, not to his employer or through higher prices for the things he buys at the store. No one "painlessly" pays this tax on his behalf; he writes a check for the full amount or pays it each month as part of a mortgage payment to his bank. He can evaluate for himself whether his property taxes have become too high relative to whatever benefit he perceives he is receiving.

In 2007, Hoosiers in large numbers began to complain that their local property taxes were out of line with benefits. We responded by reducing property taxes an average of 30 percent. In some counties, the cut was as high as 60 percent. All told, it was the largest tax cut in state history, and it gave Hoosiers the lowest property taxes in the United States.

To prevent them from becoming excessive again, we added a cap to the new law, and to our state's constitution. No Indiana homeowner can ever again be charged more than 1 percent of his home's value, no farmer or landlord more than 2 percent, and no business more than 3 percent.

But then we added an important feature by providing flexibility for spending units to seek revenue above what the caps would permit, if and only if they could secure taxpayer permission through a referendum. Higher local government spending, and higher taxes to pay for it, can still happen in Indiana; the difference is that now the spenders need the taxpayers' permission first.

In its first years, the new law has given rise to its first few dozen referenda. About half of them passed and about half were turned down. Hoosiers seem to be showing the common sense and reasonableness for which they are known. When they hear a good case for more service, they are generally willing to approve and pay for it. They are more fully engaged in governing themselves, by making mature decisions about how much government they want, and at what price.

Government by the people works best when everyone has some skin in the game and knows it, when taxes are visible and quantifiable to those paying them. When government hides its costs, it reveals its doubt that a fully informed citizenry would condone all that it is doing. Government grows fastest the more it shrinks the citizen's role in holding it accountable.

As much as the government may try to shrink its citizens, recent years have shown that we're becoming less willing to stand by and watch. In 2009, in the out-of-nowhere fashion that a wired world makes possible, a network of people who came to call themselves the Tea Party suddenly sprang to life. Unlike many alleged protest organizations we have seen, consisting of a dozen sign carriers and a couple of television news cameras, this was a genuine grass-roots citizens movement, motivated by the kind of freedom-minded citizenship this chapter has fretted about the nation losing.

The Tea Party may have been born in reaction to bailouts of Wall Street, takeovers of businesses, and the explosion of federal spending, but it rapidly evolved into a national movement worthy of the term, sophisticated not only in its tactics and communications, but in the depth of its thought. For the first time in their lives, many Americans were reminded that there is a Tenth Amendment to the Constitution that reserves certain powers to the states and therefore puts more responsibility in the hands of the people.

The response of the president and his partisans to this insubordination was comical when it wasn't sinister. First, they dismissed the Tea Party as a fictional contrivance of the Republican Party, or the Vast Right-wing Conspiracy, or somebody. Then it was a dangerous, radical operation with racist overtones. When the president's supporters were caught manufacturing false charges of racist behavior, and trying to infiltrate rallies with hate-speech signs, new criticisms had to be trotted out. Still, the movement grew.

Of course, such a rambunctious and spontaneous outfit would attract its share of quirky adherents. And it was fair to point out that the early Tea Party was long on anger and light on answers, more about diagnosis of the nation's problems than prescriptions for their improvement. It was true that, during the first election cycle of its existence, no one stood before a Tea Party rally and spelled out, for instance, how huge the changes in Social Security and Medicare would have to be to bring our debt back to survivable levels.

Yet for the first time in a very long while, Americans saw living examples of full, active citizenship by people who politely—well, sometimes impolitely—insisted that the government work for them and not the other way around. These people are determined to make their own decisions and stand on their own two feet, and they believe that others ought to do likewise.

The housewives who started the Tea Party have probably never heard of Charlie Flagg, but they have succeeded in returning some of his spirit to our country. During one confrontation in the novel, a haughty federal bureaucrat lectures Charlie, "If you don't like laws, Mr. Flagg, perhaps you should move to some country where they don't have any." To which Charlie replies, "I liked this country before it was saddled down with so many of them." In order for our country to survive the challenges it faces—both today and down the road—we must take a lesson from Charlie. We must remember the mystic chords, and refuse to be shrunk.

CHAPTER 5

The Obamacare Steamroller

The first year of Barack Obama's presidency saw the most hotly contested domestic issue to come before the American people since the Reagan reforms of 1981, or perhaps the Great Society days of the 1960s. In
our 24/7, cable channel/talk radio/everyone's-a-blogger world, Americans were incessantly inundated with claims, counterclaims, "facts," and
their prompt refutation, all about the president's proposal to change the
way health care is paid for and delivered in our country.

The struggle lasted for eleven months, and generated a debate from
which not even the most inattentive citizen could escape. The contending
interests spent hundreds of millions of dollars on lobbying, television ads,
and pseudo-academic studies. By the time it culminated in a 2,400-page
bill, unread by anyone and rammed through an exhausted Congress on a
party-line vote, the argument had drawn in countless groups and individuals, including many not previously involved in politics.

This was entirely appropriate. "Obamacare," as it came to be known,
not only fundamentally alters the terms of trade in the largest single
sector of the American economy (some 18 percent at present, and growing), but also embodies many of the reasons why the United States is now
facing an existential fiscal crisis. It was pushed through on the elitist presumption that our Benevolent Betters knew what we needed better than
we did, and with a reckless disregard for the federal government's ability
to pay its bills. As such, it thrust upon Americans all the biggest questions
we will face in the days of decision dead ahead: Do we have the discipline
to match national wants and needs? Which sector of society serves
which? What kind of people, self-determining or shrunken, do we intend
to be?

The debate is destined to continue. As health policy, Obamacare is a disaster, absolutely certain to aggravate the worst distortions and dysfunctions of America's accidentally bizarre way of paying for medical treatment. And, in an economy in which almost one dollar in five is spent on health care, health policy is also economic policy, and there, too, the legislation will be ruinous. As these effects become increasingly clear, the argument over the wisdom of the underlying law will be renewed, and it should.

The bill's purpose and likely consequences were misrepresented by its authors at every step; for that matter, it began its life as a misrepresentation. The very label "health care reform" was a misnomer, as it "re-formed" nothing of consequence. Instead, the bill perpetuated and exacerbated the worst features of the current system, the ones that combine to make American health care too expensive and inefficient.

If one had assigned a mischievous economist to design a system rigged for overconsumption and unnaturally high prices, he could hardly have done better than the way we provide health care in America today. On the purchaser's end, he would have made the product seem free, or prepaid, like a buffet dinner, so as to remove the usual consumer incentive to shop for the best price or to challenge an apparent overcharge. He would have made sure the buffet table was loaded with the most sumptuous offerings, whether the purchaser had any interest in consuming them or not.

Next, he would have provided the seller with the opportunity to maximize his revenue by forcing unnecessary services on his financially indifferent customer, all the while being paid for each service delivered: the more activity, the higher the compensation.

Finally, to ensure that the arrangement cost vastly more than it should, our designer would have built in a powerful external cost driver, in the form of an ever-present threat of lawsuits for any vendor who failed to think of and deliver every conceivable test or therapy to a given patient.

Obamacare promises to preserve all these obvious defects of our postwar health care system and make them larger and worse. It leaves our egregious medical liability system untouched. No one claims that lawsuits and the constant overhang of their possibility is not a driver of higher costs. Any honest, disinterested observer knows that the impact is enormous. Ask any physician how often he orders redundant tests or superfluous therapy just to insulate himself from being sued and the answer will likely be "daily." One 2007 study found that upward of 79 percent of doctors performed defensive medicine, ordering a test or a procedure to avoid a possible malpractice suit.[1] *The Journal of the American Medical Association* published an article in 2005 with results from a study that found that nearly all—93 percent—of doctors in high-risk fields, such as emergency medicine or obstetrics/gynecology, practiced defensive medicine.[2]

Obamacare contains provisions that seem to change the dominant fee-for-service payment model by setting up pilot programs within Medicare that will supposedly demonstrate how to reduce costs. But they are of the typical federal government variety, which almost always disappear into the memory hole after the years it takes to set them up, attempt them, and endlessly analyze their results. By the time any of these experiments have been run, the entirety of America's health care sector will have been sucked into the maw of a giant Medicare-like monolith.

Until the last few decades, people with an illness or injury went to a physician or hospital, received a bill, and paid it. Sometimes the help of family was necessary, and often the provider donated a portion of the service as an expected part of the process. But because the basic, "first-dollar" costs were borne by the purchaser, he thought carefully about when to consume health care, and any provider with a reputation for being unduly expensive would lose customers over time.

In any other economic context, this à la carte system would work just fine. The critical difference these days, of course, is the diabolical way in which fee-for-service, do-more-get-paid-more medicine intersects with the single worst element of our explosive health care costs: third-party payment. When a seller incentivized to perform as many services as possible meets a purchaser who doesn't care how much he "buys" because most of the tab is being picked up by someone else, all the usual rules and constraints of the marketplace disappear.

Throughout history, government's klutzy attempts to manage wages and prices, even when they temporarily achieved their immediate objective, have always triggered unexpected distortions elsewhere in the economy. New York City's rent controls have distorted the rental market in the Big Apple for decades in a number of ways. For starters, landlords have an incentive not to fix up apartments for which they can charge only below-market rates. Likewise, price controls on oil distorted markets in the 1970s in ways that contributed to shortages that led to gas lines. The same goes for health care. Imposing rationing or price controls on one end of the pipe leads to bad outcomes at the other end.

When the federal government imposed wage and price controls during World War II, the competition for talent led employers to discover a loophole by covering health care costs (another form of compensation, but one not treated as such by the regulators of the day). So they added to wages in this way, evading the controls, and after the war, this strange new practice survived and spread, quickly becoming the expected and "natural" way to pay for medical treatment.

The heart of our runaway cost crisis lies in the practice of third-party payment. If the biggest misnomer of recent times is health care *reform*, a close second is health *insurance*, because the perverse arrangement to which we apply that label bears no resemblance to any other kind of insurance.

Insurance is the protection we buy against unexpected, inordinately expensive events, the kind of misfortune we know will befall a few but not most of us in any given time period. Few individuals are wealthy enough to set aside sufficient personal reserves to guard against all conceivable bad luck, so we chip into a common pot, from which the unfortunate few can draw if the unforeseeable happens to them. This is the way we protect our houses, our cars, and our loved ones in the event of our untimely death.

But not our health. In that realm, and that realm only, we draw on the common pool for almost every expense, however minor, expectable, or discretionary. I sometimes point out to young audiences that their car insurance is not there to pay for oil changes, replacement tires, or worn-out wiper blades. It's there in case they have a wreck. Not so with health "insurance."

The single best line ever written about this issue came from the brilliant humorist P. J. O'Rourke, who once observed, "If you think health care is expensive now, just wait 'til it's free." What is free, or nearly so, will axiomatically be consumed in excessive quantities. Give me a coupon for unlimited pizza, and I will eat a whole lot of pizza. Only a few cents of every health care dollar is paid for by the customer out of his pocket. Former senator Phil Gramm once said, "If you only charge me a nickel for every dollar of food, I'll be overfed and so will my dog."

Although the market has belatedly begun reintroducing customer cost consciousness, in the form of higher co-payments or deductibles (the amounts policy holders must pay before the insurance kicks in), the sense and, worse yet, the expectation that the bill is going to somebody else still pervades the system.

The most disastrous consequence of this inefficient model is that it has allowed Americans to grow accustomed to the idea that, when it comes to the most personal and important purchases of all, those affecting their health, they are sheep, bystanders to a process in which they have neither the competence to decide what services to buy nor the intelligence to determine for themselves what price is too high for the value they are likely to obtain.

It is natural enough to give great deference to the medical judgment of a trusted physician; it is something else to say that people, having heard the odds of a given therapy working for them, are incapable of judging what price that potential relief is worth. But that is the implicit assumption of the accidental system we have all grown up in. It is just another way in which the personal autonomy of the American citizen has been shrunken.

I spent many years in the pharmaceutical business, a curious industry that is unique in that all conceivable risks must be tediously and, usually, excessively stated to each potential customer. During the health care debate I couldn't help but think it was too bad that Obamacare wasn't subjected to FDA regulation. It would probably never have reached the market, and if somehow it had, a disclosure of its likely or possible side effects would have killed its sales quickly.

The misrepresentations began on the day of its introduction. I was attending a Republican Governors Association meeting in Texas—an infrequent occurrence as I generally don't like to leave my post in

Indiana—when the first details about the proposed reforms began trick-ling out. The conference had concluded and I was headed for the hotel checkout when I was apprehended by a fellow governor, who implored me to join a few other Republican colleagues and discuss the new pro-posal with the press.

Seeing no way to duck the request, I joined Bobby Jindal of Louisiana, Haley Barbour of Mississippi, and a few others on the hotel ballroom stage. The other participants, Bobby in particular, were more knowledge-able than I about the implications—to both health care and our country in general—of what the president was attempting to do. My role was to comment on the fiscal aspects of the proposal, based on the time I had spent as the White House budget director a few years before. (No one would accept my truthful disclaimers about how little of relevance I remembered from that experience.)

It didn't really take an expert to spot the con job that was under way. When my turn at the microphone came, working from the few fragments available that morning, I was able to detect and point out the first obvious flaws in the bill's fiscal front.

For one, it was clear that its massive expansion of Medicaid would force huge new costs and probably taxes on the states, which share in paying for that program. I spotted one of Washington's favorite decep-tions, in the bill's accounting for ten years of taxes but only six years of spending. (Congressional convention is to "cost" bills over an arbi-trary ten-year period.) Because most of the bill's direct government spending would start only in the fifth year, while the taxes commenced immediately on passage, the first ten years could be made to look more deficit-friendly than any ten true years of operation. I wasn't clear about the details of the new "CLASS" entitlement for long-term care, but it, too, seemed to start collecting money ahead of its first spending, and thus misstate its real deficit effects when only the first ten years were looked at.

I've learned from the mistakes of experience to be cautious in the use of adjectives, but on this occasion I could already tell that any term smaller than *fraudulent* would be insufficient to capture what was about to be foisted on the country. I used the word that morning, and nothing we discovered in all the months of debate that followed rendered it hyperbolic. *Fraud* connotes a knowing attempt to mislead, and the bill's authors had to know that their assertions that Obamacare would reduce deficits and lessen rather than frighteningly worsen the debt crisis were untrue.

The same holds true for the assertion that the bill would reduce health care costs, but it was nonetheless made repeatedly. The bill itself was even called the Patient Protection and Affordable Care Act. And here's what Obama had to say at the White House after meeting with industry leaders about his proposals: "Their efforts [to reduce health cost] will help us take the next and most important step—comprehensive health care reform—so that we can do what I pledged to do as a candidate and save a typical family an average of $2,500 on their health care costs." Why the idea that expanding government into the health care market would actually reduce costs was ever given two seconds' credence is a mystery. After the bill became law, Tim Carney noted in the *Washington Examiner* that one of the Senate staffers who helped draft the bill, David Bowen, admitted that the legislation's aim wasn't to cut costs. "This is a coverage bill, not a cost reduction bill," Carney quoted him as saying at a briefing on K Street. How could a requirement that millions more citizens buy heavily subsidized health insurance, in a market of excessive and fast-rising costs, possibly lead to less rather than more spending? The Brothers Grimm started from more realistic premises.

From a credibility standpoint, the bill's best day was its first, when just a few of us, dismissed at the time as partisan cranks, protested. The phony claims made for the measure—that it would reduce costs, that it would reduce federal spending and deficits, that no one's current insurance or choice of coverage would be impacted—all began to evaporate soon thereafter. The process accelerated immediately after the ink was dry on the president's signature, and the full dimensions of the bill nobody had read became clear.

With each succeeding analysis, objective estimates of the impact on total health care spending have gone up. The Centers for Medicare and Medicaid predicted, after Obamacare became law, that overall national health care spending would increase 6.3 percent each year for the next decade. Meanwhile, the Congressional Budget Office keeps inching up its cost estimates of Obamacare, and even President Obama admits that health care costs will continue to rise. Instead of arguing that his policies will drive down the overall cost of care or reduce government spending, he has taken to arguing that without his reform, families would have spent more on health care than they will now: "We didn't think that we were going to cover 30 million people for free, but that the long-term trend in terms of how much the average family is going to be paying for health insurance is going to be improved as a consequence of health care." It would have been better—or at least more honest—for the administration to have made the case that Obamacare would be expensive, but that the costs would ultimately be worth it in order to cover millions of Americans. We could then have had an honest debate about what services government should provide and how much it should spend. But forthrightness was not to be the fuel of the Obamacare steamroller.

And just as the administration later admitted that Obamacare would make the deficit larger not smaller, health care costs higher not lower, and that the CLASS Act in reality would be "unsustainable," its overseer of the intended insurance exchanges has talked a different game since the legislation was signed into law. Joel Ario of the Department of Health and Human Services has been reported as saying that "Big companies may eventually look to dump their employees onto new state-run health insurance markets in the future. . . . Major employers won't drop their health insurance *right* away." (Emphasis added.)

But, he went on, "If it plays out the exchanges work pretty well, then the employer can say, 'This is a great thing. I can now dump my people into the exchange and it would be good for them, good for me.'" Ario neglected to mention that a deal like that has to be bad for somebody, and in this case it will be the taxpayer and, eventually, the patients who are trapped in the command-and-control, government-rationed system of medical care.

The equally absurd claims that choice would be preserved and that everyone could keep the coverage they had melted like snowflakes in May, as soon as the nation's insurers began calculating the effect of the bill's many mandates, and employers began comparing the cost of continuing their existing coverage versus dumping their employees into the new government-run "exchanges." Within months of the bill's signing, the first studies started to emerge pointing out that the reforms would actually drive up costs. Richard Foster, the chief actuary of Medicare, came out with a thirty-eight-page report in April 2010 that concluded that under Obamacare, health costs would rise more than they would have if nothing had been passed, and would come to consume 21 percent of the economy, up from 17 percent. The report projected that the reforms would lead to health care shortages as millions of Americans flooded the market, that fourteen million employees would be dropped from their employers' health insurance plans, and that new taxes would drive up the cost of private insurance for those who still had it. All this from an official within the government.

These bulletins elicited a telling, sign-of-the-times response from health care czarina Kathleen Sebelius, who issued a menacing diktat to the nation's insurance companies stating, among other threats, that insurers with "unreasonable" or "unjustified" rate increases (whatever that means) would be barred from doing business with Obamacare's coming exchanges. Citizens wondering which sector of society works for the other got an unmistakable clue from this scandalous episode.

Almost as quickly, employers started ruminating publicly about dropping employee coverage. Some plans were forced to do more than ruminate. In September 2010, McDonald's dropped a bomb on Obamacare by announcing that it might have to drop coverage for 30,000 hourly employees because of new restrictions on "mini-med" plans, which have a somewhat low cap on the total health costs the insurance covers. McDonald's, of course, is one of America's largest employers, so its announcement gave a strong hint as to what might happen to the other 1.4 million American covered by such plans. To forestall a public relations disaster, Secretary Sebelius granted a waiver to the burger chain, exempting it, for now, from the new law the administration had just rammed through.

Like the projections of true costs and the deficit impact, successive analyses of the effect on existing coverage increasingly gave the lie to Obamacare's promises. Senior citizens who had chosen "Medicare Plus" managed-care plans learned that their carriers were being squeezed out of the market.

And when the dumping begins, it may not be only private employers who take part. Governors have already begun to receive deadly serious advice that they consider dumping their state employees into the newly expanded Medicaid or into the exchanges. Nothing precludes cash-strapped state and local governments from dropping health coverage for government employees, paying the $2,000 per employee fine, and pocketing the large resulting savings. I asked Indiana's independent actuaries to calculate the effect such a move would have in my state, and they reported that Indiana would save a little over $300 million per year, a number some future governor might find highly attractive.

Even a confirmed skeptic of conspiracy theories could survey all this and wonder if maybe all the chaos that Obamacare will bring was not fully foreseen and planned by its authors. Unrepealed, Obamacare will unleash a headlong slide of more and more people into direct government-run health care, followed by millions more as smaller insurers are driven from the marketplace and the whole system turns into a highly regulated utility, virtually indistinguishable from the single-payer system the proponents plainly wanted in the first place.

Wrecking one-sixth of the economy and piling on a new mountain of debt were reason enough to cause a sense of alarm and to lead opponents of Obamacare to wage an epic, months-long struggle against it. But the issue merited the passionate debate it continues to inspire for an even larger reason. Obamacare represents the ghastly confluence of all the dangers I've described in this book.

First, it will deepen the Red Menace immeasurably. Not only will the government not be able to afford it, but it will further the exploitation of young Americans by their elders, forcing them to buy health insurance they may not want, and then overcharging them in order to cross-subsidize those who require more care. An analysis by Rand Health in 2010 found that under Obamacare, insurance premiums for young Americans would increase by 17 percent as insurers were forced to take from the young to provide for the old.

The bill will deepen the subservience of the private sector to our federal overlords. All aspects of the health care marketplace, from the products permitted to be sold to the price each participant may charge, will now be dictated by our Betters. Most of this new avalanche of controls will be devised, in the preferred Progressive fashion, by "expert" bureaucrats unencumbered by the oversight of the voting public.

Perhaps most sadly, the federal takeover of health care will worsen the dependency of Americans on "the government," as tens of millions more are drawn into this huge expansion of the entitlement state. It is estimated that Obamacare will expand health coverage to approximately thirty-four million people; more than half of that coverage will come from an expansion in Medicaid while many of the rest will end up in health care exchanges where they will be subsidized by the government (after being checked by the same system that certifies recipients for welfare and food stamps).

Meanwhile, the legislation's mandates will dictate what each recipient insures himself against. Not only are individuals mandated to buy insurance and employers to provide insurance, or pay a fine, but also the coverage you can legally buy under Obamacare will come studded with features that you may not want, need, or ever use (or afford on your own). Under the president's reforms, you must buy a policy that covers oral and vision care as well as emergency services, maternity care, mental health, and even substance abuse services. The plan must cover your children (whether you have them or not) and continue to cover them until they turn twenty-six. And you can no longer get a discount because you are young, in good health, or want limited coverage. In short, the shrunken citizen will shrink another couple of inches.

Better ways were possible. In Indiana we have chosen a path that respects the right of our people to make their own health care choices, and trusts their ability to do so. We have pursued policies that restore the true concept of insurance to the health marketplace, and in the process have restored a measure of the consumerism that presses for quality and cost control in every other economic arena.

Shortly after inauguration, as I signed up for benefits as a new state employee, I inquired whether the state's menu of health care plans included the option of a Health Savings Account. The answer was no, the

only choices were traditional fee-for-service plans and a health maintenance organization or two. I directed our personnel department to add
at least one such option by the next annual employee signup window.

HSAs are a Hoosier invention, first conceived by a remarkable gentle-
man named Patrick Rooney. Pat Rooney was first and foremost a great
businessman; he built the Golden Rule Insurance Company into a
national leader in health care and other markets. As an aside, he was also
a deeply caring citizen, who attended a nearly all-black inner city church
until his death in 2008 and founded the first charitable trust to raise
money for poor families who wished their children to be educated in non-
public schools.

Pat Rooney saw the perversities of health care financing from the
inside, and came up with a terrific innovation. He figured that a huge
amount of unnecessary costs could be cut from the system simply by
returning decisions about routine or relatively affordable care to individuals, while providing insurance only for the rare, unexpected big expenses.
With an HSA, a consumer has a personal account from which to pay medical expenses. Overconsumption would decline as people thought more
carefully about services that were no longer "free," and overcharges would
start to be eliminated as reengaged purchasers began to challenge them,
or to shop around, as they do in every normal marketplace. As I like to say,
we will never have cost control until we are all cost controllers.

From their inception, HSAs were strenuously resisted by the defenders of the now-traditional third-party payment system, and especially by
those who were working for an eventual government-run, single-payer
form. Their arguments were diverse: HSAs would work for young, healthy
people but not for those with more medical problems; people would avoid
preventive care in an attempt to husband their personal account funds;
and so on. At every opportunity, congressional Democrats threw legislative and regulatory roadblocks into the path of this innovative new
option.

But the real crux of the movement to strangle HSAs is that they
empower their users with far too much freedom. The individual policy-
holder chooses when and where to purchase health care, and in what
quantity. She can choose to forgo treatment for minor problems and con-

serve personal account funds for some more serious ailment in the future. Giving our Betters credit for sincerity, they simply believe that the vast majority of Americans are incompetent to make these decisions and must be enveloped in the protective paternalism of a health care system where these decisions are made for them by wiser, caring people, namely them.

In 2006, their first year of availability for Indiana state employees, HSAs were selected by only 4 percent of us, a little over a thousand out of the thirty-five thousand people then on the state payroll. But over the next few years, this option grew in popularity. In 2011, 85 percent of state workers were using them. Why? Because the HSAs cost both the employee and the state less money, and they were easier to manage than a traditional plan, with its blizzard of baffling, unreadable paperwork. Each month, a simple one-page statement arrives, looking much like a credit card bill but even clearer. It shows the beginning personal account balance, the deposits made by the state as employer and by the employee, and any medical payments made during the month. The resulting closing balance completes the statement. Even I can understand it—an acid test of clarity.

The results were as positive as Pat Rooney would have predicted. Medical costs for state employees were at least 11 percent lower than forecast. HSA plan members were accumulating real savings (unspent personal account dollars are the property of the member), in the amount of more than $30 million total by 2010. Notably, they were accessing preventive care at higher rates than their counterparts in old-fashioned insurance plans.

But the best news was that real consumerism had kicked in. Analyses by the state's outside actuary found that patients were avoiding emergency rooms for non-emergencies, in favor of less expensive care settings. They were using generic drugs at a far higher rate than their counterparts in traditional plans. They were shopping around for the best prices on high-cost procedures. When it's your money and not someone else's, you will always be more judicious about spending it.

It was a great surprise to learn that at 85 percent, our state government was not only the leader in HSA participation, but was almost the only one in the running. In private-sector America, HSAs (or CDHPs, for "consumer-driven health plans," as they are now more commonly called), have spread to about 10 percent of employees.

In the public sector, however, they are almost nonexistent. There, the penetration is an estimated 2 percent, and Indiana by itself must account for a significant fraction of that number. You have probably guessed the reason. The government unions despise HSAs. They free and empower the workers for whom the union wishes to speak and make decisions. Therefore unions have stifled the emergence of HSAs in every jurisdiction in which they have the clout to do so.

Too bad for those jurisdictions, and their taxpayers. While employee health costs are under control in Indiana, across the rest of the states they continue to swiftly rise. And they will continue to do so as long as health care feels free to the patient, such that he rarely asks the typical consumer questions: "Doc, is there a generic form of that drug?" "Doc, didn't I have that same test just a couple months ago?" "Doc, which hospital has the best price, and the best success record, for this procedure you're recommending?"

State employees are a very diverse group, spanning the spectrum from highway workers and clerical personnel to top executives. It cannot be said that they are unrepresentative of the overall population, or that they are somehow better able to manage their own health care decision making than the average citizen. Just in case anyone should venture that theory, we can show them a parallel, successful experience in the low-income program we call HIP, the Healthy Indiana Plan.

HIP was our 2006 initiative to bring the peace of mind of health insurance to as many low-income uninsured Hoosiers as we could. I say "as we could" because, from the outset, I defined HIP as a partial solution to the approximately 350,000 chronically uninsured low- and moderate-income citizens of our state. Having watched Tennessee's finances sink under the weight of an open-ended entitlement program called TennCare that eventually got so expensive it had to be rolled back by a Democratic governor, I was determined that our effort would be limited to the dollars available and not become a drain on our state's taxpayers.

Recognizing that we could help at most a significant fraction of our uninsured population, I set our people to the task of designing an effective means of doing so. Our Democratic opponents controlled the Indiana House of Representatives and could generally be counted on to try to block any idea of mine, no matter how good. But in this instance I was optimistic that we could work something out, as Democrats had regularly lamented the extent of the problem of the uninsured.

To pay for the program, I had settled on an increase in the tobacco tax. Indiana at the time had the second highest rate of smoking in the country, a major target of the fitness and wellness efforts I had launched and personally led. One obvious reason for our stubbornly high smoking levels was the cheapness of cigarettes, driven by a very low tax of 55.5 cents per pack that had not been changed in many years, even as most other states and all our neighbors (except Kentucky) raised theirs. This was another aspect of our proposal that Democrats were likely to find congenial, and eventually endorsed when the tax was raised to 99.5 cents per pack. And I referred those Republicans who treat any tax, anytime, for any purpose as a heresy to the words of my former boss Ronald Reagan, who said, "If you want more of something, tax it less; less of something, tax it more." I wanted less smoking in Indiana, and would be curious to hear the contrary case.

When our staff brought the first design in, it looked a lot like an expansion of old-fashioned Medicaid, just with higher income limits. I threw them out of my office (politely) and asked them to come back with "HSAs for poor people." Ultimately, that's what HIP became. Our Democratic friends would probably have preferred a more conventional approach, but to their credit they were eager to cooperate in addressing a serious problem that had bothered them for a long time.

One morning in the shower, where most of my best ideas seem to pop into my head, I devised the acronym to describe the personal accounts that would be at the heart of HIP. They are called POWER accounts, which stands for "personal wellness and responsibility." This label is meant to capture the concept that we are out to give the individual the power to control his own health care spending decisions, and that we trust him to take the responsibility for protecting and promoting his own wellness.

HIP became law in May 2007, won a waiver from the federal government in December of that year, and "went live" in January 2008. From the moment it was available, it was extremely popular. Because we use Medicaid dollars to help pay for it, we had to make a number of federally dictated adjustments to our ideal design, but the basic structure stayed intact.

Participants manage a personal POWER account, funded by their own modest premiums—averaging around 3 percent of adjusted gross income with a cap of 4.5 percent—and the state's contribution. The accounts total $1,100 per person per year. Participants manage expenses up to that amount, keeping and rolling over whatever remains at year's end. They are completely covered should expenses exhaust the funds in their POWER account. As I termed it in the marketing campaign around the time of HIP's launch, it offers "health care you can control, at a price you can afford."

Clinics, hospitals, and physicians serving low-income Hoosiers love HIP. Not only is it enabling their patients to access quality treatment more often, but those providing the care now get paid for their services, almost immediately. So our network of care organizations for our most vulnerable citizens has been substantially strengthened and consequently helped to serve their non-HIP clients.

Just as with our state employee CDHPs, we are seeing signs of consumerist behavior among the HIP population. One of the ways a patient can drive up the cost of care is to turn to the emergency room for nonemergency services. We've found that those covered by HIP turn to the ER significantly less often than those covered by the state's old Medicaid plan. For every 1,000 people, for example, covered by the old plan, 844 individuals go to the ER for nonemergency care, while under HIP, 772 do. That rate is still too high, but it seems that the twenty-five-dollar copay HIP charges for nonemergency care at the ER is having an effect. We've also found that those enrolled in HIP use preventive care and choose generic drugs (over more expensive brand-name drugs) more often than those on Medicaid, who have no financial incentive to rein in their health costs. These citizens may be low-income and often in poor health, one of the hardest populations to serve with health services, but they are proving fully capable of making their own decisions. Our program trusts in their capacity, and affords them the respect and dignity to which a free citizen is entitled.

The Indiana health care experience, which involves close to a hundred thousand people covered by HIP and state CDHPs, exposes the paternalist conceit that health care choices are beyond the ability of Americans. Tragically, the essence of Obamacare is that exact conceit, and predictably the legislation effectively kills HSAs and plans such as HIP.

By severely limiting permissible deductibles and piling on its numerous mandates, Obama's plan seeks to strangle the private CDHP marketplace. And its expansion of Medicaid will likely force the abolition of HIP, by making almost the entire HIP population eligible for Medicaid. At this writing it appears that HIP enrollees will be pitched into the Medicaid morass, like it or not. And judging from consumer satisfaction surveys that show HIP with 97 percent positive ratings, and a 99 percent renewal rate, most of them won't like it.

Obamacare reflects in crystalline form the worldview of our Benevolent Betters. It assumes that Americans are too dim-witted and too intimidated to make their own decisions, even (or, perhaps they would say, especially) in this most personal of life's realms.

It sees them as helpless victims, subject at every turn to being abused by uncaring and rapacious private interests. Obamacare's advocates' vicious, often personal attacks on one health care industry after another, even those that had naïvely attempted to cooperate in the bill's passage, revealed their commitment to this mind-set. Americans, these poor victims, must be brought under the protective wings of a system in which experts will shield them from being overcharged, choosing inadequate coverage, or selecting the wrong doctor or course of therapy. If they have chosen not to purchase insurance at all, then they must simply be ordered to do so, for their own good.

Of course, the mechanism for their deliverance must be the subjugation of the heartless and untrustworthy private sector to the altruists of government. To quote Lenin, yet another "commanding height of the economy" must be broken to the saddle of our new masters in the public sector.

Hard-core statists feigned disappointment that the president failed to pull off an immediate and total nationalization of health care on par with that of European countries or Canada. But privately they must be thrilled, knowing that the health insurance industry will most likely collapse before too long into their single-payer utopia, after a brief transition as a regulated public utility. Its product offerings, prices, and capital investments will all be tightly supervised. Businesses large and small, and even cash-strapped state governments, I predict, will find it far more affordable to pay the bill's fines and dump their employees into the public exchanges or Medicaid. Insurers, trapped hopelessly between mandated Rolls-Royce coverage requirements and the price-controlling power of HHS, will exit the marketplace in search of a business that does not require them to go broke.

American health care, distorted by its accidental payment practices and a greed-driven legal system, is at a dead end. In a dead end, the worst option is "full speed ahead." Stopping before you crash is a good first step, but eventually it will be necessary to back up to the fork where you took the wrong turn. We made the wrong turn when we disconnected health care from the discipline of consumer power, and disconnected Americans from full control over their own well-being.

Obamacare must be undone and replaced not merely as a matter of sound health policy, not merely because it promises to damage a staggering national economy, not merely because it will hasten the bankruptcy of the American government. Obamacare must be undone for the even more fundamental reason that, in its essence, it demeans and diminishes the rights of the free people Americans were intended to be.

CHAPTER 6

Taking on the Statist Quo

One glorious evening on Monday night football, the commentators turned their conversation to Bill Walsh, the legendary coach who took the San Francisco 49ers to three Super Bowl victories. Someone labeled Walsh a "genius," and Joe Theismann, himself an NFL legend, took exception to the label. "Now, wait a minute," he said. "This is football. There are no geniuses in football. A genius is someone like Norman Einstein."

I often think of that exchange because it reminds me that there is a certain brilliance to focusing on the simple basics of a task. I don't know whether winning football championships takes an Albert Einstein level of genius, but I do know that balancing a budget does not. I've been deeply immersed in numerous government budgets, and in every case the path to fiscal fitness was clear even if those in charge were not prepared to walk it. Spending only what you have isn't a matter of wit, it is a matter of will. Or, more pointedly, it can be a matter of political courage and leadership. As one European leader put it during the EU debt crisis of 2010, "We know what we need to do. We just don't know how to get reelected after we've done it."

As a people we have allowed the mind-set shared by that European leader to permeate our politics. Today we are facing a national debt crisis of our own that is fast approaching a breaking point, and we have seen very few leaders willing to do something about it. The approach always seems to be to delay until tomorrow serious spending reforms. What's worse, in many cases the recent go-go boom years fueled a spending spree that was never sustainable and always potentially ruinous.

Even while the U.S. government's debt horror show was still in production, there were plenty of danger signs on the state level, where governments are in fact subject to reality and cannot print money to cover their excesses. In 2008, California stopped paying vendors for months and issued IOUs to residents in lieu of tax refunds, thus converting individuals into involuntary lenders so it could keep the party going a little longer. Illinois and Kansas took similar steps in recent years. By the end of the first decade of the twenty-first century, states across the country were facing steep budget crunches, with California, Illinois, and New York seemingly intent on proving that Greece, Iceland, and Ireland were not modern anomalies—that bankruptcy on a grand government scale is actually possible.

This would seem to be the "Ah-ha!" moment the Skeptics of democracy have long anticipated. When state governments go begging for bailouts from Washington to avoid bankruptcy, when European countries go begging to their better-off EU brethren to avoid the same fate, and when the U.S. government takes on more debt in a few quick years than it has in its entire previous history, it might appear that there is something to the old Skeptic's warning that government by the people would last only until the people figured out they could vote themselves money from the Treasury. Skeptics have long said that once calamity comes, free institutions will have to be replaced with more workable, more authoritarian ones.

Modern Skeptics are a little less direct in their critiques of self-government. But their prescriptions for reviving the economy and conducting myriad other important endeavors are embedded with the same assumptions held by the Skeptics of old—that only by curtailing individual liberty with higher taxes, a more active government, and more public spending can the gears that drive our society start to turn at full speed once again.

But this is where we need to be thankful that it does not take a genius to balance a budget. While there are huge differences between state and federal governance, what's been going on at the state level in recent years is both cautionary and encouraging. First, states are typically required by their constitutions to balance their budgets, so they run into fiscal realities more quickly than the federal government does. This means that states can give us a hint of what's around the corner if the federal government continues to spend like a teenager with his father's credit card.

Second, as states hit the wall, we can see what fiscally ruinous policies look like before it is too late to reform Washington.

That last point is encouraging for the simple reason that we are not a static people. If Winston Churchill was right when he said that Americans could be counted on to do the right thing once all other options had been exhausted, the states offer insights into what voters will do once they see they have run out of options short of cutting spending or going bankrupt. And there are recent signs that voters are willing to impose a little adult supervision on those in charge of the public business.

In 2009, New Jersey elected as governor a tough-minded former prosecutor in Chris Christie, who has drawn the national spotlight and wide applause for refusing to sugarcoat his state's fiscal mess. We will know in a few years whether he is able to alter the trajectory of his state. Voters in Massachusetts elected Scott Brown to the U.S. Senate at what seemed like a pivotal moment in the Obamacare debate, in part because he promised to vote against the health care legislation. (Congress found a way to pass it anyway, of course.) And across the country, officials who talked honestly about the need to rein in government spending at all levels won election in 2010.

In Indiana we've seen another encouraging phenomenon. Once the stark realities of deficits and reckless spending set in, not only are serious reforms possible, but they eventually win broad voter approval.

Throughout my first term, I was warned repeatedly that our efforts to curb government spending in Indiana would doom our administration's chances at reelection. For example, at the National Governors Meeting in 2007, New Mexico governor Bill Richardson, who was then leading the charge to help Democrats win races for governor across the country, told the national press that he wasn't sure about most of the gubernatorial races, but that he could guarantee a win over Daniels in Indiana. I was supposedly vulnerable because my historically cautious state had seen an unusually high volume of "controversial" changes in three short years. He saw my administration's strict control of spending and the very public protests organized against our reforms as major political liabilities.

What he and others didn't count on was that in an era of debt and tough economic times, there are a lot of tools available for political leaders willing to cut spending. One of the ones we found most effective was that the truth was on our side—we weren't making up any of the things we'd found under the state's fiscal hood. Indeed, when I took the oath of office in early 2005, Indiana was essentially bankrupt. It was on pace to spend nearly $12 billion for the year, but was taking in just over $11 billion in revenue; it was the seventh year in a row of unbalanced budgets. In total, the state was approximately $700 million in the red. What's more, for years the state had engaged in all sorts of deceptive budget gimmickry that not only exacerbated our fiscal problems, but also allowed the legislature to sidestep provisions requiring the General Fund to be balanced at the close of each fiscal year.

These activities were abusive of the public trust, in violation of at least the spirit of constitutional balanced budget provisions, and corrosive of the good-government culture necessary for sound governance. They also eroded the individual's sovereignty by taxing him to fund activities that the state couldn't afford and shouldn't have been engaged in anyway.

Politicians can demonstrate a tremendous amount of ingenuity in finding ways to evade spending curbs. But, as it turns out, Indiana politicians were not even forced to be particularly clever.

The state's balanced budget provisions date back to the 1830s and '40s, when Indiana went deep into debt as it built canals. Those canals turned out to be bad bets, and paying for them nearly broke the state's balance sheet. To guard against reckless borrowing again, provisions were written into Indiana's constitution barring it from taking on debt for pretty much anything other than hard capital assets (such as roads and buildings).

In recent years, one favored tactic for getting around borrowing restrictions was to pretend a debt wasn't actually being incurred. This was typically done by skipping payments to state pension funds. In reality, skipped payments are a debt on the future, because fiduciary duty will eventually compel the state to make up for a missed payment much the way a bank forces a homeowner to make up for a missed mortgage payment. Another favored tactic was to force others to take on debts that would indirectly fund the state's spending habits. This was done by delaying payments to public schools, colleges, and other entities until additional tax revenue rolled in. The victims here would have to wait six months or more for their state funding, and in the meantime would keep their lights on by taking out short-term loans. The 2008–10 recession saw states all over the country trot out similar tricks to "balance" their budgets.

Our administration quickly concluded that stamping out such financial subterfuge was essential to putting the state on sound footing. It would make it harder to balance the state's budget, but I forbade late payments and required the state to put the proper amount of funds into its pension programs. We made it our mission not only to square spending with revenues but also to catch the state up on its overdue bills, all within the four-year term granted to us by the voters.

Operating with the extra burden of these principles, we expected a very difficult slog, and we got one. But along the way something interesting happened. The system responded to the calls for fiscal integrity. Most residents seemed to know that we were operating in a tough fiscal environment, so drawing hard budgetary lines drew out the creativity and understanding of many Hoosiers. In the end, we managed to haul the state out of its ditch of debt, and we did it much faster than the "experts" said was possible.

Four years later, the operating deficit and unpaid bills were eliminated, and the state had $1.3 billion (just over 10 percent of a year's budget) in "rainy day" reserves. Overall debt, including that from highway bonds and other past capital borrowing, had been reduced by 40 percent, and the state had its first AAA (the highest possible) credit rating ever, making it one of a handful of states to hold that distinction. Thanks to those reserves, and to continued frugality, Indiana was one of the few states (almost the only one without energy-driven revenue) to navigate the recession without raising taxes of any kind.

Genius was not a factor. Halfway through my second term, a reporter asked me how we had turned things around. "Prepare to be dazzled," I said. "We spent less money than we took in." Total state spending had been held almost flat, growing at about 1 percent per year for six years, one-third the rate of inflation, while revenue caught up and surpassed it.

And, after four years of hard decisions, controversies, and turmoil, our administration was rehired by the people of Indiana, returned to office with the largest number of votes ever cast for any candidate for any office in the history of our state—this in a year when the opposing party's presidential candidate was winning Indiana's electoral votes.

So how did this improbable turnabout occur?

Well, it's important to note that none of Indiana's fiscal problems could be blamed on the economy. In 2004 the Great Recession was still almost four years off and the real estate bubble was fully inflated. Revenues were not shrinking but growing, albeit slowly. Indiana's budget crunch was entirely the product of deliberate decisions to spend more money than the state had. During the first half of the decade, state revenues increased on average between 3 percent and 4 percent. Spending, on the other hand, increased at an annual average rate of 6 percent. No one should need "Norman" Einstein to tell him that kind of arithmetic would lead to trouble.

At bottom the problems were age-old ones. Milton Friedman once explained why government spending tends to be wasteful. A person who spends his own money (or even other people's money) on himself, will likely show some respect for each dollar spent, Friedman said. But when it comes to spending other people's money on other people, a person's financial discipline all but disappears. Add to this the fact that government spending can increase a politician's popularity by demonstrating his concern for the environment or some other popular cause and you have plenty of incentives to open the spending spigots. What's more, while each item in the budget has its defenders, rare is the single budget item that is large enough to provoke a taxpayer revolt against it. The political incentives are nearly all wrong for cutting spending, which is why Ronald Reagan was on to something when he said, "A government bureau is the nearest thing to eternal life we'll ever see on this earth."

So, from the start, we had our work cut out for us.

Our plan was straightforward: Make private-sector job growth a leading goal of government policies, while also changing the culture within governmental institutions in ways that encouraged thriftiness and a healthy respect for the liberty of individual Hoosiers, and do it without letting up on environmental protections or taking away essential government services. Wiping out the practice of skirting spending restrictions was an early, vital step. Another important early step was my decision to rescind the executive order dating back to 1989 that had swept state employees into unions without their consent. Essentially, I decertified the state's public employee unions and thereby made it possible to shift employees around, assign them new tasks, and make other moves that brought efficiency and cost savings by changing the inner workings of government without union consent. It was a hard decision, but it gave us both the ability and the credibility to put out one of the leanest budget proposals the state had seen in more than half a century. That proposal won support in the State Legislature and set the stage for spending reforms across all layers of government in the years ahead.

One tool that I had at my disposal was the power not to spend money budgeted by the General Assembly. On the federal level, this is called the power of "impoundment" or "rescission." It is a powerful tool because it enables the chief executive to react to changing budget circumstances and stop agencies from spending money the government doesn't have. Unfortunately, Congress effectively stripped the president of this power, along with others, in the post-Watergate period that tilted the federal scales toward easy spending.

I appreciated the power to save unspent funds—which in Indiana is called the power of "reversion"—because it not only made budgetary sense, but also changed the politics of government spending. It's hard to hold any one legislator responsible for a budget tipping into deficit. Consequently, few legislators become sharp-eyed budget hawks. But a governor (like a president) is both visible and subject to election outside of a gerrymandered district. He has the platform to draw attention to needed cuts and a political incentive to follow up.

What's more, I found that legislators were happy to let me do the dirty work. They were able to vote for higher spending than the state could afford (thus pleasing some constituents) and then let me be the bad guy while lamenting my cuts, if it was politically expedient to do so. In other words, it worked out well for them. But I never minded as long as we got the results we were looking for.

There is no question about the effectiveness of such powers in willing hands. Between 2005 and 2010 we reduced spending below that approved by the Indiana General Assembly by a total of some $1.9 billion, while some executive branch agencies have made 25 percent reductions since

2008. Unspent and secure in the state's savings accounts, those dollars came in handy in the Great Recession as protection against tax increases and radical cutbacks in necessary services.

Many reductions triggered yelps from the special interests most affected, but it was fascinating how few cries of real pain filled the airwaves. The average citizen just didn't feel a cut in government lease costs, centralized procurement, or the number of National Guard armories. Now whenever someone claims that a cut will severely impact citizens, I can respond, "You'd be amazed how much government you'd never miss."

Effective and indispensable as impoundment has been in our case, one must acknowledge the legitimate balance-of-power issues it raises. Strict constitutionalists, among whom I have always counted myself, often challenge the practice as a violation of the clear assignment of the spending power to the legislative branch. The problem is that both state and federal legislatures have repeatedly proven unwilling to impose the simple discipline of matching dollars out to dollars in. With full respect for these reservations, I can testify that without this tool, Indiana would never have staved off the fiscal disaster that has befallen other states. And I have to observe that reinstatement of some similar power in a president prepared to use it vigorously would be of tremendous value in repairing our shattered federal finances.

Less Spending and Better Results, Too

Wasteful government spending, however, isn't just costly to the bottom line. It can also have a negative impact on the people it is supposed to help. Reversing the damage from this kind of spending requires more than the power not to spend a portion of funds authorized. It often requires rethinking how government services are delivered.

I was reminded of this not long after taking office when I received a call from the innovative young man we had hired to run our prison system.

"Do you know we're paying a dollar forty-three a meal for prison food?" he asked me.

"No," I answered. "Is that a lot?"

"It's a heck of a lot," he said. "Where I came from, it was ninety-five cents a meal, and I'm pretty sure the food was better."

He went on to explain that we'd been cooking the meals in twenty-seven different kitchens, each of which bought its own food in small quantities. He asked me if he could outsource meal preparation to get us a better deal. He might as well have asked if I minded if he stopped wasting taxpayer money.

A few weeks later we contracted with a large catering company, the kind that provides food at convention centers, sporting arenas, and military bases. The cost per meal dropped to 98 cents, which may not sound like a big savings. However, multiply it by 23,000 prisoners who eat 3 meals a day, 365 days per year, and the simple decision to contract out food preparation produced a fast savings of $14 million per year. Over time, that savings grew to well over $20 million a year. And here is the most important part: the food, as measured by nutritional content and prisoner feedback, did, in fact, improve. While spending less money, we got better government.

Most people assume that the vast amount of money the government spends goes to paying state workers. But that is often not the case. We analyzed Indiana's sprawling social services bureaucracy and found that approximately ninety-two cents out of every dollar spent passed through one of more than a thousand nonprofit and for-profit entities.

This isn't a bad thing in and of itself. People who operate under the competitive pressure of the marketplace almost always do it better than the monopoly we call government. It's been well said that if you can find a service in the yellow pages, government probably shouldn't try to do it itself.

So, over the years, we extended the simple concept we applied to prisoner meals to prison health care, medical services, and education. (We found that the best paid teachers in the state, many of them earning over $125,000 per year, were teaching our criminals, so we gave the job to the faculty of our state community college, at an enormous savings.) We also applied this concept to state hospitals, parks, custodial services, administrative functions—anywhere it made economic sense—and found again and again that service levels went up as costs went down. It turns out that focusing on fiscal discipline also forces government to focus on effectiveness and quality of output.

Even in the realm of education, we found that a tight adherence to budget discipline and a full understanding of why organizations behave the way they do can help boost results without increasing costs.

When it comes to education, the services offered by government are often too expensive, too inflexible to the needs of all children, and too slow to embrace change. There are some very good public schools, but when a public school system is failing its students, it is often too difficult to reform it without first fundamentally changing the structure that led to its failures.

There is also an additional problem with an educational system that is designed to minimize parental choice and maximize bureaucratic power. In the best of circumstances, such systems foster a culture of dependence among parents, not individual responsibility. Few decisions are more basic to parenthood than how a child is educated. To interfere with that choice is to step between a parent and a child. And today we have more riding on educational outcomes than at any point in our history.

In a modern, technology-driven economy Americans will increasingly be forced to succeed based on the skills best acquired in organized learning settings. We simply can't afford to allow the government to impose a one-size fits all educational system on our children when we know that expanding educational freedoms will help instill a necessary sense of individual responsibility, help us discover the best way to educate each and every child, and lead us to a system that is focused on quality rather than cost. Education is a civil rights struggle for our time, and to succeed as a modern society we have to get this one right.

So in Indiana, we took every opportunity to improve education by expanding parental freedom and flexibility. We did this in a number of ways. School choice is often a hotly contested issue when it involves allowing public money to be spent on private school tuition. So one step we turned to first was to expand public school choice by enacting a new law that allows students to transfer to any public school district without paying tuition. The response was amazing. School districts started advertising their graduation rates, test scores, and other academic achievements in order to attract new students. Competition works in education as everywhere else in life.

We also expanded charter schools, which gave parents new choices within the public system and, as underappreciated as it usually is, gave many parents a new avenue for getting involved in the education of their children. It is not uncommon in a charter school to find very active parents working to make sure the school has what it needs to succeed.

Finally, working within the public system, we designed an innovative program that gives enterprising students who graduate high school a year early the money the state would have spent on their education had they stuck around for a final year. Students can use this money only to further their education, so the program rewards hardworking teens by giving them a leg up on paying for college.

To make real strides in education, however, you have to think outside of the box—or, in this case, outside of the public system. In 2011 we pushed legislation that would give families who have tried public schools and found them unsatisfactory the power to take the tax dollars used to educate their children and spend it on sending their children to any school of their choosing, public or private. Parents making less than $62,000 can take advantage of the program; this takes in well over half of all Indiana households. Effectively, Indiana is the first state with universal school choice, because most parents above that income threshold already have the resources needed to send their children to the schools they want them to attend.

These reforms alone will not produce the excellence we need, and our program has included a host of other changes, such as new standards for teacher licensure, annual A–F grades for every school and district, and replacing teacher tenure and pay by seniority with rewards and job protection based on classroom performance.

But empowering poor and middle-income parents with the ability to pick their child's school will provide a healthy impetus for system-wide improvement, while raising those parents' personal dignity by entrusting them to make that choice, rather than having it dictated to them.

By tackling every major problem we could identify, we guaranteed that some initiatives would work out better than others. Sometimes reforms would fall short or simply go awry or just not give us the results we needed. When that happened, our practice was to swallow hard, admit we were wrong, and try again.

Saying Oops

One of the words people in public life find hard to say is *oops*. In my view, pretending that all is well when it plainly is not is another way to disrespect the judgment and maturity of our fellow citizens. To me, admitting an initiative isn't working, and finding a way to fix it, is part of treating the voters like adults. It's also a way of arriving at government that remains focused on its core responsibilities at a price we can afford.

One big "oops" I had to issue as governor stemmed from a letter that was awaiting me when I took office in 2005. It was from the U.S. Department of Health and Human Services and basically informed me that Indiana had the nation's worst welfare system. If we did not improve it, the letter warned, the state would be assessed massive financial penalties.

The letter was, unfortunately, on target. Our welfare system was rife with error. Many of those who qualified for benefits were denied them, while those who didn't meet the criteria were nonetheless being put on the welfare and Medicaid rolls. Unnecessary delays and fraud plagued the system. And nearly everyone was unhappy with the way things were working.

We quickly realized just how bad the problems were. As part of a sweeping ethics reform, we created an inspector general and implemented new protections for whistleblowers, moves that helped apprehend dozens of welfare criminals and send them to jail for handing out or receiving money illegally. Site visits to welfare offices revealed a chaotic mess. Antique, green-screen computers from the 1970s sat amid floor-to-ceiling stacks of boxes stuffed with paper. I asked our researchers to take pictures. Otherwise, I knew no one would believe later how bad the system was.

We spent a year analyzing the problems and assessing our options. It was clear that fundamental change was necessary—no amount of money would be able to get that system functioning properly. What we needed was a modern information back office, along with new front-line processes to interact with the public in a timely and accurate way.

Our analysis showed that trying to rebuild the existing back-office system inside government would be the most expensive of all the options, costing several hundred million dollars more than outsourcing. So we launched a competition and then selected a consortium of companies, led by IBM, to do the job. The contract promised millions of dollars in savings from the status quo, and far more compared to the state's attempting to fix its problems within the existing bureaucracy. As in any outsourcing, we insisted on protecting incumbent employees. Approximately 99 percent of the relevant state workers voluntarily chose to go to work for the consortium, which offered better pay, better benefits, and more opportunities for advancement than the old state system had. Those who did not were offered new government jobs. In addition, our negotiators secured a side agreement to bring a thousand new jobs to new customer service centers in our state.

Great, right?

Well, no. IBM's new system design proved too complex for the task. It produced just as many errors as the old one, and in some cases more. It didn't help that the system had to handle an exploding caseload because the recession was displacing a large number of workers and, in 2008, epic floods had inundated the southern half of the state, displacing even more people. But we accepted no excuses, and made none to the public. So, in 2009, I cancelled the IBM contract and put the state into direct supervision of the partner firms. We kept the features of the IBM approach that worked well and jettisoned the elements that failed. The new hybrid system we put in place, as this book was being written, is being rolled out with dramatically better results than the system we started with.

Our partisan opponents pounced on all of this as a "failure of privatization," even though they'd remained silent while the previous all-government system racked up its worst-in-America record and stole money from poor people. Much of the media coverage was inaccurate, incomplete, and irresponsible, parroting the partisan attacks.

In my view, the experience validates the practice of bringing private solutions to bear on public needs. When IBM wasn't meeting its contract obligations, we fired the company. You can't fire a state bureaucracy. When we were not satisfied with the results we were seeing, we were able to move quickly to replace the vendor with one who performed far better. Also, although the pro-patronage lobby hates to admit it, the back office of our welfare system is still privately run. In other words, contracting out is attractive for the same reason that charter schools are: if the public does not get the result it deserves, political leaders can revoke the charter and find another provider who can do better.

Our struggles with welfare modernization demonstrated that Hoosiers can act with a maturity the political class often assumes is beyond them. When you adopt, as we did, a "limited but active" approach to government, choosing not to shy away from problems, and trying lots of new ideas along the way, there will be mistakes, or at least efforts that fall short of their objectives. On several occasions I have had to own up to an unacceptable result. (I keep a list of goofs in my desk drawer, and it's not a short one!) But at work or at home, I have never found *oops* a particularly hard word to say.

My approach is similar to what I learned on the baseball diamond as a mediocre high school infielder. It is always better to charge the ball, instead of "letting the ball play you," as my coaches used to say. This gives you a better chance of making the play, because even if you mishandle the ball, you often have enough time to recover and throw the runner out at first. I have also always liked Lord Keynes's formulation "When I find I'm wrong, I change my mind. What do you do?"

When I fired IBM, I admitted responsibility for a flawed attempt and pledged to learn from the experience and do better. My fellow citizens weighed the issue, saw through the partisanship and sloppy journalism, and shrugged it off. To the disappointment of our attackers, they behaved like responsible citizens.

Busing in the Orphans

That wasn't the only time Hoosiers were asked to play the role of adult supervisor in sorting out impassioned and partisan attacks aimed at driving us away from reasonable reforms. In fact, you might say that the arc of any successful good-government initiative involves entering the fray, trying to meet distortions with facts, and then leaving it to voters to decide the merits of your actions after the results are in. That's exactly how one of the most egregious examples of the politics of protest played out for us in Indiana. Only, in that case the opposition trotted out orphan children to rally against us at the Statehouse when we made plans to close the Indiana Soldiers and Sailors Home.

The home dated back to the aftermath of the Civil War, which had orphaned thousands of children across the country. Many states took steps to care for these children. Indiana created its Soldiers and Sailors Home in the small community of Knightstown. At its peak, this residential school housed nearly a thousand young people. There are many heartwarming stories of the way it helped launch alumni on lives of high purpose and achievement.

At some point, however, the school bore no resemblance to its former self; the last Civil War orphan had long since entered history. Government agencies are famous for modifying their missions in order to survive, and the home's mission had morphed several times over the decades, with apparently no oversight by anyone. As orphans became harder to find, the home struck up alliances with the state's veterans' organizations to identify new entrants. The intent was noble at each stage of the home's evolution, but over time it became impossible to tell exactly what need the place was filling.

The student population came to include many kids with two parents, sometimes of reasonable income, whom someone decided needed a change of scenery. While many of the dwindling student base came from very low-income families, others did not. While many had deeply troubled backgrounds, others' lives seemed far less problematic. There was no rhyme or reason as to who got in and who didn't.

Of course, no one was complaining. Veterans' groups liked being involved, parents appreciated being able to send their children to a school for free, Knightstown loved hosting the home (it sat on a beautiful campus, much of it forested), and the administrators were determined to keep their jobs. It was a good deal for everyone, except the taxpayers.

In 2008 an in-house efficiency team began looking into the home's operations, probably the first time anyone had seriously done so, and found that with enrollment having dropped to just over one hundred, with no change in the number of employees, the ratio of staff to students had reached one to five. At an annual cost of around $10.2 million, the state was spending $91,205 per student to provide a "free" boarding school. We could have sent twice as many youngsters to Harvard for less. The state had a host of other options for problem children in or near their home communities, all of which were far less expensive.

For me, especially when faced with perpetually tight budgets, closing the home and placing the children in alternative settings was an obvious thing to do. However, in government the obvious is often elusive.

The ensuing controversy reminded me of dozens like it I have seen over the years, where a "statist quo" fights to keep in place wasteful systems that have long since outlived their usefulness. In this case an entrenched bureaucracy spent public time and money lobbying for its own perpetuation. It rallied good-hearted and well-meaning advocates to its side, in the form of the veterans' groups, which were rightfully proud of their relationship with the home and those who had attended it over the years. Alumni, understandably emotionally attached to a place they felt had served them well, were enlisted to pour out their stories. Legislators fulminated and vowed to protect the status quo at all cost.

Worst of all, the adults conscripted the children, who were bused to the Statehouse to pose for the cameras holding "Save Our Home" signs. All of this was like catnip to the media, which dramatized heartrending individual anecdotes and ignored minor details such as the thousands of dollars per student that went toward free room and board.

The stage was set, and all that remained was for our administration to play its assigned role of being stampeded into capitulation. Yet we declined the part. Instead, we gritted our teeth and rode out the clamor. We made customized individual arrangements for each student, at a huge savings to the state. I hit on the idea of moving a similar program, our National Guard Youth Challenge, from its Spartan facilities at a military base to the Knightstown campus, where it now turns around seriously troubled young lives. And Indiana's budget was better off by millions per year.

In our budget, $10 million is not chump change, but it's not a game changer, either. It would have been easier to just let the home slide along. Andrew Carnegie reportedly began the annual planning sessions for each of his enterprises by saying "Okay, boys, what are we going to get rid of this year?" Rotating funds from low-performing or less important purposes to higher priorities is among the principal duties of leadership, and businesses often shrink from the change it brings. Government almost never gets rid of anything. In the age of debt, however, it's necessary to take on obsolete government activities and prove that we can, in fact, throw something away once in a while.

Committing "Unnatural Acts"

Whether in the private or the public sphere, we Americans distrust bigness, and we dislike monopolies most of all. We have systematically regulated them, and dismantled them wherever possible. Government is the last great monopoly. Regulated neither by some higher authority nor by competition, it tends to behave as all monopolies do, by overcharging and underserving its customers. Measured by no stock price, market share, or profit-and-loss statement, government thinks in inputs, not outputs. How much is our department's budget for this year? How can we manage to get more for next year?

Coming from the business world, I had to learn after entering public service that efficiency is not merely unusual in government, it is countercultural. In this setting, finding ways to spend less money works against an agency's interests. "If we get through this year on less money than we were given," the thinking goes, "someone is liable to decide we don't need any more than that next year." The best indicator that this is a widespread phenomenon is that in the last month or two of a government's fiscal year, agencies tend to ramp up their spending to make sure they leave nothing on the table.

In Indiana, we caught on to this tendency after monitoring spending rates in our first budget year. By year two we'd made it clear to the head of every agency that anyone caught attempting a "June balloon" of last-minute spending (the state's fiscal year ends on June 30) would face stiff consequences.

As a monopoly, government always needs an accountability implant. In the absence of competition's inherent pressure for efficiency and improvement, incentives have to be artificially inserted. I learned how important and how hard this is while serving as President George W. Bush's director of the Office of Management and Budget for the first few years of his administration.

Each December, President Bush assembled his executive branch appointees, some two thousand in number, to thank them for their service and to lay out his goals for the coming year. One year, he asked me to say a few words before he spoke to the crowd. I took the opportunity to talk about a spending initiative we had under way called the President's Management Agenda, and began by saying that I wanted to talk about "unnatural acts." I figured that using that phrase would at least ensure that everyone was paying attention when the president stepped to the podium. Noticing an opportunity to extend the joke, I turned to Health and Human Services Secretary Tommy Thompson, who was seated to my left. "No, Tommy," I said, "not the kind [of acts] you give those grants to study."

It all got a good laugh. But the point was this: saving money, improving performance, terminating ineffective activities, and so forth do not come naturally in the public sector. The President's Management Agenda aimed to upend the federal government's overspending, underperforming culture. We would set performance metrics to track how effective each spent dollar was at reaching predetermined goals and then reward employees or agencies that performed well. We were also going to subject government spending to private competition and push for every dollar to have a specific target attached to it. The idea was that we'd be able to reinforce programs that performed well and reform or eliminate those that did not.

No presidential administration I know of tried harder to build a results culture in the federal government than the Bush administration. Over a five-year period, of which I was its director for the first half, the federal Office of Management and Budget made an effort to arm Congress with a way to scrutinize spending rationally. Program by program, roughly one out of five each year, OMB analysts went through the entire federal budget and assessed the effectiveness of each spending activity. The thinking was that, regardless of political ideology, legislators ought to know which programs are working, and therefore support efforts to spend money more effectively.

In each of the budget submissions whose preparation I oversaw, my colleagues and I recommended the termination of a host of federal programs. Some were demonstrably ineffective. Others were pursuing missions that had clearly become obsolete in the years or decades since enactment. But if Congress ever agreed to a single meaningful termination, it has slipped from memory.

Not even national emergency made a difference. After the 2001 terrorist attacks, I gave a speech at the National Press Club making the case to pay for the new war on terror by cutting back less vital programs. Since it was just two months after the attacks, I had hoped to win bipartisan support for the idea in Congress. I noted in the speech that already there were signs that Congress would reflexively add to the deficit during the time of national emergency. After all, it had arbitrarily doubled the $20 billion request the president had made to deal with the new situation. I invoked John Jacob Astor's apocryphal line as the *Titanic* went down: "I rang for ice, but this is ridiculous."

Rereading the talk a decade later, I was reminded that I had used words such as *adult* and *maturity* that only seem more fitting with the passage of time. I called for abandoning "business as usual," which I defined as simply piling new debts on top of old once new expenses came due.

Business as usual won. And remember, all this was under a Republican Congress.

Even though the years of my OMB service were unusually eventful ones, and I was in the middle of some high-profile national issues—the passage of the 2001 tax cuts, the No Child Left Behind education bill, and the 9/11 aftermath, which included funding for New York City, compensating victims' families, rescuing the airlines, and creating the Department of Homeland Security—like most cabinet officers, I was quickly forgotten when I returned to private life. Over the intervening years, almost the only memory that has resurfaced now and then is from my much-publicized budgetary battles with members of Congress, reduced in most accounts to a single extemporaneous line.

As I've often said, I was never in an argument with a member of Congress in which they wanted to spend less money than I, on behalf of the administration, did. Having served previous sentences in Washington—in the 1970s as a Senate staffer and in the mid-'80s Reagan White House—I was not naïve to the native customs. I knew, for instance, that the typical posture adopted by a witness before a congressional committee was obsequious and deferential, regardless of the insults or the fatuousness of what was being said to or about the witness or his point of view.

There is a plausible theory that such deference is only practical, that it avoids antagonizing a powerful member or, worse yet, showing him up in any way. And the institution and its members do deserve proper respect, which I believe I maintained on all occasions. But I also knew that the "rope-a-dope" mode (after Muhammad Ali's famous defensive crouch) employed by most witnesses or people lobbying Congress in other ways had a second, perhaps subconscious motive, and that was to protect one's future job prospects. For that large number whose next job, and the ones after that, was going to be in Washington, talking back to a congressman, especially about one of his pet programs, could be career-limiting.

But I had no intention of ever working in Washington again. I had severed all ties with the business from which President Bush had plucked me, and no idea what kind of work would come next, but I knew it wasn't going to be lobbying or in any other way dependent on chummy relationships on Capitol Hill. So I chose, at least on select occasions, to talk back to the dons of the Budget or Appropriations Committee in a slightly unconventional way. (After a while, I discovered that a small cult of C-SPAN junkies had become fans of my congressional appearances, apparently because they were a bit livelier than the usual fare. I got an increasing number of "give 'em hell" letters after each such hearing.)

The members of the Appropriations Committee, who are often

described as a third party of government, and who are united across partisan lines by their affinity for spending taxpayer money, were my most frequent and vociferous debating partners. It was after one contentious hearing, in the 9/11 aftermath, that I was asked by the press about the appropriators' insistence on voting far more money than the president had requested. I offhandedly commented, "Their motto is 'Don't just stand there, spend something.'" Years later, people still replay that line to me.

Banal as the comment may be, it does sum up the problem that brought us to this point. The new House majority of 2011, and the aroused electorate that put them in power, is the most promising political development of recent times. Their grasp of the debt crisis and their commitment to addressing it seem firm, but their leverage is limited. They still confront a pro-spending Senate majority and an administration that openly asserts its right to claim one-quarter of the entire economic output of the country for federal spending. Grim as further delay is, the bariatric surgery our bloated federal establishment needs is almost certainly a couple of more danger-filled years, and another electoral upheaval, away.

I believe it is coming. The American people, as they have again and again in our history, have begun to rouse themselves to meet a national threat and to keep our republic. People who differ in background and cultural outlook are coming to the same conclusion on the biggest issue of our time. I believe they are ready to be summoned to demand the necessary changes, but the window for action is closing.

The Ride of the Efficiency Raiders

Fortunately, we have some evidence that not every effort to cut government spending is doomed to failure. In Indiana we benefited from the simple fact that all of us in the new administration were new to state office. No Republican had been governor of the state in the preceding sixteen years, so we started out asking a lot of basic questions that apparently no one had asked for a long time. For example, why did the state own twenty-one aircraft and have four different operations to maintain them? Why did we have seven separate departmental print shops? And why did we need thirteen thousand vehicles, more than one for every three state employees?

Our young efficiency raiders searched for answers to these questions, often by paying visits to relevant agencies. In one case, they found employees working for overtime wages in one print shop while other workers in the print shop next door were playing cards because they had nothing to do. In another case, our efficiency crew went through state garages putting pennies on the tires of vehicles. If the pennies were still there a month later, we said, "Give us the keys." It was my treat, during my first year in office, to serve as the amateur auctioneer as we sold off the one thousandth unneeded state vehicle. By 2010 we had reduced the aircraft fleet by fourteen for a total of seven in our hangars, and the number of state vehicles by several thousand. I knew that even small reductions helped bend the state's spending curve downward. Left unchecked, spending increases compound on top of one another year after year. Today's small cut is the future's large saving.

In business there's a saying: "If you're not keeping score, you're just practicing." On arrival in state government, we installed metrics in every department that were linked, wherever possible, to our paramount goal of private income growth. We ditched the antique step-and-grade pay system the state had long used and replaced it with performance pay on a bell curve. Gone were the days when the very best worker and the very worst in an agency were treated identically. The top few percent of state employees, after full and fair evaluations, received the largest raises in state history, in some cases double-digit increases back to back. The poorest performers were given a chance to improve or move on.

Management was given funds to award spot bonuses for exemplary work, and was encouraged to emphasize employee actions that saved tax dollars. Once a year, we honor with public service recognition awards, coupled with substantial cash payments, those state employees who do the most to save the state money.

Progress came gradually, but after several years the difference was palpable. In the biweekly updates I receive from every key department head, it is now routine to read of innovative money-saving approaches developed by state workers. The savings are often quite modest in the context of a $13 billion budget, but taken together they have been essential to our staying above water.

Maybe the best measure of Indiana's improvement is that more is being done with less. Because we measure everything, we can say with certainty that, in almost every respect, service levels are better than before. Citizens who are owed tax refunds now get them back in an average of sixteen days, versus the thirty-one days it took a few years back. And a building permit now takes only thirteen days to get.

And all of this has occurred while state spending has risen less than 1 percent per year, only one-third the rate of inflation. Most tellingly, these enhanced services are being driven by almost 20 percent fewer employees. Indiana in 2011 has the fewest state employees per capita in the nation, fewer than we had in 1978. We were startled to realize that with no adjustment for inflation, total personnel costs (wages and benefits) for Indiana state government were $159 million lower after six years than they were upon our arrival.

The baseball immortal Satchel Paige used to say, "None of us is smarter than all of us." The most conscientious legislature and governor by them selves will not be able to deliver for taxpayers nearly so well as they can when assisted, and often led, by an aligned army of dollar stretchers. It is to these productive, economy-minded public servants that most of the credit for our state's solvency belongs. They share it with the fair-minded, mature people we call Hoosiers, who gave change—often massive change—a chance, and who judged it, and our administration, on results as reviewed through the lens of citizens' common sense

Assuming the Best of Us

Much of life is about mutuality. Marriages, business contracts, and other relationships originate in some understanding of each party's obligations, and each party's favorable assumptions about the other. There is usually an element of faith involved; the other party may disappoint you, but we often take that chance because things just might work out. Besides, simply showing faith in another person can sometimes have positive consequences of its own. Anyone who has raised children knows that assuming a level of responsibility and trustworthiness can often engender or cultivate the growth of those very qualities in a young person.

If our republic depends on the prevalence of Americans who accept the duties of citizenship and the risks of liberty, our public policies should assume that we are still that kind of people. I believe that one reason Hoosiers have shown a maturity about public spending, and a willingness to support limits on the size and scope of government, is because, at least in recent years, their government has acted as though it sees them as adults, as the bosses and not the vassals of public institutions.

To ensure that the state wouldn't lapse back into its bad habits, we worked to embed political incentives in the system that would encourage elected officials to remember whose money they were dealing with. One way we did that was with an automatic taxpayer refund.

This refund is a simple mechanism that could have a significant impact over time. As proposed, it provides that, whenever budgets are balanced and the state's "savings account" or rainy day revenues exceed 10 percent of the coming year's spending, the excess will be refunded per capita to taxpayers.[1] Previously, nearly all of the incentives were lined up in favor of additional spending. By voting for a new spending item, for example, legislators could go back to their districts and point to a shiny new bridge or government building they had provided. Now when the legislature doesn't spend all of the money available to it there is a quantifiable item everyone can point to. That gives legislators a strong incentive to keep the refunds flowing. And after taxpayers get used to receiving their refunds, the first year the legislature doesn't provide one, more than a few taxpayers will want to know why. The refund may never be a large amount of money for any one person, but the opportunity to create it and display it in every citizen's tax return should give future legislators an incentive to stop spending at a level where the refund kicks in.

My hope is that the refund program serves to remind officials just where the money comes from. I ensure that this is so by reminding lawmakers of a phrase that traces, like so many great lines, to Mark Twain. In regards to the contents of the state's coffers, I told them, "Remember, it's tainted money. 'Taint yours, and 'taint mine."

Does treating citizens like dependents and victims over time make them less self-confident, less self-reliant, less "virtuous" in the sense that Jefferson and Madison and Adams warned against? It sure seems that way. Does treating citizens as fully capable, responsible decision makers make them more confident, self-reliant, and maybe more assertive in their citizenship? There is a large element of faith in this outlook, but what evidence there is in Indiana suggests it just might be so.

Truth be told, I have a little more confidence now than I had a few years ago that it is in fact so. After all of the things we did to take on tough challenges, tangle with special interests, and eliminate wasteful programs that led our opponents to portray us as callous and uncaring, we stood for reelection in 2008. A year earlier the pundits had all but written us off, and as the election year wore on, many of our opponents hoped that Barack Obama's campaign would swamp our efforts at reelection.

After all, throughout the Midwest, governments had chosen differently than we had. Over the same period in which Indiana spending was virtually flat, expenditures in Ohio, Wisconsin, and Michigan shot through the roof. Right next door, in Illinois, Governor Pat Quinn won election in 2010 while the state was $13 billion in debt, six months in arrears in paying its vendors. After his election, Governor Quinn, who first came into office after Governor Rod Blagojevich was indicted on corruption charges, claimed he had "a mandate to raise taxes" and then promptly proposed a 75 percent increase in the state income tax and a near-doubling of taxes on business.

But in Indiana, even as Obama became the first presidential nominee of his party to carry the state in decades, we won reelection with the largest number of votes ever cast for a statewide candidate in Indiana. We won with a margin that stunned many of the political pundits who, a year or two earlier, were ready to write our political obituary. Is there something in our bountiful Indiana groundwater that produces a different outlook from that of our neighboring states?

The record leading up to 2005 says no. The conclusion I draw is that our citizens responded to honest talk about our problems, actions that were consistent with the talk, and, finally, concrete results. They heard all the usual special interest criticisms about heartlessness and callousness and a lack of compassion, but they weighed them fairly against the diffuse public benefits of stable finances and lower taxes. Then they made a grown-up judgment.

In my first inaugural speech, viewed on closed-circuit television by thousands of schoolchildren, I said, "The young people of Indiana are watching us today . . . watching now to see whether we who are already adults will behave like it. Whether we have a fraction of the fortitude our ancestors had in such abundance. Whether we will rebuild the barn, pay our debts, and leave the family business strong, so that they can carry it on and pay the bills when their turn comes." We never deviated from this outlook.

Adulthood in citizenship involves more than simply supporting policies of fiscal discipline. It includes taking more responsibility for one's own life and for the success of one's community. So we have spoken steadily to Hoosiers about their own responsibilities apart from what government can do. The organizing metaphor of that 2005 inaugural was the old pioneer custom of the barn raising, in which every member of the community had a part. Again from that speech: "When trouble came, and it came often, our forefathers didn't use words like *sacrifice*. And they certainly didn't divide into little groups and demand to be excused from taking part. . . . They would not recognize our problems as daunting. They'd say, 'Wipe your nose. Let's get to work.'"

In office, we have designed policies that have assumed the dignity and the capacity for full citizenship of every Hoosier. When we changed health insurance to restore more discretion to the individual, when we returned the power to choose a child's school to her family, when we placed with the voters the power to allow property tax increases above a set amount, when we established a ceiling on state tax collections beyond the level of solid solvency, we were saying to each voter, "You are an adult, and a citizen in full. We trust you. Now you decide."

Most people I've met have a fondness, often a love, for the state in which they live. I'm that way, passionately, about Indiana. I love its natural beauty and its traditions but I love its people most of all. I have witnessed their decency, kindness, willingness to help one another in times of trouble. After eight years of travel, a hundred overnight stays in their homes, thousands of coffee shop and tavern bull sessions, I feel qualified to praise them and I have countless stories to back it up.

But I am not starry-eyed about our progress as a state, which is spotty and partial, or about us as a people. We have behaved in selfish, indulgent, and shortsighted ways in our recent past. The story of our recent improvement, and of our relatively sound management of the public's business compared with that of other states, is simply that we have engaged in a somewhat more mature dialogue of citizenship. I hope that the outcome encourages those pessimistic about the readiness of Americans everywhere to listen to calm reason, accept the need for tradeoffs, and set our nation back on the course of greatness of which we are fully capable.

CHAPTER 7

The Road Back

We have seen how the desire for dominance among today's statists trumps even the interest they should have in a strong private sector that is capable of generating the tax dollars they long to spend. Our Indiana experience with infrastructure, a national problem of special seriousness to our state, helped me understand how the urge to power outweighs in its victims even the most sincere intention to address public needs.

For me, the lesson started at a charity golf outing in Warren County, Indiana, sometime in the summer of 2003. An unknown, first-time gubernatorial candidate—that would be me—stopped by the event in a rural area, because it was one of the few Warren County occasions at which even as many as one hundred or so unsuspecting voters could be found in one place.

I introduced myself to a guy who said he worked for the state highway department. When I said something about how important his work was to the state's economic future, he replied, "It's all a joke, you know."

"What's a joke?" I asked.

"Our highway program," he responded. "We don't have a third the money it would take to build what we've paid to design and what people have been promised."

When I returned home, I asked our volunteers to check into the highway worker's contention, and they confirmed that, if anything, he had understated the mismatch between needs and resources. The state and federal gasoline taxes that had funded roads, bridges, and other transportation projects were falling woefully short of what was needed to maintain, let alone expand or improve, the nation's vital economic backbone.

It's become a cliché to say that our nation faces an "infrastructure crisis." But usually a phrase becomes a cliché for a reason. By any measure, the United States is hundreds of billions of dollars behind in maintaining the capacity and quality we need for economic growth, and the gap is widening every day. Nationally the issue came to the forefront of people's minds with the collapse of the I-35W Bridge in Minneapolis in 2008. But for years the gap between what we've needed and what we've built has run into the billions. The American Society of Civil Engineers has estimated, for example, that 27 percent of the nation's bridges need to be replaced, and that traffic jams cost Americans $78 billion a year as they sit idle for billions of hours collectively. Freight delays cost the economy billions more in lost revenue or productivity. Figure 7 illustrates the totality of our infrastructure gap.

By now it's clear that I believe in a strictly limited scope for government and that I think that much of what government does today is neither necessary nor consistent with our liberties or national well-being. On our watch, Indiana has moved to the third lowest in per capita state spending and to the fewest state employees per capita in the country.

But the provision and upkeep of first-rate public infrastructure is a core duty of any responsible government, clearly within the sphere of government's legitimate purposes. It furnishes the backbone to which men and women of enterprise can attach their investments; it is a major part of government's role in promoting the flourishing of the private sector. This was a central tenet of Republicans stretching all the way back to Abraham Lincoln, and I for one think it still should be.

For my administration, improving our infrastructure was an especially urgent priority. The creation of more and better private-sector jobs was our central, transcendent objective. Indiana's central location (our state nickname is "The Crossroads of America" because more than two-thirds of American consumers live within a one-day truck drive of our borders) means that we have as great a stake as any state in first-class transportation facilities. When we quantified the shortfall that highway worker alerted me to, we found it came to at least $3 billion, seven times the state's annual average new construction budget.

Our first legislative session was consumed with balancing the state books and meeting immediate campaign promises to begin enhancing

Figure 7 | **Five-Year Infrastructure Investment Needs**

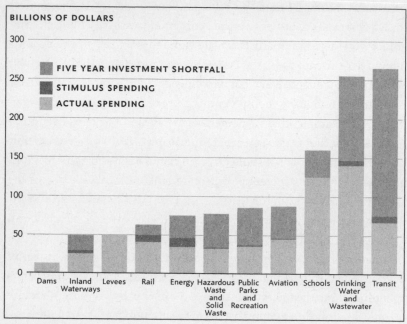

Source: 2009 Report Card for America's Infrastructure, American Society of Civil Engineers.

the state's business climate, improving the protection of abused children, and cleaning up a lax ethics environment. But at a news conference just after that first year's General Assembly adjourned, I was asked, "Governor, that was some session. What's next?" Without hesitation, I said, "Infrastructure. That's our second deficit." With the tightest budget in fifty-five years, and what proved to be the most successful tax amnesty program any state has ever seen, we were on our way to fixing the operating deficit in the state's annual accounts. Now we had to find a way to close a gap of equal significance in our largest capital account.

We set out on a search for a solution to this immense dilemma. Little did I suspect what a firestorm it would bring on, or what a lesson about the lust for power it would teach.

Through the summer of 2005 our finance team, led by two brilliant businessmen I had somehow lured away from my old place of employment, Eli Lilly and Company, worked to identify every conceivable option that might enable us to close the infrastructure gap. As is our practice, I ruled out nothing, telling the group to consider anything that might work.

By summer's end the team had produced a list of more than thirty actions we might take. These ranged from imposing special fines for the most flagrant moving violations to outright increasing the gasoline tax. At the end, it became clear that unless we tripled the state's tax on gasoline, an economically counterproductive and therefore senseless idea, there was no option or even combination of options that would come close to producing the money we needed to fix our roads—except one. Like many states, Indiana has a major highway that was originally constructed as a toll road. Once the principal means of building roads (in pioneer days almost all roads were built by private capital and financed by charging their users to travel them), tolling has been used less often in recent decades.

The Indiana Toll Road, opened in 1956, offered an intriguing possibility as a solution to our transportation deficit. The closer we looked at it, the more obvious it was that, in state hands (which is to say, in politicians' hands) it was what any first-year business student would recognize as an underperforming asset. Amazingly for a business with a largely captive customer base, it was losing money, barely covering its operating expenses but not covering its depreciation or appropriate capital costs.

I had first become fascinated by the Toll Road during the sixteen months of constant travel that led to my election in 2004. In what turned out to be a futile attempt to make inroads into the Chicago-dominated bastion of northwest Indiana, I visited this overwhelmingly Democratic area over and over, frequently traversing the Toll Road.

The last toll booth before you head west toward the Illinois line was what grabbed my attention. It cost fifteen cents, which is a challenge to pay these days, when not many of us carry dimes and nickels. Watching a patronage worker sit there collecting coins made me wonder, what does it cost us to collect a toll?

After winning the election, I asked my staff that question. This being government, nobody knew the answer. So I politely (well, maybe not so politely) asked that they go figure it out. A couple of weeks later the answer came back: "We think it's about thirty-four cents." When I finished chuckling, I remember saying, "I have a better idea. The honor system! Close the toll booth, and we're already nineteen cents ahead. Put out a cigar box and every so often some good soul will chuck in a quarter or two just to be nice."

As we searched for a way to build the roads and bridges Indiana needed, we knew that, around the world, most of the large new projects were being built with private capital, or a mix of private and public funds. These so-called "P3s," for "public-private partnerships" are now more the rule than the exception in Asia, Europe, and the developing world. The United States, in so many ways the world's leading innovator, lags behind in this area. Under these partnerships, many existing roads, bridges, and other public facilities are operated by private companies who are more efficient in running them and have private funds to upgrade and maintain them better than the governments that contracted with them for the operations. There is nothing remotely radical about this idea; these are simply a new form of regulated public utility, like our electric companies, few of which are owned by government. P3s everywhere operate under very strict contracts that regulate every aspect of their performance and control the prices the public can be charged for their use.

You may be wondering, "Why was the Indiana Toll Road losing money?" Feather-bedded, slack management was one big factor. But the biggest reason was that its prices had not been raised in 25 years. In that quarter century, the price of a gallon of milk rose from $0.92 to $3.00, a loaf of bread from $0.19 to $3.00, and a median home from $22,000 to $177,900. But the last toll booth before Chicago was still just $0.15.

So next you'll ask, "Why were the tolls so out of date?" The answer is because politicians set them, and politicians never want to risk irritating a voter if they can avoid it. If the road crumbles, if it gets congested because there are no funds to add lanes, if it continues with a prehistoric toll booth system years after other such roads have no-stop, electronic payment systems—all these things were the case—well, let the next governor figure it out.

Long before we decided on the move that became the biggest such transaction in American history (by a factor of two), I had told our team we were going to modernize the tolls on the Indiana Toll Road (ITR). At least we could maintain and improve the road and, maybe occasionally, have a little money left over.

But the more we studied the ITR, the more we saw a larger opportunity. The Toll Road was run so poorly (and would have been so difficult to fix internally) that there was a tremendous upside to turning the road over to private management. Said another way, there was enormous "trapped value" in the ITR, value that government would never unlock but that a private bidder might; a private bidder might therefore pay us a large sum of money for the opportunity to do so. Plus we knew the companies that built and ran roadways elsewhere in the world were eager to get into the American market.

The Democratic mayor of Chicago, Richard Daley, had recently demonstrated the efficacy of such an approach by leasing the Chicago Skyway to a Spanish company, Cintra, which was backed by the Australian Macquarie Bank. In payment for a ninety-nine-year lease, Chicago reaped $1.8 billion, a figure that certainly caught our eye.

So, with that attractive precedent and the absence of alternatives, I announced that Indiana would entertain offers to lease and operate our Toll Road. There was nothing to lose by asking, as nothing would oblige us to accept an offer that wasn't a net benefit by a wide margin for our citizens. We had valued the road, in government hands, even under unreasonably positive assumptions (such as the assumption that politicians would raise tolls with inflation each and every year in the future), at $1.3 billion. If we didn't receive a bid well in excess of that figure, we would just go back to the drawing board.

The investment advisers we worked with said that it would take a year to gather bids, evaluate them, and reach an agreement. That wouldn't work for us. For starters, many road projects were already long overdue, and some repairs couldn't wait much longer. Second, I was worried that waiting would cost us in two ways: moments where you can act decisively in politics are fleeting; and a delay could give the financial markets a chance to turn against our getting a top-dollar bid. So we demanded a schedule that made the Wall Street types gasp, but that ultimately must have set a new land-speed record for such transactions. From issuing a request for proposal to receiving a winning bid took just 117 days. I've always called on our administration to move at "the speed of business, not the speed of government," and in this case, I think we outran even business standards for nimbleness.

Looking back now, it's a good thing we did. We could hardly have hit a sweeter spot in terms of the financial markets than the spring of 2006. Interest rates were low (too low, as we would find out later) and, as mentioned, the zeal of bidders to break into what they thought would be a vibrant U.S. P3 marketplace was intense.

Moreover, I knew that the Republican legislative majority we had carried into office with us in our big 2004 win might be short-lived. We needed legislative approval for any deal we might strike, and even at that point it was clear that the GOP was facing national headwinds. The Bush presidency faced a second off-year election during an increasingly frustrating war in Iraq, so I knew there was a chance that our narrow Indiana House majority might tip back the other way.

That's just what happened, and the financial markets softened as well. If we had taken the bankers' advice—or that of the old pols who told me to take things slow—to have a legislative committee think about the proposal, to let the public get used to the idea, et cetera, a gigantic opportunity would have been blown.

So much has happened in our gubernatorial years that I'll need a scrapbook to recall much of it. But one moment I'll never forget is Friday afternoon, January 20, 2006, when five of us assembled to open the ITR bids. I had told myself I wouldn't consider anything under $2 billion, and probably nothing much under $2.5 billion. But that was almost twice what the road was worth under government management (even under rosy assumptions), so I thought the chances of receiving a high enough bid to make the transaction worth it were just so-so.

So imagine my surprise to see a high bid of $3.85 billion. It was high-fives all around. What a thrill to think that we could not only close but eliminate the state's "impossible" infrastructure shortfall, put thousands to work building projects we could never otherwise have afforded, and create a great new backbone for Indiana's long-term economic future.

As I began looking for votes for our "Major Moves" plan, a label I came up with in (where else?) the shower one morning while singing a Hank

Williams, Jr., song of the same name), I naïvely thought that, with such a blowout bid in hand, bipartisan support would be easy to come by. Our Democratic friends differ with us on many issues, but I thought that building infrastructure, employing principally the union members with whom they are allied, and benefiting cities and towns where the majority of mayors were Democrats seemed like a straightforward call for them.

I wasn't the only one who thought so. On Monday morning my very large office was packed with legislators, road builders, construction trade union leaders, and journalists, all present to hear what kind of interest our RFP had generated. When I said the words "$3.85 billion" there were gasps, exclamations, and applause. I guarantee you there wasn't a person in the room who didn't believe at that instant that the bid would be embraced by statewide consensus.

The exact opposite happened. The next several months turned into a long war, a difficult period in which this matchless opportunity—"the jobs bill of a generation," as I called it—was very nearly thrown away. Indiana almost tore up a $4 billion (actually, it was more than $8 billion once you added in the commitments the private company made to improve the Toll Road itself) lottery ticket. At the end, not a single Democratic House member and only two Democratic senators (both courageous members of the Black Caucus who put jobs over partisanship) voted for the Major Moves bill.

Why? Well, partisan politics played a role. The Democratic Party soon discovered it was easy to inflame state residents by playing to their fears in hopes of turning voters against us in the upcoming elections. Our critics claimed that we were "selling the Toll Road," which of course was false. The state would continue to own the road, and always would.

They also claimed that the windfall from the lease would be "gone in ten years." That was also untrue: after the Toll Road's debt was paid off, the rest of the proceeds would go into long-term transportation investments; the more than two hundred additional projects we would be able to complete with the proceeds from the transactions would reap benefits generations into the future for all who drove on the road or who depended on businesses served by our highways and byways.

They also claimed that we hadn't gotten a good deal. That was the most absurd line of all. We got billions of new dollars—no taxes, no borrowing—and a better Toll Road, too. But on and on it went anyway.

The xenophobic charge that we had turned the road over to "foreigners" made the most political hay. Misinformation (and disinformation) ran riot. Attending a soldier's funeral during that time, I was asked by one teenage boy, "Why'd you give our road to the Russians?" The more confused the public got, the more outrageously false our opponents' attacks became. Good short-term politics mattered more to them than the long-term public interest. As they admitted to political writers, they might love roads, but they hated the idea of Republicans building them, and maybe getting credit for having done so.

I came to see that politics was not the only, and probably not even the biggest, reason our Democratic friends were willing to trash a breakthrough so obviously in the public interest. Their visceral antipathy to the private sector, and their determination to keep maximum power and control in governmental hands, shaped their attitude even more.

This understanding dawned on me not in my home state but in Washington, D.C., when I confronted the power-over-performance mentality in its purest form. Against my inclinations, I accepted a request from Governor Ed Rendell, Democrat of Pennsylvania, to help him appeal to Congress for new thinking about infrastructure. Like his party colleague Mayor Daley, Governor Rendell was not doctrinaire about his infrastructure problem and was hopeful he could pull off a success similar to what we did in Indiana.

The governor told me that, according to his engineers, hilly Pennsylvania was home to as many as ten thousand substandard bridges. What a burden to take to bed every night, to worry that somewhere a structure might collapse, with terrible human consequences. Governor Rendell was working toward what would eventually be an offer of $12.8 billion, more than three times the Indiana figure, to lease the Pennsylvania Turnpike.

Shortly thereafter, joined by Governor Tim Kaine of Virginia, another P3 pioneer, I entered a congressional hearing room with hopes of some sort of constructive discussion. After all, as I said in my brief opening remarks, we all agreed on the dimension and urgency of the problem, and there must be multiple possible approaches we could consider. Here were two governors of opposite parties who agreed that private partnerships could be an important part, though certainly not all, of the solution.

Silly me. The rest of the hearing was a duet of diatribe in which Democrats James Oberstar of Minnesota and Peter DeFazio of Oregon took turns bashing me for even contemplating building roads in any way other than with government taxes and under government control. Oberstar, the chairman of the House Transportation Committee, went so far as to promise to "work to undo" any public-private partnership if given the opportunity. For the record, it is worth noting that governor Rendell wasn't able to complete his deal before his moment of opportunity evaporated and the private company that had bid billions withdrew its proposal to run the Turnpike.

Thanks to the Major Moves transaction, Indiana is now a national leader in the vital mission of building transportation facilities. While some of our sister states are grinding roads back into gravel for lack of the wherewithal to repair them, we are midway through a record building boom, with several years of new construction at three times the historic run rate. More than two hundred new investments, including some huge projects that sat on the drawing boards for decades, are under way. It is a success that people of all political persuasions ought to be able to celebrate.

The fact that they do not, that the same congressmen I faced at that hearing went on to propose new prohibitions on P3 activity, teaches the dispiriting lesson that the will to power overbears even the sincere desire to address a truly critical national issue. I don't doubt that the likes of Representatives Oberstar and DeFazio would like to see America build the roads we need. They just cannot abide the idea that it might happen through even partially private means, without the states and localities having to come to Washington and kiss their rings for the money. (As it turned out, Representative Oberstar's ring is no longer available for smooching; he was soundly defeated by an upstart challenger in the 2010 election.) In a test between power and performance, between results for the public and preserving government's growing position as master not servant, too many of today's public "servants" choose to serve themselves and not the rest of us.

It took a shocking disregard for the public interest to call for turning down billions in found money and denying our state its one chance to build a twenty-first-century infrastructure. It would have been absurd to throw our Toll Road transaction away because of a blind commitment to a big government ideology or, more crassly, to save a few hundred government jobs and the union dues flowing from them. Believe it or not, I have an even more extreme example.

During the transition period before we took office in 2005, our volunteer team tasked with assessing the Department of Corrections came to me with an alarming report: "We're going to have to build at least two more prisons in the next couple years." I can't remember my exact reaction, but I'm pretty sure it started with "Are you crazy?" Our most immediate need was to cut government spending in order to avoid bankruptcy, not to build more items that would come with recurring costs.

Besides, there had to be a better way. As I had pointed out in my campaign, the state had already built a large and costly new prison in New Castle, Indiana, which was sitting almost entirely empty three years after its construction. Meanwhile, hundreds of Indiana felons were being housed in other states at enormous expense. By now you're asking, what were they thinking?

As usual, the answer started with maintaining maximum government payrolls. It turned out that, under the archaic corrections processes—the term *management* would not be accurate—of that time, it cost nearly sixty dollars per day to house an Indiana prisoner, and a broke state could not afford to open New Castle on that basis. So the state found other jurisdictions as far away as Oklahoma who would do the job for forty-five or fifty dollars, awaiting a time when it could staff New Castle under the collective bargaining agreements then in effect.

Needless to say, those agreements would never have permitted the action I had called for: bidding out the management of the new facility to the nation's growing (everywhere but in the Indiana of that era) and highly sophisticated private corrections marketplace. When we did so, the winning bid came in well below $40 per day. What had been a million-dollar "white elephant" at New Castle opened under private management and has had a stellar record, with zero escapes and fewer injuries than Indiana's traditional prisons. In 2010 it became the first facility in Indiana history and one of the few anywhere to achieve a perfect 100 percent score on its national accreditation inspection.

Incidentally, when we "brought our boys home" and opened the site, the economically struggling city of New Castle became home to several hundred new jobs—private-sector jobs. And, by the way, seven years later, Indiana has still not been forced to build another prison. It turns out that when your goal is to maximize the efficiency of your assets rather than the size of your government payroll, very different outcomes are possible. When you give first priority to results rather than politics, to taxpayers rather than government unions, to delivering government services through whatever means make the best business sense, the public interest wins.

Clarity of Purpose

In December 2004, a month after I was elected Indiana's next governor, I assembled the first few dozen men and women who had agreed to serve in the "New Crew." They were the truly impressive lot I had dreamed of. We had our share of young whizzes, but also people who had built and sold businesses and retired from major business roles, and other distinguished professionals. Since our party had been in the wilderness for so long, there was nobody with state governmental experience, and that turned out to be a blessing, as businesslike newcomers turned agency after broken agency upside down and made them work vastly better in serving the Hoosier public.

Still, all this was impossible to predict back then. My goal for the day was to provide clarity to those who would lead our good-government endeavors over the next four years, at a minimum. I told them, "Every great enterprise I ever saw had a very clear purpose, and everyone in the organization knew what it was. It was on the wall, the annual report cover, maybe the laminated ID card everyone wore. Pick your favorite buzzword—*mission, strategic objective,* it doesn't matter—but every team member understands it and their unit's role in producing it.

"So here's ours. We are here to raise the disposable income of Hoosiers.

Whatever your area of responsibility, we will be working with you to identify what you can do, or do better, or do faster, or maybe stop doing altogether, that makes it more likely that the next set of jobs comes to Indiana
and not anywhere else. That those jobs are more diverse, and pay more
on average than the jobs of today. Then we are going to see to it that the
workers holding those jobs get to keep more of the money they earn,
through lower taxes. If we do those things well, all the rest of Indiana's
problems will begin to become more manageable, and we will leave a state
of greater freedom and happiness than the one we know today."

Assembling a leadership team committed to economic growth and
placing the private sector first is one thing. Changing the culture of government bureaucracies from indifference or even hostility and into one
of active support and collaboration with job creators is a taller order. So
we commenced work on that goal on day one.

On the afternoon of that first day in office, I went to the largest meeting
room our Indiana Government Center has to offer, where I had invited
the entire staff of our Indiana Department of Environmental Management (IDEM) to gather. I walked in to find a crowd of several hundred,
augmented by an indeterminate number more participating over speak-
erphones at sites around the state.

I told the crowd that I had come to let them get a look at their new
coworker, and to give them a sense of our expectations for the work they
would be doing over the next four years. I started by telling them what we
did *not* intend to do, and that was to weaken or soften in any way any of
the environmental protection rules in place. I commended them for
choosing the careers they had, and endorsed wholeheartedly the agency's
mission as essential to preserving the natural inheritance of our state and
the quality of life that Hoosiers deserve.

But, I continued, I had some specific expectations about the way IDEM
and other agencies went about their work. I said I expected their regulatory activities to become "fast, consistent, and collaborative." I had heard
dozens of horror stories of interminable delays, of job creation being
postponed for long stretches while IDEM refused to say yea or nay. I
reminded them that "Time is money" is not a mere figure of speech, and
that it could be expressed with equal validity as "Time is jobs."

I told them that our transition team had counted almost five hundred overdue air and water permits awaiting decision, some of them pending for as long as twenty years, and that that was unacceptable. Going forward, they would be measured on the time it took them to make decisions, and this would be a major factor in future pay raises and promotions. (It took six years, but the backlog of air and water permits was completely eliminated. And since every new permit reduced the amount of pollution allowed, this will lead to a dramatic improvement in air and water quality in our state.)

I finished by saying, "Those people you are regulating out there are not the enemy. They are your neighbors. Their greater economic success will be a boon to their communities and to all of us in a state that has been sinking economically.

"The vast majority of them are eager to do what is right. Those few who willfully disregard our laws, we'll throw the book at, but most are just as committed to a cleaner Indiana as you are. So if they are not in compliance, your job is not to lurk in a tree across the creek waiting for them to mess up so you can jump out and whack 'em. Your job is to help them understand what is required to comply with our rules, as quickly and economically as that can be accomplished."

We worked ceaselessly to foster this same attitude in every corner of Indiana state government. I will not pretend that every one of our 28,000 state employees (down, incidentally, from around 35,000 on that first day of work, and now the lowest number since 1978 and the fewest per capita among the 50 states) has embraced the goal, but the spirit has spread widely. Indiana today has a public sector that understands it is there to serve and not to rule, that remembers who's the boss and who pays the bills, and that looks constantly for ways to enlarge economic opportunity for all its 6.5 million employers.

So we established at the outset our objective of strengthening the private sector and private income. That has been our central purpose ever since. We look after public safety, especially the safety of children, and let nothing interfere with that duty. In our first year, even while slashing spending and balancing the supposedly out-of-control budget we inherited, we doubled the number of child care workers, halving the highest caseloads in the nation and beginning a process that took our system from "worst to first."

But always we are looking for ways to encourage the growth of the Indiana private economy. We have enacted every law and taken every executive action we could think of to lower the cost of doing business in our state, taking every step we could conceive of that might have a positive bearing on our business climate.

Over time we built a culture in which it is broadly understood that, if Hoosier jobs are at stake, whatever you might do about it goes to the top of your in-box. When it's getting Indiana's proposal in front of a company first, or turning around a permit quickly, or ensuring the construction of a new highway exit ramp to a factory site, it is pretty obvious what kind of action we need and who should deliver it. But the stories I love best are the ones in which a more obscure corner of state government had its chance to help a neighbor get a job and came through.

One of my favorite stories of this kind involves our Board of Pharmacy. When the market-leading mail order pharmacy Medco was deciding where to put its giant new high-tech facility, Indiana was a finalist along with Kentucky. In the end, Indiana was selected, and Hoosiers received 1,400 jobs averaging over $70,000 per year. I asked the Medco leadership what we'd done well and not well in pursuing the investment. On the positive side, they finished their answer by saying, "And then, of course, there was your Board of Pharmacy."

I was glad to hear it but puzzled. So the Medco officials explained that to operate this massive nationwide pharmacy required several dozen different licenses. Kentucky had told them that their board met quarterly and that the agenda for the next meeting was full, but that they were pretty sure they could get Medco's applications scheduled for the meeting after that. If all went well, Medco was told, they would get their licenses a few weeks after that, months after the start of the process.

I asked, "What did our folks say?" It turned out that the Indiana Board had called a special meeting for the next week, on the first day legally possible, and issued all the licenses a few days thereafter. Ever since, I have enjoyed visiting with my coworkers in other departments and telling them, "If the Board of Pharmacy can play a key role in landing fourteen hundred great new jobs for our citizens, don't think you won't have your chances."

Building a pro-growth, pro-private-sector culture takes more than pep talks. On the old business principle of "If you're not keeping score, you're just practicing," we monitor how long it takes to turn around a tax refund, grant a building permit, or decide on an environmental approval. We know how competitive our global marketplace can be and that often the United States loses out to China because of the length and expense of getting permits to open a new facility. James Fallows, for example, reported in *The Atlantic* in November 2010 that permits that took years to get to open a new manufacturing plant in the United States were particularly harmful. Fallows quoted an American government official working in China: "In America, it takes a decade to get a permit for a plant." Meanwhile, in China, "they build the whole thing in 21 months."

At every cabinet meeting, I position the president of our Economic Development Corporation at my right hand, and every meeting begins with his report, and his request to any other department present for any cooperation or expedited decision that might help land the next investment.

We try never to let anyone lose sight of the main objective, and we reward those who contribute most effectively to it. We replaced the antiquated step-and-grade compensation system with one based on performance. We junked the unfair system in which the most diligent, effective workers in state government were treated exactly the same as the laziest and least productive. In the bell curve process we installed, the best employees have received the largest raises in state history, in some cases at double-digit levels in consecutive years.

We implemented spot bonus programs for exceptional achievements in between pay adjustments, and major cash prizes for the most exemplary accomplishments leading to more efficient use of taxpayer dollars.

One graphic example among scores I could provide will suffice to illustrate the extent of the change our people brought. It came in one of the most hated organizations in any state: the Bureau of Motor Vehicles.

It seems a fixed rule that these agencies, with which virtually every American must deal on a frequent basis, are sinkholes of lost time and

incompetent customer service. For wasted time and maddening mistreatment (not to mention fraud: until we cleaned them up, Indiana's license
branches were a nationally known capital of phony driver's licenses), the
Indiana Bureau of Motor Vehicles took a backseat to no one. I used to say
that Hoosiers went to the license branch with a sack lunch and a copy of
War and Peace and hoped not to finish both before their name was called.

This was intolerable, not just because of the time and money wasted,
but because it was another factor holding back economic progress. Many
businesses—car dealers, trucking companies, etc.—have a regular need
to be serviced at the BMV. And every minute that a citizen spends at a
license branch is time that could have gone toward helping his company
make a buck.

Delivering a necessary, widely used public service with competence is
a bedrock duty of public servants spending their neighbors' money, but
it is also a very healthy factor in earning the public's confidence and support for other reforms and changes. After we had transformed our bureau,
to the astonishment and delight of its millions of customers, Hoosiers
started saying, "Well, if they can fix the BMV, they can fix *anything*."

As practitioners of limited but active government, we try not to let
skepticism about Big Government become contempt for *all* government.
The massive challenges facing Indiana, after several decades of economic
decline and many years of drifting negligence in state government, could
be faced only by forceful, active public administration. Major change
became much more feasible once the public began to trust that, once in
a while, government actually gets something right.

During our transition from Election Day to inauguration, probably no
personnel decision took up more time or required more deliberation than
who would be BMV commissioner. As newcomers to state government,
none of us knew anything about the agency from the inside, but as frequent
victims of its hours-long visit times, miserable customer service, repeated
mistakes requiring return trips, and so on, we knew we would soon be the
owners of Indiana's worst-performing and most hated enterprise.

One of the transition volunteers assigned to study the BMV was
a young businessman whose background included retail experience. I
remember his first report: "What you have here, Mitch, is 170 Dairy

Queens." He went on to describe a chain of essentially retail outlets, with almost all transactions occurring on-site, with walk-in customers usually paying in cash. Our research revealed several reasons for the bureau's legendary awful results: redundant paper processes; hundreds of thousands of dollars in cash sitting uncounted in unlocked drawers on any given night; and a culture in which there was no incentive to serve customers well or improve efficiency.

The transition was a thrilling time for me in large part because of the amazing array of idealistic people who stepped forward, most at substantial personal sacrifice, and offered to help us revive our state. One of those was the CEO of Galyan's, a major sporting goods chain that had recently been sold, freeing its leader to move on. This able and determined first-time public servant got the "BMV miracle" started. He was the pioneer in uncharted territory, but his successors became the settlers in the new land of a high-performance, award-winning agency.

The turnaround took more than two years and involved hundreds of changes in process, technology, and personnel. One of the first things we did was close branches. The state did not need 170 Dairy Queens. Many of them had little or no business, while others were swamped and making people wait for hours. Once established, none had ever been closed, even if population patterns shifted away from the town or area in question. Meanwhile, an antiquated and hopelessly inadequate computer system only exacerbated the mass confusion and error rates for which the agency was infamous.

From a business standpoint, it made perfect sense to close the least used branches and put the savings toward the first of the huge improvements needed to modernize the system. A careful capacity assessment said we needed at most around 130 branches, and many of them in different locations from the ones we had. Anyone who ever proposed closing a post office knows what happened next.

Under state statute, any such closure was subject to a process that included public hearings. These predictably turned into highly emotional affairs, in which the affected towns or areas interpreted the bureau's proposal as an insult or a marker that they were no longer important. Nearby merchants protested that there would be fewer potential customers drawn to their vicinity (as though forcing citizens to travel to a given location were somehow a valid public activity). Local and state legislative politicians piled on, pledging their eternal loyalty to saving the treasured branches.

Our well-meaning businessman commissioner was totally mismatched with this part of his job. He was just out to make the bureau work well. Never having operated in a political environment, he could not understand how people could so vehemently denounce what were so obviously sound decisions. He let his exasperation show on more than one occasion, and took many shots in reward for generally excellent service.

Still, we stood behind him, politely declined demands for his firing, and persevered with the closures, which liberated some $10 million per year, enabling the BMV to modernize its computer systems and begin renovating dilapidated branches and building attractive new ones that were closer to where Hoosiers live today.

The most crucial of the reforms, however, came from rethinking the entire delivery model from our customers' standpoint. We asked, "Why should a free citizen have to spend one more minute than necessary getting his government's permission to drive a car?" The best way to start reducing this "time tax" was to save Hoosiers the burden of going to the branch in the first place. A host of changes, including highly user-friendly online and mail services, made it possible for most transactions to happen outside the branches.

As in any major change effort, we made our share of mistakes. Someone got the idea to take down the clocks from branch walls. I never was clear what the rationale was, but it generated a deserved level of derision for the few days before we heard about it and told the bureau to "put the damn clocks back up." A bigger blunder came in the summer of 2006, when the agency attempted to launch its new computer system without fully testing and debugging it. A series of failures and snafus forced a shutdown, a restart, a personal apology from me, and the resignation of our commissioner, for whom the episode proved the final straw.

I could rattle on about the continuous stream of improvements that the agency has made, proving conclusively our maxim that "government is not a business, but it can be a lot more businesslike." But all one needs

With then mayor of Indianapolis, Dick Lugar (right), 1972.

Aboard Air Force One with President Reagan while a senior adviser, 1986.

With Mayor Giuliani (right) at Ground Zero, one week after September 11, 2001.

With President Bush in the Oval Office, 2002.

A typical meeting with my employers at a breakfast stop in St. Joseph County, Indiana, 2007.

With a little Hoosier during the first day of construction of the Fort to Port Highway, one of the hundreds of infrastructure projects made possible by our toll road transaction. Building roads for her future, 2008.

Breaking ground for Medco's 1,400-employee mail order pharmacy and research center, one of the more than 1,000 new investments won by Indiana's new Economic Development Corporation, 2009.

Welcoming Honda and thousands of jobs to Indiana, 2008.

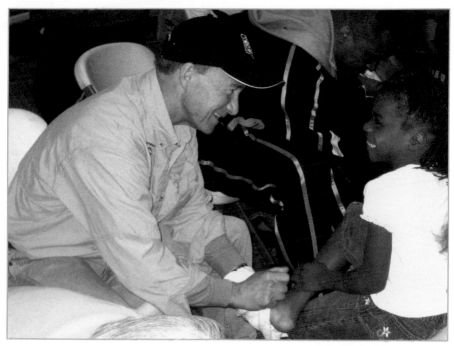

Washing my new friend's feet so she could try on her new sneakers, donated through the Samaritan's Feet program, 2010.

Visiting Indiana troops at Camp Speicher in Iraq, 2008.

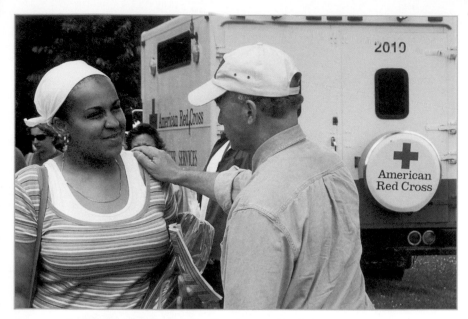

Speaking with a victim of Indiana's worst floods in a century, 2008.

Signing the Healthy Indiana plan to provide self-directed health insurance to low-income Hoosiers, 2007.

An overnight visit to Doug Gerber's farm near Richmond, 2006.

A surprise congratulatory visit to one of the branch managers who made our BMV turn-around possible, 2010.

With citizens advocating to make our property tax cuts permanent, 2010.

At the Peru Circus Parade, one of countless summer parades, on my custom
State Flag Harley Davidson, 2008.

to know for our purposes is that Indiana's BMV has won the international award for the best such agency two of the last three years, the only jurisdiction ever to win it twice. In the fourth quarter of 2010, the average customer satisfaction rating in an Indiana license branch, measured three different ways, was 97 percent; the average total visit time was 0.6:59. That's in minutes and seconds, not hours and minutes.

None of these changes would have been possible under the collective bargaining straitjacket we jettisoned on day one. That's the difference when you approach government as the servant and promoter of private life and not the other way around.

I've had one experience over and over as governor: a businessperson will come to discuss an issue or problem or a new investment he is contemplating. At the meeting's conclusion, in almost identical words, it's almost certain he will inquire, "Now, what can we do for the state? How can we be a better 'corporate citizen'?"

I always respond the same way: "Make money." Just go succeed at what you do and make money. If you do, you will be able to hire somebody else, and give them a better chance in life. You will have profits and therefore pay taxes to support those activities we must do together through the agency of government. You will have some money left over to give to the United Way and all those good causes we love. That, I always say, is our first definition of corporate citizenship. If you don't make money, you won't be able to do any of those good things that make for a better state.

In our little corner of America, we see the role of government not as dominating and ordering around a private sector that exists at our sufferance and mainly to fund our wise decision making, but as protecting and promoting the parts of life that really matter. That is a very different conception from what our national leadership represents. Choosing between Government the Master and Government the Servant is the fundamental, future-altering decision Americans must make in the days directly ahead.

CHAPTER 8

Our "Raison Debt"

Man is often described as a social animal, but that does not mean we are naturally given to communal action. Virtually every attempt to organize societies or even local communities on communal principles has collapsed in failure, usually not long after it began. One of the most famous, the New Harmony project, was attempted in the far southwestern corner of Indiana in the 1820s. Today, all that remains of the experiment is a fascinating historical site but no proof that a collectivist community—even one buttressed by the bonds of a shared religion—could survive.

This is not to say that humans are incapable of common purpose. Often we simply lack the will. Arguably, the most effective acts of cooperation happen not when people are conscripted or enslaved into service but when they are individually and personally moved to commit themselves to some common endeavor. Love of neighbor, or tribe, or nation, is among the most compelling motivators, for good or ill.

Hoosiers believe we have a gene for cooperation. The tradition of the barn raising, when neighbors came together to do the backbreaking work of constructing a new barn for one member of the community, has such a proud history in our state that I chose it for the central metaphor of my first inaugural address.

Even though the tradition of barn raising has been relegated to our memory, our communal spirit has not dampened with time. I have witnessed it in action on many occasions, especially during my tenure as governor when I would stay as an overnight guest of a state resident. One occasion in particular comes to mind: the time I spent at Doug Gerber's home. I met Doug in 2005, a few years after he was hit by a train while driving his tractor. The accident left him near dead and in a month-long coma. He awoke to find that his neighbors had planted his crops and fed his livestock while he was in the hospital, and they continued to do so during the entire summer and fall while he recovered. When Doug offered to pay them back, he recalls, "No one would even take a cent for the diesel fuel they used."

Humans are imperfect, and often selfish or cruel, but we sell our species short if we fail to recognize our unique capacity for empathy, our ability to put ourselves in the place of others. This is what sets us apart from the lower orders of God's kingdom and suppresses our basic instincts in favor of a higher moral order. Adam Smith dissected this trait best in his *Theory of Moral Sentiments,* which opens "How selfish soever man may be supposed, there are evidently some principles in his nature, which interest him in the fortune of others, and render their happiness necessary to him, though he derives nothing from it except the pleasure of seeing it.... The greatest ruffian, the most hardened violator of the laws of society, is not altogether without it."

That said, the most powerful communal project, and the most frequent in human history, is war. Wartime elicits the greatest selflessness of which mankind is capable. Often it involves the ultimate sacrifice, the laying down of life itself for the common good as it is perceived by those participating.

Again, free and voluntary action usually wins out over that coerced by kings or despots. It has been persuasively argued that democracies, once aroused, make the most deadly and implacable of military foes, and it was perhaps said best by Dwight D. Eisenhower on the day Germany invaded Poland in 1939: "Hitler should beware the fury of an aroused democracy."

Not surprisingly, then, people hoping to rouse their fellow citizens to some mutual cause are prone to invoke military images. Here in the United States, President Lyndon Johnson declared a "War on Poverty" to justify an explosion of government spending on new social welfare programs. President Jimmy Carter labeled the quest for energy independence the "moral equivalent of war."

Today's America faces two dangers that rise to the level that can honestly and without exaggeration be said to threaten our national survival. The first is the emergence of Islamist religious fanatics in potential possession of weapons of mass destruction. Briefly, this menace united the country in the days after the New York City and Pentagon attacks of 2001. What is striking about this unity, though, is how quickly it evaporated. Within months, partisan battle resumed in Washington, and by 2003 the country was almost as divided as it was before the attacks. The division was striking enough that singer Darryl Worley noted it in a song that topped the charts that year about 9/11 titled, "Have You Forgotten?" For many Americans, as the tenth anniversary of the attacks nears, the answer to that question is plainly yes.

To be sure, the prompt action to enter Afghanistan and eliminate the safe haven from which the Al Qaeda murderers had operated enjoyed strong public support. So, in its early stages, did the Iraq intervention, understood by all participating nations as likely to uncover weapons of mass destruction, either ready or being developed for possible delivery to terrorists.

But within a short time, large segments of American opinion had turned against efforts to deal effectively with this continuing, rising danger. With a straight face, many declared that the real threats lay in American conduct: using military tribunals to try military enemies or turning to enhanced interrogation techniques to obtain information. These were steps taken in every military conflict and were far more humane than those the enemy uses at each opportunity. But they were nonetheless seen as more outrageous to much of the American left than the terrorists' ongoing attempts to kill Americans.

So, over the past few years, some national leaders have gone to great lengths to downplay the threat of, or dismiss attempts plainly to identify, the enemy. Attorney General Eric Holder went farther than most with a set of verbal contortions during a congressional hearing in May 2010. Republican representative Lamar Smith of Texas asked Holder if he considered radical Islam one of the factors that led specific terrorists to attack the United States. The attorney general responded that there are a "variety of reasons ... I think you have to look at each individual case." When pressed, Holder reiterated his belief that there were several reasons why al Qaeda operatives attacked America before finally allowing that, "Some of them are potentially religiously based." Holder simply refused to acknowledge the plain truth that certain fanatics were motivated to attack us by a radical interpretation of their faith. His comments would be comical in another, less deadly, context, but if we are to unite in the face of a common enemy we need leaders who tell us the facts directly and without flinching.

Even the military has colluded in the obfuscation. The official report on the Fort Hood massacre, in which a radical Muslim with direct ties to a terrorist network and who shouted, "Allah Akbar," as he killed thirteen innocent men and women, made absolutely no reference to the murderer's religious affiliation and motive.

This is worth pausing to contemplate. At various times in our history, hostile acts of far less viciousness aroused Americans to demand immediate reprisal. The explosion that sank the battleship *Maine* in the Havana harbor comes to mind, which may not have even been an attack but that nonetheless led us into the Spanish-American War. The German sinking of the *Lusitania*, which helped turn public opinion toward entering World War I, also comes to mind.

More than three thousand Americans have already been slaughtered in our homeland, and thousands more in nations abroad, but the undiminished effort to murder more of us, openly shared and supported by governments such as Iran's, has not sufficed to create and maintain the kind of unity, or the sense of national identity, required to generate shared sacrifice.

If the life-and-death danger of Islamist terrorism is not enough to bring Americans together, what are the chances that we will unite against the second threat, which is much more abstract and is posed not by a foreign enemy but by our own past and current imprudence—especially when so many of us benefit, in the short term, from our spending and borrowing excesses?

Regardless of the odds, the answer to whether we will unite must be yes. To admit otherwise is to accept that we are permanently and fatally shrunken as citizens, that we are incapable of grown-up public conversations and adult decision making, that the Skeptics were right.

The threat here may be faceless and not literally life-threatening, but on the other hand it is more certain than those we have risen to defeat in the past. Nazi Germany and Japan were deadly in their actions and intentions, but they were each an ocean away and not in a position to immediately conquer the American homeland. The Soviet Union presented a constant danger to annihilate us with nuclear weapons, but the risk that it would ever do so in the face of annihilation itself appeared, and proved to be small.

Today's clearest and most present danger is the Red Menace, and unlike past threats it is not an ocean away and we cannot hope to negotiate with it or deter it. It is as implacable as an iceberg, as unreasoning as an insect. Procrastination won't buy time for any miraculous change. We either deal decisively with the threat, or simply let it ruin our nation, our standard of living, and our way of life.

Wars are often fought simply for defensive reasons, for the single purpose of survival. But the greatest causes are usually a mix of sacrifice and aspiration. America's surmounting of its challenges offers not merely the staving off of disaster but the promise of a very bright future, one of prosperity that is greater than today's, peace more secure than we have known, and world leadership restored to a level that benefits not just us but all nations.

When it comes to our debt, the positive, aspirational common cause around which Americans must and can rally is a growing economy. Without this we will remain forever insolvent—no matter how many programs we try to cut or taxes we collect. Late in 2010, writing about "The West and the Tyranny of Public Debt" in *Newsweek*, Jacques Attali hit on this point by listing eight things a government could do to "escape disaster" from too much debt. He included defaulting on loans, increasing taxes, waging war, and allowing inflation to go unchecked, and concluded that "only one of them is both plausible and desirable today: growth." He went on to write that "A growing economy (which raises tax revenue) permits the absorption of debt and restores sustainable public finances. . . . The West needs to wake up now, shake off the yoke of public debt, and take the path of liberty." Attali also noted several examples where a heavily indebted government did not handle its debt load well: France in 1789, Venice in 1490, Genoa in 1555, Spain in 1650, and Amsterdam in 1770 all ended up far worse off for not having embraced a path of greater economic prosperity.

For validation that growth offers a path to salvation, look no further than President Obama's own budget forecasts. His 2011 submission says the economy will grow at an average rate of 3.4 percent per year over the next decade. This will be a tall order. First, it is more than a full point above the rate at which we started the decade; the growth rate in the first year of 2010 was only 2.8 percent, so there is already ground to make up. Even more daunting is the fact that 3.4 percent is a higher growth rate than the American economy has achieved over any decade since the 1950s. Each percentage point by which we fall short of that assumption would add another $3 trillion to our debt ten years from now.

Also, considering that Obama's budget forecasts unsustainable debt loads, a 3.4 percent average annual growth rate is what it takes just to produce disaster! The deficits forecast by the Obama budget total $7.2 trillion over the ten-year period, with a resulting national debt of $16.7 trillion, or a Greek-like 87 percent of GDP. By the administration's own assumptions and calculations, the nation needs substantially faster private sector growth than is now in prospect. And, as I can testify from helping prepare three national budget proposals, their underlying assumptions usually lean toward the rose-colored end of the reality spectrum.

Please note that, again, this conclusion is not ideological but mathematical. The most devout statist and the most committed fan of limited government have an equal stake in achieving a long boom of almost unprecedented vigor and duration. There is no way the president and his allies can possibly realize their dream of a European welfare state that funds enormous new social spending without this boom. And, without a dramatically stronger economy, those of us who favor a dominant private sector served by a supportive, subordinate government have no hope of success.

The growth imperative is shared equally across the age groups of society. The young and not-so-young each have an enormous stake. For young people, nothing short of a long boom can save them from a crushing, lifelong and life-limiting tax burden. The Peterson Foundation, for example, has calculated that unfunded obligations owed by the federal government amount to a debt of $483,000 for each household in America. As John Fund noted in the *Wall Street Journal*, that's ten times the median household income. The Tax Foundation estimates that realistically financing our nation's debt through tax hikes will force a spike in everyone's tax bill in the years ahead as the Baby Boomers retire. Under its calculations, for example, those in the 10 percent tax bracket today will eventually have to be taxed at a rate of 24 percent, those in the 15 percent tax bracket will pay 36 percent of their pay in taxes, while the top tax rate would have to increase to 85 percent. Those rates are economically self-defeating and likely politically impossible, and one reason why a former comptroller general of the United States, David Walker, recently said to young people at the University of Maryland, "Things are being done to you, not for you."

Yet it is not as though older Americans can shrug the threat off as "the kids' problem." For those in their middle years, an ample supply of adequate jobs today and any assurance of a livable retirement tomorrow are unlikely without a major recovery, starting soon.

So, when the inexorable arithmetic, confirmed by the assumptions of the Obama administration's own budget proposals, proclaims the indispensability of resounding private-sector growth, national policy surely must have moved to a "job-one," no holds barred, all-hands-on-deck prioritization of measures to produce it, right? As George Carlin used to say, *"Au contraire, mon frère!"* At the very moment when any other objective must be set aside or assigned second place to its revival, the Obama administration launched the most comprehensive assault in our history on the vitality of the free enterprise system.

President Obama has become famous for his reliance on the teleprompter, and correspondingly for making his most revealing statements when no teleprompter is handy. He will long be remembered for telling a concerned citizen that his central goal was to "spread the wealth around." The obvious predicate for this comment is that there is plenty of wealth now, and the task is to redistribute it according to a higher concept of justice. Whose concept? Leave that to the president and the fraternity of our Benevolent Betters.

In the first months of the new administration, the attacks on the free economy came swiftly and ferociously. But that was just the beginning. "Inheriting," as they monotonously put it, a creaking, staggering national economic wagon, the administration began heaping new burdens on the only vehicle that could pull America "out of the ditch"—another presidential cliché—let alone fund the new spending schemes they were proposing during a national bankruptcy.

The health care "reform" bill was the most publicized of these attempts but, with all its flaws, not necessarily the most economically backward. That distinction probably goes to the "cap and trade" plan aimed at controlling world climate temperatures by reducing the amount of carbon dioxide emitted by American businesses.

By now, libraries have been filled with claims and counterclaims about the trend of world temperature, the cause of whatever changes are occurring, and the best measures for dealing with either the cause or the consequences of these changes. Despite having read reams of this material, and followed the continuing debates as closely as a layman can, I do not pretend to be certain on any of these questions.

But one doesn't have be an expert to conclude that the Obama climate change legislation was an ill-conceived mistake that will accomplish nothing more than to further damage, if not cripple, the national economy. Reading the bill as an open-minded agnostic when it comes to climate change, I could not find the common sense in a policy that would inflict immediate, immense, and certain costs on a suffering economy in the hope of producing distant, infinitesimal, and highly uncertain changes in world temperatures. This was factually groundless, ideological, feel-good government at its worst.

Believing as it does in its superior wisdom, and its right to dominate and dictate to the private sector, such government stops at nothing to do what it wants to do. Cap and trade's rejection by Congress, on a strongly bipartisan basis, did not stop a zealous and willful administration from pursuing it outside the democratic process, through the science-bending actions of the Environmental Protection Agency. The EPA today claims the right to regulate carbon, and agencies as far afield as the Fish and Wildlife Service were directed by executive order to incorporate "climate change" into all decision making, thus erecting a new set of barriers and delays in the path of people attempting to put their fellow citizens to work.

Writing in the *Wall Street Journal*, I pointed out that "Politicians in Washington speak of a reawakened appreciation for manufacturing and American competitiveness. But under their policy, those who make real products will suffer. Already we observe the piranha swarm of green lobbyists wangling special exemptions, subsidies and side deals. The ordinary Hoosier was not invited to this party, and can expect at most only table scraps at the service entrance." Nothing that has happened since makes this conclusion any less clear. Indeed, the legislation's nickname of "cap and tax" is an appropriate summation. The bill would have put a cap on the economy, while imposing massive new taxes on carbon that would have driven the price of energy through the roof. The imperative of national growth, and its centrality to the survival-level challenge of the Red Menace, means that a massive new cost, a tax in all but name, on energy and the jobs that rely on it is a luxury we cannot afford.

The attempt to rewrite the nation's labor laws was even worse. In the case of climate change, we can at least acknowledge the passion and sincerity of those who have convinced themselves that they are staving off catastrophe. No similar excuse can be made for the proponents of the so-called card check legislation. It was a naked payoff to political allies that would have piled another mountain of costs and antigrowth requirements on our groaning economic wagon, causing a major loss of jobs with absolutely no corresponding benefit. And we are lucky the legislation hasn't, as of yet, been enacted. But given an opportunity, we can fully expect that card check would reemerge as a top priority of this administration.

The idea, permitting workers to be unionized without a secret ballot, is the desperately sought grail of dying private-sector unions, which have fallen from a 1950s peak of 35 percent of all employees to about 7 percent today. Even in Indiana, once the third-most-unionized state in the country, and still the most manufacturing intensive (meaning that manufacturing is a larger share of jobs and income here than anywhere else), unionism outside government has plummeted to about the national average.

Our state has leaped from sixth to second in auto production in the last few years, but it is the workers of Toyota, Honda, and Subaru and their suppliers who have lifted us. Indiana output by the Detroit Three ("Big Three" became a misnomer years ago) shrank during that time. And the workers of our growing companies have been unreceptive to unions that would take away part of their pay, spend it on purposes about which they are not consulted, while insisting that jobs be kept narrow and boring, and that the most hardworking, productive employee be treated no better than the slacker next to him on the line. If given card check, unions might be able to sweep many of these workers unwillingly into unions, and thus diminish their productivity and dim their future earning potential.

The list of new antigrowth regulations either imposed or in process by the Obama administration goes on and on, and is too depressing to recount in full. A strategy to survive the debt tsunami and renew the promise of America would not only avoid such counterproductive steps but also adopt a diametrically different approach.

Right before Obama's inauguration, the president-elect took a highly positive and encouraging step toward bipartisanship and cooperation by inviting the nation's governors to meet with him to discuss our national difficulties. I found it more than just a generous gesture, and said so. It seemed to reflect a promise by the new administration that the federal government alone would not be the engine of recovery, nor the locus of all good ideas for a national comeback.

We met in Philadelphia's Independence Hall. Next to the discussion with the president, the day was memorable for affording me my only opportunity to meet Illinois governor Rod Blagojevich, who was assigned the seat next to mine. I had made absolutely sure to arrive ahead of time, taking no chance of being impolite to our new president, and every other governor did likewise except the governor of Illinois. He came blowing in literally three minutes ahead of the Obama motorcade, which left only a moment for small talk.

Trying to be friendly, I innocently brought up the fact that Obama's election as president gave the governor a chance to mint a new senator for his state and said, "Well, your phone must be ringing off the hook with that vacant Senate seat appointment coming up."

"Yeah," he replied, "every SOB in Illinois thinks he ought to be a United States Senator."

Five days later, FBI agents arrested the governor on charges that he had sought bribes to make the appointment.

Looking back after two years of the new administration, the most telling and significant moment of the morning came when the group discussed the best ways to jump-start (or, as we all learned to say, "stimulate") the economy. I planned to propose what I thought was the constructive idea at least to temporarily suspend federal regulations and mandates that make government construction projects take too long and cost too much. Some, such as the Davis-Bacon requirement that union wage scales be used on all but the smallest projects, are well known, their enormous cost in time and money well documented. But maybe the best examples drew on my own infrastructure experience, most notably our Toll Road lease bonanza.

Virtually all major transportation projects are paid for with a mix of federal and state dollars and are therefore subject to federal approval of specifications, environmental impact, and other matters. Securing these agreements can consume months or years, inevitably adding to costs along the way.

Armed with more than $3 billion in cash from our transaction, Indiana was in the unique position of being able, on occasion, to build a major road or bridge with our own money, free from all the usual federal restrictions. Our engineers reported to me that, working on our own, we could get the job done in two-thirds the time and at two-thirds the cost.

Many governors go to these meetings eager to declaim, but I almost always keep my mouth shut. At this meeting in particular, held in the wake of a massive Democratic Party triumph, I thought my little moratorium idea might get a better reception coming from someone in the president's own party. So I mentioned it to the meeting's host, Governor Ed Rendell, my pro-infrastructure ally, and asked him to make the suggestion.

Ed did so, and it touched off a good discussion, as other governors (I kept quiet) chimed in with supportive comments and their own frustrating experiences. The president-elect expressed an interest in the notion and asked the governors to send him a list of requirements that would get in the way of stimulus infrastructure spending.

Under Governor Rendell's leadership, I'm told, the list was prepared, but that's the last I ever heard of it. As far as I know, not a single regulation was ever suspended or even waived anywhere, and that is one reason the $787 billion "stimulus" package, which had a small part dedicated to infrastructure, did so little for the economy and took so long actually to be spent. At this writing, two years later, a reported $168 billion of the money is still unspent.

Fiscal policies and tax reform tend to dominate our news, talk shows, and commentary because they spark hard-fought battles in Congress. But the all-out pro-growth commitment we must make to save the American project will depend at least equally on a national agreement to relax, or waive, or suspend for a time, many of the single-purpose rules that are strangling growth and costing us jobs. In the process, these rules, as laudable as their intents might be, are often subverting their own objectives.

The most critical, and politically the most difficult, are restrictions that stymie job creation in the name of the environment. As much as anyone, environmentalists need the economy to grow if they are to have a chance at realizing their goals. Accustomed to opposing almost any new economic activity—industrial, manufacturing, power production, infrastructure, agricultural—environmentally minded citizens should begin to think more carefully about the overall long-term effects of their absolutism.

Because of the deep commitment almost everyone feels to conserving and protecting our natural heritage, anyone who proposes an activity that is even alleged to be dangerous is put on the defensive. The burden of proof is always on the pro-growth side, which has to prove that creating a new job won't hurt the environment. I predict that this, not the reduction of long-entrenched spending programs, will be the hardest set of tradeoffs Americans will have to weigh, the most difficult of all the grown-up decisions we will have to make.

Some environmentalists appear to nurture the visceral illusion that a less developed, less wealthy society would be a cleaner one. (*Devout* is a literal term here; for many, environmentalism has taken on every aspect of a theology, a transcendent belief admitting of no doubt or disagreement, to which dissidence is not merely error but evil.) Their view seems to be that, if we could just stop building things, stop expanding things, stop developing things, we would be healthier and so would Mother Nature. But it's a false conclusion.

There are some ways in which, in the short term, poor equals green. When the world economy crashed into deep recession in 2008 and factories and businesses were closing left and right, CO_2 emissions, the fixation of those for whom man-made climate change is both irrefutable fact and the worst of dangers to society, plummeted. So did the levels of the true pollutants, genuine health hazards such as sulfur dioxide, nitrous oxide, lead, and mercury. The most effective way to reduce a factory's emissions is to shut it down.

But impoverishment is neither a humane nor a smart long-term means of protecting the environment. Poor countries are never greener ones. The world has never known more filthy, degraded ecologies than those of the former Soviet Union and much of today's developing world. Without the wealth that a growing economy produces, consumers have no way to pay for modern, cleaner cars. Companies do not have the money to install the extremely costly technology needed to make today's clean air and clean water even cleaner.

Yes, I said "clean." If you are a recent product of the public schools or a regular moviegoer, you may be concerned that your family's health is at risk from dangerous levels of bad stuff all around you, and that the problem has been getting worse. With the most limited of exceptions, this is nonsense. And according to environmentalist Bjorn Lomborg, the doomsday scenarios are "fundamentally wrong." The truth is, by every measure, the air I am breathing right now and the water I will drink or swim in later on are dramatically cleaner than what I was exposed to, and somehow survived, in my younger days. This is true of anyone, regardless of his age.

I often make this point to Indiana high school students, who are almost always amazed to hear it. It's another example of miseducation by today's school systems.

We pay a frightful price in lost jobs and economic opportunity for what I think of as the mad pursuit of zero. When, at great expense, we have reduced the amount of a given pollutant to a few parts in a bajillion and it produces no meaningful health benefit, we reduce the amounts even more. But the more of these tiny changes we implement, the more it costs. We may spend $100 for the first 99 percent improvement, $1,000 for the next half percent, and $10,000 chasing the final half percent, when there is absolutely no additional measurable protection to be gained.

I don't mean to suggest that we stop moving forward, only that we do so thoughtfully, and with an eye to the critical need to grow our economy, provide opportunity for Americans, and, incidentally, generate the funds we need to pay for further environmental improvement. In Indiana we have made enormous headway by clearing out a backlog of some 450 expired air and water permits. In some cases, these had been pending for more than 20 years. I came to understand why the businesses involved were not complaining: new permits invariably require lower limits and tighter restrictions than the expired version, so as long as they could continue operating under the old permit, they were saving money. When, in early 2011, the last of these antique permits was rewritten, we had reduced collective emissions by thousands of tons per year. In 2010, Indiana also hit a benchmark in air quality. For the first time since the passage of the 1970 Clean Air Act, all ninety-two counties in the state met all applicable federal clean air standards. In 2004, air tests had revealed that twenty-three counties and one township didn't meet the federal standards.

And yet, just as invariably, our local environmentalists could be counted on to remonstrate and litigate these new permits endlessly, all the while delaying reasonable and substantial progress in air and water quality.

My most stunning encounter with environmental absolutism began during the Fourth of July holiday in 2007. After a long, rigorous semester that included Indiana's biannual long legislative session, my wife, Cheri, and I were headed to West Virginia for our annual weeklong vacation. We hadn't driven two hundred miles when I got the first of two phone calls that would take a lot of the fun out of the getaway. The first was to inform me that citizens incensed about their local property tax bills were demonstrating on the Governor's Residence lawn. That challenge ended in a great triumph for taxpayers when we enacted the biggest tax cut in state history, reducing Indiana property taxes to the lowest in America and capping them at 1 percent of a home's market value.

The second call was to let me know that a new economic project, one that I had announced with great excitement and satisfaction, was under attack. The project in question was a major expansion and modernization of British Petroleum's refinery in Whiting, Indiana, which was scheduled to be the largest single capital investment in state history.

I had multiple reasons to be excited. First, at $4 billion, this investment was going to generate thousands of construction jobs for several years. It would then create hundreds more permanent positions once the refinery opened for operation.

Second, Whiting is on Lake Michigan, in northwest Indiana. This has been the hardest part of the state to attract jobs to. Culturally close to Chicago in both economics and politics, and with a reputation for governmental corruption and labor union aggression, our northwest corner is a place employers are more likely to flee than invest in. So I was thrilled to have landed a major new source of jobs for our people.

Finally, the purpose of the refinery's reconfiguration was to allow for the processing of Canadian oil sands. This enormous new energy source, in a nearby, friendly country, had great potential to reduce our dependence on the oil of Iran, Venezuela, and the OPEC countries, which has been the source of so much economic and security-related strife in our country. Gasoline had just passed three dollars per gallon, at the time a recent record, and lack of refinery capacity was identified as the biggest reason for the run-up. No new refinery had been built in the United States in more than twenty years, and this facility would not only promise new jobs and lower fuel prices in our region but also give Indiana a chance to play a constructive role in easing our nation away from both expensive gasoline and the clutches of sheiks and charlatans. What was not to like?

I found out.

Even though the new plant would produce less pollution than the previous one, even though our environmental agency had meticulously dotted every *i* in issuing the necessary permits, and even though the federal EPA had then approved the issuances, all hell broke loose. Chicago politicians of both parties began competing to see who could do the best Green

Preen, who could bluster the loudest and act the toughest with BP and with Indiana. With a blindfold on, you could tell from their rhetoric that these people were from Chicago: "We are not here to bargain, we are here to negotiate BP's total surrender," one was quoted as saying. The politicians were abetted by a sensationalizing *Chicago Tribune,* whose editors must have been too preoccupied to check their facts.

Hypocrisy was not an obstacle. If the jobs had been on the Illinois side of the border, you can bet the press would have come to a different conclusion. The City of Chicago was (and is) depositing fifty times more ammonia into the water than the BP expansion would. Ammonia does no harm, by the way; fish excrete it, too, and it biodegrades quickly, but why let ninth-grade science get in the way of a hot press release?

The BP plant emissions would be way under the EPA's allowable limits, which are always set with a gigantic margin of safety to start with. As I noted to myself at the time, "We are being asked to arrest someone for driving 30 mph in a 45-mph zone."

It ended well. The more the politicians and press ranted, the more determined I became not to be bullied out of a completely safe and economically important project. Later, after we had persevered and endured months of abuse for it, the project moved forward. BP made some environmentally meaningless but very expensive adjustments to its plans, so the plant and its products will cost more than was necessary, but the project went forward. The politicians, surprised that we were not going to turn tail, lost interest and slunk away. The jobs appeared, the new energy supplies will eventually come to be, and the public interest was served.

BP's CEO later told me that, in any other state they operate in, he is certain the authorities would have abandoned the project rather than be criticized for being insufficiently "green." It was my latest and most powerful reminder that the greatest debate ender in our politics today is the charge that someone or their stance on an issue does not meet the standards of environmental fundamentalism.

The nation's tremendous progress in cleaning and safeguarding its environment should be celebrated as a triumph of effective public action, but no one wants to say it. Right-wingers would hate to admit that government ever gets anything right. Passionate environmentalists are impatient to move on to the next control or reduction, for its own sake. And bureaucracies are genetically incapable of declaring any mission ever accomplished, for fear it will interfere with their next budget increase.

As much as I applaud our nation's tremendous progress in cleaning and safeguarding our environment, America cannot conceivably surmount its debt crisis without emphatically giving economic growth first priority. And without doing this, we cannot preserve the promise of upward mobility for those who start on life's lower economic rungs. There is absolutely no reason this should interfere with continual improvement of our natural environment. In fact, the wealth that a long boom would produce is indispensable to that improvement.

Still, achieving that long boom will require sustained pro-growth policies very different from those now in place, and that, in turn, will require a very broad new consensus among the American people. Given the utterly sincere, quasi-religious devotion with which many Americans now approach any issue with environmental implications, that consensus will be very elusive and easily subverted.

Spending and debt reduction will be hotly debated, and agreement for big change will be hard to forge and sustain. But at least people have an innate grasp, recently revived and reinforced, of the dangers of too much debt. A consumer study in late 2010 by Javelin Strategy and Research, for example, found a stunning behavioral shift. The percentage of households using credit cards plunged from a high of 87 percent just three years earlier to only 45 percent today. It is not far-fetched to believe that Americans who have modified their own behavior so dramatically would also modify their political attitudes, provided the facts of our national indebtedness are shared with them. But learning to weigh the value of jobs and growth against charges, however unsupported, of environmental risk will be the hardest of all the adult conversations that await us.

We Have to Be Optimists

Every American, none more so than the poorest among us, now shares a common, critically urgent interest in a long boom of growth and investment here in our country, and therefore in every action that might lead to one. This will necessitate new thinking by each of us, and some willingness to subordinate, if only for a while, other goals and prejudices.

An obdurate insistence by every stakeholder that every penny of their favored spending program is nonnegotiable will consign us to doom. Similarly, uncompromising resistance to new ideas will almost certainly lead us to suicide. Yet most observers express deep doubt that our current politics, with its polarized parties, single-issue zealotry, and slash-and-burn tactics, can produce the boldly different action our imperiled situation demands.

One has to admit that the pessimists have a lot of evidence to cite. But I come to the opposite conclusion for two reasons.

One, optimism is the only operating assumption that ever makes sense in life. Like the old coach's saying, "If you think you can, or think you can't, you're right." We can face up to the political difficulties of making big change as long as we have a theory, a vision, a faith, that free people will not in fact slide into sloth, borrow and spend themselves into bankruptcy, or reject any compromise or second preference that might be necessary for the good of all.

Nothing unites a people like a common enemy. Nothing brings out the best in people like the chance to do something important for others, especially those dear to us. As I once said to Hoosiers, "We never enlarge ourselves more than when we immerse ourselves in a cause larger than self."

The enemy is real and imminent. It is the debt we have accumulated, and it presents a danger as mortal to the nation as the military enemies of the past. Unmet, this enemy will eventually affect our physical security in a literal way, but because it represents a threat to every single American, it has the potential to bring us all together. Because each of us will have to take a hand in defeating it, it *must* bring us together.

Defeating this enemy should not be seen as a depressing, negative act of sacrifice. It will not be a mere matter of staving off disaster. The flip side of our current struggle is that an America that cleans up its fiscal act, that rekindles the growth of its still-dynamic private sector, that in so doing revivifies in its people a sense of personal dignity and proud citizenship, will be the great nation of the twenty-first century.

The program of action that leaves a better, freer, more prosperous country to our children will be not a dreary but an ennobling endeavor. To take but one example, if Baby Boomers are seeking a great cause to be remembered for, a legacy of their own, here is their opportunity.

On Election Night 2008 in Indiana, after four years of tough, often unwelcome decisions, and many innovative actions that stirred controversy or were simply written off as impossible, our administration was rehired by the greatest number of votes ever cast for any candidate for any office in our state's history. Speaking, as I almost always do, extemporaneously, I asserted that night that the results of the election proved that Indiana had the kind of citizens a democracy must have. I said that, going forward, elected officials will come to look at our administration being returned to office and will conclude, "You know, these Hoosiers, they're grown-ups. You can tell them hard truths. You can talk about tradeoffs. You can say we can't do everything at once. And they'll understand. You can propose a new idea and they won't shoot the messenger."

What is true of Hoosiers, I know is true of Americans everywhere. To say that Americans cannot rally around a common cause insults their character and shortchanges their maturity. Appealing to their best instincts, emphasizing those dangers and those opportunities that can unite us, and always, always leveling with them as the intelligent, autonomous, non-shrunken citizens they were meant to be can lead to things others say can't be done.

The common enemy is here, and therefore the great common cause. It sells Americans short to despair that we cannot make the changes necessary to overcome that enemy. It will take a broad consensus, a recently unseen large majority, to take the bold steps of victory. We must marshal that majority around the single imperative goal, the unifying purpose: of putting our national family finances back in order. Call it our new "Raison Debt."

CHAPTER 9

Can We Talk?

The formidable difficulties of renewing the democratic spirit and some sense of national unity are compounded by the poisonous nature to which our national discourse has descended. It is not just Alinsky acolytes such as the president who have embraced the politics of personalization. It seems that everyone these days has joined in the game of attack, demonization, and even criminalization of political differences.

It is tempting to dismiss any dismay at today's political tactics as fanciful, ahistorical squeamishness. It is certainly true that American politics was never "beanbag"; even our earliest campaigns, such as the Adams-Jefferson contest of 1800, were characterized by slanderous untruths and underhand practices.

But it is a long distance from James T. Callender's broadsheets attacking John Adams to the highly refined smear and slime tactics of the present. All parties at the crime scene are complicit.

Ambitious candidates are far too ready to defer to the new mercenaries who dominate most current elections. A sure sign to me of a mediocre officeholder in the making is the candidate whose first announcements are about who he has hired to handle polling, fund-raising, media advertising, or "general consulting," whatever that is. These are the mercenaries—the guns for hire—who dominate the conversation of most elections. People who believe they must buy credibility through the reputations of others are unlikely to know their own minds, let alone assert them when given bad or dishonorable advice.

The mercenaries, with no particular stake in any program of public improvement, and who most assuredly will not be around should a winning candidate attempt to implement one, tend to recommend negative tactics as the first and foremost element of any campaign. Their highly formulaic, repetitive, and boring attack ads germinate in a compost of laziness, indifference to principle, and contempt for the intelligence and standards of the voters they believe they can manipulate.

Laziness is human enough, and reworking the same obnoxious body slam ads year after election year is a lot easier than creating new and fresh material. As long as the pliable candidate is willing to accept that this is the route to victory and glory, the mercenaries can keep reselling the same old elixir over and over.

Messages that attempt to convey much substantive content, let alone a constructive new idea, are disdained by the mercenaries as ineffective and in any event plagued by the "tyranny of twenty-eight," that being the maximum number of seconds an advertisement has to express the point it wishes to make.

One suspects, however, the mercenaries' real objection is that, in order to distill to a few sentences the essence of a meaningful policy proposal, one must first invest the effort to understand the issue. There's just not time to do much of that when you have to catch a plane to the next client, where, if all goes well, you can sell a close variation of the same negative ad you've just produced.

The worst contributor to the mercenary mind-set is the assumption that the typical voter is indifferent to real ideas, or too dense to grasp them, and certainly too close-minded to entertain a proposal or viewpoint he hasn't told a pollster he already holds. The voter is, in short, a child, and children are easily persuaded to shy away from bogeymen. Hence, the first objective of any campaign is to "define" one's opponent in some scary or despicable fashion before he does the same to you.

In the television era, our politics was, as we now say, "toxic" enough. The Internet explosion, which has opened and democratized the process in some ways, has unfortunately only exacerbated the lethality of the toxin. Half-truths or non-truths can now go global before the target first hears about them. Mark Twain taught that a lie can travel halfway around the world before the truth gets its boots on. These days, it can make the full trip. The kind of quality control once exercised by newspaper editors or TV/radio bureau chiefs is nonexistent in the i-world. Even after a charge has been successfully refuted, it remains uncorrected and infinitely accessible by Googlers, who have no way of knowing that the information their search just turned up is total bunk.

No one has proven more willing or skillful in the art of smash-mouth politics than the president and his close allies. As we have seen, the Alinsky playbook to which they subscribe calls specifically for the personal demonization of opponents. In one of those revealing remarks for which he has become known, the president once urged a partisan audience to "punish our enemies." This from the man who promised to transcend our political dividing lines.

The elections of 2010, culminating as they did in a resounding repudiation of the incumbent party, dragged our dispiriting discourse down to new depths. Facing strongly adverse public opinion on the substance of their policies, the national Democratic Party made a conscious decision to try to change the subject from stimulus bills, the national health care takeover, and the horrifying deficit and debt levels to the unacceptable personal qualities of their Republican opponents.

In virtually every race, highly personal and usually unsupportable charges dominated Democratic communications. The consistency of the pattern could not be missed. In late September, the *New York Times* reported on its front page that "Democratic candidates across the country are opening a fierce offensive of negative advertisements against Republicans, using lawsuits, tax filings, reports from the Better Business Bureau, and even divorce proceedings to try to discredit their opponents and save their Congressional majority . . . these biting ads are coming far earlier than ever before. . . . many Democrats are deploying the fruits of a yearlong investigation into the business and personal histories of Republican candidates in an effort to plant doubts about them and avoid having races become a national referendum on the performance of President Obama and his party."

During the election season, Democratic rhetoric went, in *Star Trek* parlance, where no man had gone before. California gubernatorial candidate Meg Whitman was branded a "whore," Tea Party favorites Sharron Angle and Christine O'Donnell a "bitch" and "crazy," respectively. Campaign advertising plunged lower, if this is possible, than the rhetoric. In one ad, a Republican Senate candidate was accused of "worshipping false gods" and branding Christianity a "hoax." A candidate for governor was said to have murdered cats and dogs, and a House candidate in Florida was labeled "Taliban Dan" by his opponent and accused of wanting to impose a "radical fundamentalism on women."

This slime-'em-and-smear-'em strategy expressed itself at every level of government, at times becoming almost comical. One Indiana GOP candidate, a small-town pharmacist making his first electoral bid, was attacked for weeks for having somehow assaulted Hoosier workers by sending jobs to China.

More often the attacks were anything but funny. This same candidate, who was not the owner, but just an employee of the pharmacy, was the target of an especially vicious tactic. A female Democratic campaign worker was recruited to go into the pharmacy—the candidate was not working that day—with a prescription for the morning-after pill. From there she went straight to a print shop, where a photograph of her hand holding the prescription was converted into a direct-mail postcard attacking the candidate as an abortionist and a hypocrite for having claimed to be pro-life. The postcards were in voters' mailboxes within three days of the campaign worker entering the store.

Indiana's most respected political journalist termed the practice "political pornography." In case the word seemed overblown, he reminded readers of the dictionary definition of *pornography*: "The depiction of acts in a sensational manner so as to arouse a quick intense emotional reaction." He cited numerous examples of Democratic tactics in Indiana legislative races, such as a lawyer who was falsely accused of malpractice, a coal miner who was said to have poisoned the environment, and the pharmacist who supposedly sold on-demand abortions. Another mailer attacking that pharmacist showed a baby being handed a pharmacy receipt. It is satisfying to report that the besieged pharmacist won the election, handily, as did those in the other examples just given and almost all Indiana Republicans subjected to such ridiculous abuse.

Apparently it's never too early to start preparing your attacks. In early 2010, I finally had a chance to visit the Ronald Reagan Presidential Library in Simi Valley, California. As a Reagan administration alumnus, I was provided with an extensive tour of the beautiful facility, including a walk through the downstairs vault where documents from my White House days are stored.

"Funny you'd pick today to drop by," said Ronald Reagan Presidential Foundation executive director John Heubush. "We just got a big document request about you."

"From whom?!" I asked.

"Oh, from the Democratic National Committee. They want every piece of paper with your name on it."

This struck me as particularly odd, given the fact that I had been reelected only a year prior and had indicated an intention not to run for future office. Why would the DNC consider me worth checking out? In October 2010, ABC reported that the DNC also filed a Freedom of Information Act with the Pentagon seeking all communications any agency of the army had with nine Republicans who apparently it thought might run for president. I was one of the nine. It seems that the attack artillery begins loading its magazine years in advance of even a highly theoretical campaign.

After the rout they experienced in 2010, one might assume that elected Democrats and their supporters in the media and blogging world would at least pause for breath and a little reflection. Instead, they dialed up the stridency and redirected their anger toward the voters. Even before the Election Day (though the outcome of at least the House falling to the GOP was clear) one Internet outfit labeled 2010 "The Temper Tantrum" election, and a respected columnist for a major newspaper wrote that voters were acting like "a bunch of spoiled brats." After the election, neither President Obama nor other Washington Democrats recalibrated their approaches much. Nancy Pelosi even hung on to a leadership post in the House, an unusual occurrence for a deposed speaker.

Those on what we call the right have been disparaged for years as mean-spirited, angry, and generally nasty. But, with full recognition of their many excesses and abuses, in fact they are creampuffs by comparison with the Dobermans of the left, weaklings in the blood sport of our current politics. I have advised those with whom I agree not to attempt to match our opponents' invective, but rather to concede the field of hate speech to them, striking instead a contrast through a more temperate and positive politics that assumes the best in our fellow citizens and speaks to the "better angels" of their nature.

Much of the vitriol wells up around the so-called social issues, and to an extent that is understandable. Viewpoints on abortion, gay rights, gender, and race are often deeply and personally held, and criticism of one's opinion tends to be translated as criticism of one's character. The implicit, and sometimes explicit, message is if you disagree with me, you must be a bigot, a racist, or a baby killer.

It does not belittle at all the importance of the social issues to point out that, in terms of the survival of the American experiment, they do not rival the Red Menace and the related dangers we face from our overwhelming debt. Of course, strong cases can be made for some relationship between traditional moral norms, which tend to promote intact, enduring, self-providing families, and better economic performance. But no course society might choose, either in law or custom, on these questions will matter nearly so much as whether we deal effectively with our fiscal crisis. Our debts imperil our republic in a way that no other issue, foreign or domestic, does. If we collapse fiscally and economically, it really won't matter very much what legal status we confer on gay cohabitation, or whether we continue to operate de facto quota systems in hiring and government contracting.

The Skeptics would already have detected, in our affluence, our increasing dependence on the largesse of others, and in our ignorance of our national institutions and principles, insuperable barriers to dealing with our challenges. They would have seen us as having fallen too far from the virtues on which democracy itself depends. They would have concluded that we had divided fatally into a majority of takers who now expected their neighbors to subsidize them, and the subsidizing minority that was powerless to prevent their further exploitation.

Piling our social divisions atop these barriers to change only makes a hard task harder. By definition, grasping all the "third rails" we will need to grasp to restore national solvency will require a broad consensus, a majority far larger than those supporting any position or set of attitudes on the social issues. We will save our republic only if we band together across our other dividing lines. People who disagree strongly about other important questions will somehow have to decide to come together around the overriding, mortal one.

Part of recognizing and creating such a broad, common purpose is to set aside, at least temporarily, lesser things. Wartime brings about coalition governments, including parties that immediately before the conflict were in fierce dispute, and that usually resume their debates as soon as the conflict is over and victory secured. Entire nations have set aside bitter enmities in order to defeat common foes.

Is it possible that, as one step toward the rescue of our republic, we might declare a sort of truce on our other differences? It might be tacit, perhaps not even acknowledged by the parties to it, none of whom would need to alter their positions in any way. I choose the word *truce* here specifically because it must be totally mutual, it involves neither surrender nor even retreat, but simply a decision to stand down for a time.

The demand to legalize gay marriage, in spite of the widespread public unreadiness and discomfort with the concept, is probably the best example. At the very least, legislative or referendum battles over this question create a distraction from the imperative work of reducing spending and averting fiscal catastrophe. In many cases, they lead to an atmosphere so hostile that people who might, and one day soon must, agree on fiscal matters cannot or will not even talk to each other.

The endless debate over abortion is another such issue. Its intrusion into the Obamacare debate was a godsend to the president and the bill's other proponents because it took attention away from the bill's even more dangerous provisions. For weeks the abortion issue dominated coverage of the struggle, leaving many citizens with the impression that the risk of more abortions was the biggest or even the sole defect with the president's atrocious measure.

I am no conspiracy theorist—I've been around government enough to know that supposed grand designs and strategies are often just the actions of people improvising and hoping for the best—but I was tempted during the debate over Obamacare to believe that the president's allies had cooked up the abortion flap as a clever way to obscure and distract voters' attention away from the bill's thousands of horrific provisions, and from its intended takeover of one-fifth of the entire economy.

Race is another issue that warrants a stand-down. Although it runs counter to the self-interest of many interest groups and cottage industries to admit it, America has made vast strides away from the disgraceful racism that ran through our history. Discrimination still exists in places, but it is rightly and promptly stomped out wherever it reveals itself. No behavior one can name is as certain to be condemned and harshly punished. The violation need not take the form of physical harm or threats; it need not involve any action at all. It can be as minor as a negative comment blurted out in anger or a joke told in poor taste. Society has agreed almost unanimously to outlaw racism and never to condone any whisper of its return.

Meanwhile, discrimination has long since ceased to explain much of anything about the heartbreaking disparities between black and white, or, tellingly, black and Asian Americans. Perhaps the late Patrick Moynihan was premature by decades when, back in 1970, he suggested that we move to a posture of "benign neglect" of racial questions. But continuing to expend energy on them today only keeps apart Americans who should be uniting against a common foe. The economic collapse to which our debts will lead will fall on black and white alike. In fact, black Americans have the most to lose from it.

The same goes for gender. The rise of women to fully equal status with men was a great triumph of the last half century. The women who led that movement performed a tremendous service not only to their sisters but to our entire country, as womanpower began making much bigger contributions to our economic strength and productivity and became an underappreciated source of competitive advantage in international economics.

Today, *patriarchy* is an almost comically outdated term. Young women are now far better educated than young men. They are graduating from both high school and college at higher rates, and making higher grades in the meantime. Not surprisingly, then, in a knowledge-based economy, young women are beginning to out-earn their male counterparts. In the nation's top 366 metropolitan areas, the gap is 8 percent. Young women lead in pay in thirty-nine of the largest fifty cities; men out-earn them in only three. Men, who tend to work in fields such as manufacturing and construction suffered a disproportionate share of the recession's job losses, compared with women, who are more prevalent in health care, education, and government.

And, most fundamentally, women outlive men by five years. If one were starting a gender equity movement today, it would clearly be on behalf of young males. Obviously, I'm not calling for one. Men will have to remedy their own deficiencies. We should celebrate the nation's great success in removing the historic barriers to women living to their full potential, and turn together to the real threats of our era. On one front, we have achieved truly perfect equality; if America goes bankrupt, the sexes will share the misery in very equal measure.

Again, a truce is not a surrender. No one need change his viewpoint or concede error. Advocates can continue appealing for support, but perhaps without castigating or demeaning those who disagree.

After I first made this, I thought, innocent, modest, and offhand suggestion in an interview in mid 2010, the "truce" notion created quite a stir. Along with a flood of positive comments, there began a sustained chorus of disagreement from people who felt it reflected some indifference on my part to social or cultural concerns. Some misread the idea as directed solely at conservatives rather than all sides of these disputes; most failed to catch that I was thinking about questions beyond just traditional marriage and the right to life.

Of course, the irony of the situation is that the harshest criticisms came from those with whom I agree on those questions. I accept this as a measure of their commitment to principle, and perhaps to my inability to fully explicate my idea. But, in view of the sustained critiques, it was interesting when the *Wall Street Journal* fashioned a national survey question about the "truce," and found that Republican primary voters supported the concept by a margin of 65 percent to 8 percent.

I suppose no one should propose that others relent a bit from their own deeply felt convictions without disclosing his own. Just for the record, I have been a reliable advocate of the right to life. During my gubernatorial service, my administration commenced regulation of abortion clinics, which had for some reason enjoyed a special status of non-inspection not permitted to other health clinics or even veterinarians' offices. We also enacted an "informed consent" law that requires that women who seek abortions be provided with specific information at least eighteen hours before undergoing the procedure. The information that must be disclosed to them includes possible risks of having an abortion or carrying the baby to term, that alternatives to abortion are available, and that the father is liable for support regardless of marital status. It also requires that the name of the abortion doctor be disclosed along with other information. A 2011 enactment added notification that the unborn child can feel pain, and, consistent with scientific advances, moved the deadline permissible for abortions back to twenty weeks.

On gay rights, I expressed support for the traditional definition of marriage, and for the protection of Indiana's existing statute against judicial overthrow, but I also issued an executive order barring any discrimination by state government on the basis of sexual preference.

Race and gender records are always more open to interpretation, but our administration put extra effort into successfully raising the level of minority contracting, and into the recruitment, appointment, and election of women and minorities into significant public positions.

These thoughts are offered with deep respect for the advocates on both sides of each of these issues. I know from lengthy experience that almost all of them are sincerely motivated by principle and by idealism. I would not argue further with anyone who rejected these ideas, or in particular with anyone who did not share my alarm about the fiscal and economic predicament of the country.

I submit the suggestion temporarily to set aside our social issues only as a matter of prioritization in the face of what I believe to be a genuine emergency, and in the cause of assembling the extraordinarily broad coalition that will be needed to do "the impossible." If America goes broke, suffering will come to gays and straights, men and women, pro-life and pro-choice advocates, and to people of all races. The steps necessary to fight our way out of this desperate corner will happen only if a broad swath of Americans come to trust each other, and to accept the good character and motivations of all partners in the enterprise of rescue.

My experience with elected office is limited to three campaigns (one primary and two general elections), two four-year terms, and one state. Admittedly, what worked in that limited context may not apply elsewhere. But for what it's worth, we waged these campaigns without running a single advertisement or giving a single speech denigrating the background, character, or motives of any opponent. In fact, the most positive feedback I ever received from the nearly ninety ads run in those campaigns was for commercials in which I said complimentary things about the personal goodness and worthiness of our competitors.

This pattern was probably easier because we chose to operate our campaigns without any "consultants" and almost no public opinion polling. Late in the last of the three races, the talented and wonderful woman who managed the few surveys we did take called to ask me a favor.

"Sure, Chris," I said. "What can I do?"

She answered, "I've worked for you for five years, and we've never met face-to-face. I'm coming to the state to see my mom. Do you mind if I drop by?"

I was startled and embarrassed, and rectified my shortcoming, but it was an indicator of the extent to which we had charted our own course, and kept ourselves free of outside influence.

Chris would not likely have pushed me to attack opponents, but she is the exception to the general rule. For most of the mercenaries, this is the first and the most constant counsel. Maybe it's all they know. I agree with Peggy Noonan, our most thoughtful commentator on the quality of national discourse, that negative advertisements have become "boring [and] unpersuasive." Sure, they may contribute to a victory, but at what price? The winner is stamped as just another ranting, negative politician, and those who preferred the other candidate are left seething with animosity. That is not a formula for getting much of anything done after the swearing-in, let alone the kind of huge changes America needs to make now.

Once in office, after some early slips into tit-for-tat harshness of rhetoric, I learned that cheek turning is more effective than name calling, and have held to the practice with very few slipups. It is not always easy, when confronted with purely partisan obstruction, falsehoods, or personal insults. I once remarked that I thought I might bleed to death from biting my tongue too much. But success in the only realm that matters, making large-scale, concrete change in the public interest, is far more likely for those who practice a politics of goodwill, civility, and restraint in the presence of its opposite.

Noonan, too, assigns much of the blame for our gridlocked process to the political professionals who "divide us cynically, needlessly, for small and temporary partisan gain. It is too late for—we no longer have time for—the old ugliness. Once, perhaps, we could afford it. Once, the stakes were not so high."

She goes on "[W]hat we need most right now in our national political life is a kind of patriotic grace, a grace that takes in the long view, apprehends the moment we're in, comes up with ways of dealing with it, and eschews the politically cheap and manipulative." What is most impressive about these words is that she wrote them before the full impact of the recession was apparent.

Might our national leadership attempt to spark a patriotic grace, first in the pursuit and then in the conduct of high office? If so, it would be a sharp departure from the President Obama who urged supporters to "punish our enemies." But then, maybe today's politics permits nothing else. In his earliest days as a national figure, the president sometimes spoke eloquently of rising above the muck. As Peter Wehner observed, "Obama himself has become what he preached against: a deeply divisive politician who . . . is painting his opponents as individuals people should run from."

The first president I served, Ronald Reagan, had a different approach. He lectured the more hotheaded of his staff (I confess to having been one of them on occasion) more than once, "We have no enemies, only opponents."

President Reagan is also remembered for coining the Eleventh Commandment: "Speak no ill of another Republican." As we bear down on the debt iceberg, when all hands will be necessary to avert disaster, maybe we need to invoke a twelfth: "Speak no ill of another American."

We Can't Afford Everything

On Election Night 2008, I expressed hope that our record electoral win would make some difference in the way future Indiana candidates approached us as citizens. Perhaps wishfully, I said, "Now ultimately it's for others to decide what lessons if any to take out of what you have accomplished these four years and these last few months [the reelection campaign]. But I think we can venture to hope there will be some lingering lessons drawn. I hope future candidates for public office in our state will look at 2004 and 2008 and say, you know what, maybe clean and positive works. After all, that Mitch guy got away with it."

As proud as I am of my fellow Hoosiers, there is no reason to believe that, in their proven capacity for mature citizenship, they are any different from or better than the large majority of their fellow Americans.

Our national politics would be enriched by more discussion of the largest issues and far less attention to trivial ones. It would be much more bearable if it became more civil, and more conducive to effective action after the election when the victors took office. But we can scrape by without those two developments. What we must have, on the other hand, is a much more candid, more grown-up discussion of our national choices, while there is still time to make some.

The era when politicians promised ever-rising spending to every group in sight, and pretended either that the nation could afford it or that someone else could be taxed enough to fund it, must end. In its shrinkage of freedom and of the citizen himself, over-promising is an antidemocratic policy, and doomed to failure. As Margaret Thatcher said of such a philosophy, "The problem is eventually you run out of other people's money."

My fellow Republicans have been more responsible than their Democratic counterparts, but only slightly. They know that attempting to raise taxes to finance a burgeoning public sector harms an economy and, as it does so, prevents the collection of the desired revenue. But to drift into the viewpoint that opposes any tax, at any time, at any level, is illogical and unjustifiable. Hewing inflexibly to this position when the nation faces fiscal catastrophe is worse; it is the triumph of blind ideology over patriotism.

During the Obamacare debate, Republicans pounced gleefully on a Democratic suggestion that doctor and hospital reimbursement rates should be limited as a means of offsetting the bill's new costs. They denounced this "slashing of Medicare" in terms virtually Xeroxed from the three-by-five cards of a generation of Democratic scare-mongering.

To me, it was not a proud moment for our party. Oh, one had to take some sardonic satisfaction watching the Democrats get a dose of the snake oil they had been peddling for so long. And the policy was flawed: cutting the rates would only drive more doctors out of treating Medicare patients. But the truth is that Medicare is going to have to change, and we are going to have to find ways to spend less on it, or it will devour the American dream, head and hoof. Hollering that "Medicare must not be cut" perpetuates the public misunderstanding that will have to be corrected soon; my allies may have gotten some short-term tactical points, but they disserved the nation's long-term interests as they did.

Every elected official knows the hazards of truth-telling. Every proposal that might even slightly, temporarily, or hypothetically disadvantage a single individual is sure to be met with a heavy dose of demagoguery. But we cannot concede that the public will always and forever fall for the pitch that the lunch is free, or that somebody else will pick up the tab. Many of those who are the least confident about calling for specific spending cuts are those who have never actually tried. I have found that Hoosiers, or at least a large majority of them, will listen to reasoned arguments about priorities, tradeoffs, and the public interest inherent in maintaining sound finances.

One of the two most useful work experiences I ever had (both in the private sector, incidentally) was the three years I spent as CEO of the Hudson Institute, a nonprofit research organization founded by the legendary Herman Kahn and considered one of the original "think tanks." In a hundred-employee, multimillion-dollar enterprise with no endowment and a limited base of unrestricted donations, we had to sell our research services to businesses, governments, and the occasional foundation. In my time there I learned a lot about what it takes to manage a small business constantly trying to devise new products, find new customers, meet the payroll, and stay current with its creditors.

While I was tending to the business of Hudson, I was enormously fortunate to imbibe daily the intellectual work of my colleagues, and the intellectual heritage of the institution. From its inception Hudson Institute had been known for its iconoclasm, its contrarianism, and its bent for coming at problems in new and unexpected ways. Its reports often came to conclusions at odds with the views or interests of its clients, which was referred to at the institute as "biting the hand that won't feed us again."

At Hudson, I learned that, by the time an idea is conventional, it is generally out-of-date and wrong. That change in society is discontinuous, so that extrapolation from current trends almost always leads to incorrect forecasts. Life at Hudson was a constant search for new and different approaches to the business, public policy, or other questions posed to its renegade scholars. By studying technology, searching for the next discontinuity, and maintaining their skepticism about any conventional wisdom, Hudson was the first to foresee the rise of Japan, the end of the 1970s oil crisis, and the complete discrediting of the "limits to growth" thinking of a few decades ago.

Such "perpendicular" thinking, as I came to call it, can of course lead to mistaken conclusions, and Hudson had its share of egg laying. But it is also essential that someone in a decision process strive to examine alternative views of the problem at hand and different ways in which it might be tackled. The best businesses try to create room for "skunk works" thinking that might lead them to a breakthrough before their competition finds it. In the exhausted terminology of our day, they try to think "outside the box."

The competing parties in today's American politics have each been living in very small boxes. But occasionally one finds oneself outside of them, as I discovered one night in Washington in 2010. Fittingly, the experience was occasioned and shaped by a tribute to Hudson Institute and to its illustrious founder Herman Kahn.

My task for the evening was recalling and paying tribute to Kahn's prescience and his willingness to think unconventionally. I quoted from Hudson's stunningly accurate 1983 book, *The Coming Boom*, in which Kahn and his co-authors suggested, among many ideas, a total rewrite of

U.S. tax policy, replacing the loophole-ridden income tax with something more likely to encourage "entrepreneurship, investment, and growth."

This is exactly what a nation facing trillions in debt should be thinking about, and that is all I set out to say that evening in my speech. But in one of those it-can-only-happen-to-me circumstances, a few hours before I was to give the speech an old friend drew my attention to one particular sentence in Kahn's book. That sentence included, along with the idea of a flat tax, the term "value added tax." If my friend hadn't spotted and e-mailed it to me, I'd have praised Herman's provocativeness some other way. Merely quoting it, offhand, and expressing appreciation for the open-mindedness behind the idea, put me in the Washington lobster pot.

Now, there is nothing all that radical about a consumption tax, of which a VAT is one variety. Very similar ideas have been offered by such free market advocates as Larry Lindsey, Glenn Hubbard, the American Business Council (the association of high-growth enterprises), and the entire Fair Tax coalition. The invaluable congressman Paul Ryan included a version in his comprehensive Roadmap fiscal blueprint. A consumption (sales) tax is the number one revenue source for America's state governments, including Indiana, where it comprises more than 40 percent of all receipts. Taxing spending rather than work and investment, as the income tax does, is more conducive to the sort of growth we need so badly.

I don't happen to favor a VAT, not because it is bad economic or social policy but because of the purely practical risk that it might be increased too easily. Still, it's not an illegitimate idea for a nation in an emergency to consider, or at least it shouldn't be. Given the shape we're in, *no solution* should be dismissed out of hand. Regardless, I wasn't, at the time, trying to offer prescriptions for our debt crisis or advocating anything in particular. I was merely pointing out that, long ago, this great man Herman Kahn had offered up constructive thoughts that might be of relevance and possible usefulness today.

I picked the wrong town to do that in. Instantly, a cavalcade of castigation descended from people reacting to a report in the online publication *Politico*, which cited one alleged expert as saying I had placed myself "outside the bounds of acceptable modern Republican thought," "beyond the pale," and "disqualifying." (Those particular quotes all came from one source, but were echoed around the blogosphere, from a diversity of commentators whose only thing in common was that none of them had actually heard the speech.)

This is not the spot to argue the fairness of any criticism, or the merits of consumption versus income taxation. I tell the tale for what it demonstrates about the nature of public conversation, at least at the national level, these days. I derived three lessons from this experience.

Number 1: "Fire, Aim, Ready!" People who had no idea what I had actually said were only too happy to expound on its impermissible heresy. In today's Washington it's natural to sound off now, lest some reporter choose to go with someone else's sound bite instead. If it turns out that you were ten miles off base, your error will quickly be buried under tomorrow's avalanche of commentary. Meanwhile, your name will have made it into print! Now the next reporter's call is that much more likely.

Number 2: "All Politics, All the Time." Someone once said the trouble with socialism was that it leaves you no free evenings. Today's Washington never takes a night off from campaign politics, and can't quite comprehend those who do. The young *Politico* reporter behind the original article has been acculturated to view everything through the lens of political tactics. Of my speech, he wrote, "Taking on his party's shibboleths is certainly nervy, even for someone who has positioned himself to become the tell-it-like-it-is candidate. The question becomes whether the strategy is savvy or naïve." It seems never to have entered his mind that, first of all, I wasn't calculating some political effect from my comments. I was paying tribute to a man, and a way of thinking about issues, that we ought to bear in mind as we confront today's problems.

I don't blame the young reporter. This is the only world he has known. He was led by his short experience to assume without question that any statements I might make anywhere were part of a "strategy." Isn't every public appearance and utterance contrived for optimal political effect? Isn't the whole point of public life for my sound bite to trump your sound bite?

If I had been out to promote any particular tax policy, or been a candidate for something, I probably would have bubble-wrapped the statement in qualifiers and caveats, to placate the political thought police. But that only underscores the inflexibility of the third lesson.

Number 3: "Stay in the box, or else." Herman Kahn and his ilk were deeply committed to free institutions, but this commitment never prevented them from following the facts where they led, and working to come up with different ideas that might enhance the nation's prospects. Perhaps the Hudson Institute's most famous book was *Thinking About the Unthinkable*, which dealt with the truly ghastly topic of nuclear war and asserted that even that most terrifying of subjects should not be out of bounds of common discourse. It seems that the zone of what is "unthinkable" has been expanded, and that is unfortunate.

We have drifted in our politics into a place where often the worst enemies of pro-freedom change are its supposed adherents. So often those for whom a given reform does not go quite far enough aim more fire at its proponents than at those who favor no change at all, and often play right into the hands of the "statist quo."

Multiple diagnoses have been offered for this trend. Gerrymandered, noncompetitive districts produce legislators who play to the extremes and compete on purity rather than results. The 24-7 cable and blogosphere media environment certainly features and often overexposes the most strident voices and viewpoints.

This is not another plea for some form of squishy "moderate" compromise that sees split-the-difference, "one from column A and one from column B" approaches as somehow virtuous in and of themselves. The proposals we have enacted in Indiana and those advanced in this book for our nation are by any measure dramatically different from those favored by the party in power. They are not "halfway measures."

It is rather to suggest to our allies that, when freedom and the American project hang by a thread, and time is short, results must trump rhetoric, and that concrete action is all that matters. Two examples from our state's experience illustrate the point.

When we set out to reduce Indiana's property taxes, we spent weeks examining all possible options. We even looked closely at the possibility of abolishing property taxation completely, or at least for homeowners. This concept appealed to me intuitively, for its boldness and clarity and because it would sharply distinguish Indiana, as we have constantly sought to do, from all our sister states. Our team came at the issue from every direction, but was forced to conclude that total elimination could not possibly be the answer.

The problem was the math didn't work. In order to wipe out local property taxes totally, we would have had to more than double the state sales tax, or double the state income tax, or some equally onerous combination of the two. There were many other problems—for instance, such a system would have made every city, town, county, and school district a complete ward of the state, essentially ending local autonomy—but the fatal flaw was in the numbers, and the fact that the costs of such a step would have crushed our state's rapidly improving status as an attractive place to invest and create jobs.

A very sincere and well-organized citizens' group had grown up around the idea of total elimination. They labeled themselves Let Us Vote, and asked for a statewide referendum on their plan, although such a referendum would have accomplished nothing under Indiana law. The General Assembly would still have had to enact the new statute later.

We met over and over with the Let Us Vote advocates. We showed them the simple facts about the impracticality of their approach, and the gaping holes and wildly unrealistic assumptions in the "analysis" they claimed to have done. We tried to get them to share our excitement at a workable plan we had fashioned to slash property taxes by more than one-third, to what would prove to be the lowest level in America, and to cap them permanently. It wasn't good enough.

During the months that followed, the repeal-or-nothing crowd continued criticizing our initiative as though it were valueless, and they urged legislators to reject it in favor of . . . well, in favor of what was not clear—presumably to do nothing and try later for their utopian and unworkable dream. Their continued opposition was tacitly welcomed by our Democratic opponents, who hated the idea of a huge tax cut and a limitation on the ability of local governments and schools to raise taxes at will, but were politically cautious about saying so. For a time, the Let Us Vote crowd was the loudest, if not the largest, lobby against our reform.

We prevailed and enacted the largest tax cut in state history. More-

over, we protected all future Hoosier taxpayers against unbridled spending increases at the local level. The repeal-or-nothing group dissolved
and, in fairness, as far as I could tell, supported our administration's subsequent reelection strongly. But, for a time, this signal achievement was
endangered by good folks who not only agreed with our low-tax, limited-
spending policies, but agreed so strongly that they almost derailed any
progress at all.

The early months of 2011 brought another bout of "save us from our
friends." As the year began, friends of freedom had grounds for great optimism. Weary of working uphill against Indiana's backward-looking, reactionary Democratic Party and its House majority, I had made a big effort
to recruit a host of new and attractive candidates for our legislature, most
of them running for their first public office. We had worked hard to support and elect these people, and aided by the national Republican gale of
2010, we won a massive victory, sweeping away the Democrats' 52–48
House majority and driving them down to forty seats, their lowest level
in decades.

With great optimism, I presented to the new General Assembly another
broad set of reforms, all ideas we had espoused for a long time: local government modernization, to remove outmoded and redundant offices and
layers; criminal justice reforms, to strengthen penalties against the worst
criminals while moving less dangerous offenders to lower-cost places of
incarceration; and, especially, a comprehensive program of educational
improvement.

While "conservative" by any description, this last part of our agenda
included all of President Obama's so-called "Race to the Top" initiatives:
to begin meaningful assessment of teachers, based on performance rather
pure seniority; higher standards and real accountability for schools and
districts; a plan to turn around the most miserably failing of our schools;
an expansion of charter school options; and so on.

But we went even further. We offered a bill not to eliminate collective
bargaining, but to narrow it to wages and benefits. Indiana school contracts routinely handcuff administrators and principals on matters such
as when teacher meetings can be held, whom a principal can direct to

monitor recess, or even what color walls or room temperature the teachers' lounge can be.

We also offered a bill to permit low-income parents who were not comfortable with the public school options, either traditional or charter, to direct a portion of the funds to be spent on their child at the nongovernment school of their choice. As a growing number and diversity of Americans have concluded, this is the civil rights issue of our time. It is certainly the position most consistent with liberty and the personal autonomy that lie at the heart of our republican form of government.

Our Democratic colleagues, of course, despise all these ideas. Perhaps I should not say "of course," because in most of America, beginning with the Obama administration, charter schools, more accountability, performance over seniority, and the like are now topics of broad consensus. In many states, Democrats are leading the effort to reform our unacceptably lagging public education system. In our state, where the teachers' union and our Democratic Party are as one—it is difficult to tell which is a subsidiary of which—all of these mainstream ideas are still anathema.

By themselves, even the teachers' union, with all its compulsory dues income, political muscle, and ability for teachers to use paid days off to politic or lobby, would not have been likely to block change that a huge majority of Hoosiers had voted for. But then our allies handed the union a huge gift. As stunned as our opponents were by the size of our 2010 victory, and its historic majorities in both the House and Senate, a few Republican legislators decided to make a lunge not for the major pro-taxpayer, pro-education changes we had run on, but for a fundamental change no one had run on: to convert Indiana into a "right-to-work" state.

There is nothing either illegitimate or radical about such a law. It is expressly permitted under federal labor law, and is already the rule in twenty-two states. It merely says that no worker can be compelled to join a union and pay dues as a condition of employment. To most Americans, this seems only fair: polls, including in Indiana, routinely find majorities approaching three to one favoring such a law.

In addition, we know for a certainty that the absence of this worker protection costs Indiana jobs. As we shaped up Indiana's business

environment, and moved to top-tier status on every ranking of attractive-
ness to investment, our new Indiana Economic Development Corporation began achieving a 90 percent win rate in direct competition with
other states for new jobs. At the same time, we discovered that, as often
as one out of four or five times, we were not even getting a chance to
win; we were being excluded from consideration because the company in
question insisted on only opening a new facility or expanding an existing
one in a right-to-work state. So this is an issue worthy of debate.

Still, to me and many others, 2011 was not the time, for two reasons.
First, this very momentous proposal had not been advocated or debated
in the election season just concluded. No one could claim a mandate or
even the voters' agreement with it. Second, and just as key, anyone could
see the potential of this issue to inflame all the private-sector unions, who
had no interest in opposing the other changes that made the year's session so potentially successful. The course of both responsible legislating
and of political prudence was to commence perhaps a year of exploring
and developing the right-to-work idea among Hoosiers, who are likely to
favor it once they hear the facts and arguments, and then consider an
attempt to enact it in 2012 or 2013.

But the enthusiasts, egged on by a national organization and a few suddenly giddy business interests, could not be deterred. I found myself
flayed in various corners as too timid or insufficiently pure of viewpoint.
As I sat through a National Governors Association meeting in Washington in late February, hundreds of hostile faxes flooded the Marriott Hotel
front desk from clueless people around the country who had no idea that
the damn-the-torpedoes course they were demanding might lead to the
demise of other legislation they likely supported with equal fervor.

The right-to-work advocates insisted on pushing the idea forward, getting as far as passing it through a House committee. Then, predictably,
all hell broke loose. Private-sector union members descended on our
capitol building in large (though consistently wildly overstated by themselves and the media) numbers.

The Democratic House members, with the exception of a single brave
member whose conscience would not permit it, got the pretext they had
been dreaming about to overturn the election results and wreck the ses-

sion. Having already collected their entire year's salary, they walked off the job, meaning that the chamber's two-thirds quorum requirement could not be met and no business could be transacted. The Democrats went to Urbana, Illinois, apparently so that the State Police could not follow them and bring them back to work. This was amusing, as I made it plain immediately that I had no intention of diverting a single state trooper from protecting the safety of Hoosiers for such an errand. Many citizens pointed out that maybe our Democrats just felt more at home in Illinois, since they shared the spend-'til-you're-broke, tax-to-the-max approach to government that prevails over there.

Now, nothing is easier than setting up a union rally. Compulsory dues mean there is plenty of money to hire buses, print highly professional signs, and pay "protesters" as needed. Our unions used Craigslist to recruit bodies at an offering price of $7.50 per hour. (Good thing they weren't subject to one of those "living wage" laws they argue for.) Most construction workers don't work in the winter anyway, and many teachers abandoned their classrooms to substitutes to come yell against change. Still, they gave the AWOL Democrats their needed cover, and raked in day after day of media coverage, much of it merged with news of Wisconsin governor Scott Walker's courageous attempt to curb the excesses of government unions in his state.

The teachers' union could not believe its luck. The entry of all the private-sector unions enabled the flight of the Democrats, and a cosmetic merger of two completely different agendas. Even after the right-to-work bill was withdrawn, the emboldened Democrats promptly issued a set of eleven bills they wanted killed before they would return to work. Their list began with all the education reform proposals. That the first four of these were the programs of their own president seemed to be of no interest to them.

The Democrats finally came back to do their duties. And it is possible that the disgust of Hoosier voters and the $250-per-day fines that the House Speaker reluctantly and belatedly imposed on the legislators will compel them to respect the democratic process in the future. For many weeks it appeared the education reforms we'd had a good chance of enacting at the start of the year could be a casualty of this thoroughly unnecessary fight. We have lived through another case in which demands for unachievable perfection—the right-to-work bill had zero chance of passage through both our Houses in 2011—risked wrecking real results and enormous potential progress.

Occasionally I read where some self-appointed arbiter on the right has attacked someone else as a "RINO," or "Republican in Name Only." I have never had this shopworn phrase aimed at me, but I have often seen it applied unfairly to others who looked to me to be striving simply to advance freedom's cause as far and as fast as they could.

In any event, I have come to identify another species in our political ecosystem, the RIMO. It stands for "Republican in Mouth Only" and it describes that fairly numerous class of people who have never cut a dollar of spending, never lowered real taxes by a single dollar, never effected even one reform in the size of government or the way it serves taxpayers, or made any other actual change in the real world. They just . . . talk— except that occasionally their talk, aimed so often not at opponents but at their nearest allies, winds up blocking real progress in protecting or promoting the very freedoms they claim to believe in.

The fellows who carp from the sidelines are the fantasy football players of our public life. They sit in the relative safety of their homes, at their computers, rating and often denigrating the real combatants, those who take the hits and get the bruisings pushing for actions that really matter. The fantasy fans are more interested in the individual statistics of the real combatants, who, by contrast, must often be willing to sacrifice their ideological rankings and personal reputations in pursuit of the only result that matters to the fans: team victory.

The breakthroughs necessary to discipline government, restore national solvency, and reinstate freedom among Americans will require the realism to move now, as far and as fast as possible. If the measures achieved are less than optimal, we can always come back with the next round. But stalemate means ruin. Stalemate means that the statist quo wins. Keeping the republic will require the unity of the likeminded, an agreement that action now comes before imaginary, unattainable perfection, and a welcoming willingness to treat anyone who supports the basic, paramount end goals as a friend and comrade.

The same old formulations, even those with the most theoretical validity, will likely not suffice to rescue the American project from the perilous fiscal corner into which we have painted ourselves. Absent a thunderous Republican win and mandate, probably on a scale beyond President Obama's 2008 victory, the choice is likely to come down to new action or no action. Occasional politics-free evenings on which we set aside "gotcha" tactics and explore options, if only to discard some and refine the rest, could be helpful. It's time to take counsel of the old British saying "Now that the money has run out, we shall have to begin to think."

In the national conversation ahead, those who would suggest ways to ward off the Red Menace and revivify the American dream must resolve to address our countrymen as grown-ups, which is a facile way of saying "citizens in full." This means laying out the arithmetic of our fiscal crisis unsparingly. It means offering solutions that hold water. It means acknowledging honestly that, no, we cannot do everything we would like to do for everyone, all at the same time. That, yes, some important objectives will have to be paused or subordinated temporarily while we save our nation from ruin.

To me, grown-up public conversation includes the willingness to say, "oops," to admit failure when it happens, and to try again. It includes the candor to concede that one's own ideas may not be the absolutely optimal ones, and the openness to accept criticism and constructive alternatives that improve those ideas. Benjamin Franklin wished, in his closing remarks at the Constitutional Convention, that anyone who still had apprehensions about the work ahead in building a new republic "would with me, on this occasion, doubt a little of his own infallibility." We, too, must on occasion doubt our own infallibility, if we are to find solutions to our pressing problems.

Finally, and fundamentally, it means assuming the best about Americans. It means choosing to believe that we still are a people prepared to listen to calm reason, to see through deceitful demagoguery, to choose positive appeals to those that slander and demean, to accept the necessity of rational trade-offs in the interest of our children and their futures. To slip into the contrary assumptions is subconsciously to join the Skeptics, and to make the task of keeping our republic even harder.

In a February 2011 speech at the Conservative Political Action Conference (CPAC), the nation's largest gathering of conservative leaders, I put it this way: "History's assignment to this generation of freedom fighters is in one way even more profound than the tests of our proud past. We are tasked to rebuild not just a damaged economy, and a debt-ridden balance sheet, but to do so by drawing forth the best that is in our fellow citizens. If we would summon the best from Americans, we must assume the best about them. If we don't believe in Americans, who will?"

Of course there are risks involved. There is still plenty of voltage in the third rails of our politics, there are still audiences receptive to slime and smear, and there are still many who will hold wishfully to conspiracy theories and empty promises of something for nothing. But we must accept these risks if we are to rally the nation to the big changes required, and to assemble the broad and diverse consensus it will take to achieve and sustain those changes.

Elsewhere in the aforementioned speech I said, "All great enterprises have a pearl of faith at their core, and this must be ours: That Americans are still a people born to liberty. That they retain the capacity for self-government. That, addressed as free-born, autonomous men and women of God-given dignity, they will rise yet again to drive back a mortal enemy."

So, let's talk.

CHAPTER 10

Change That Believes in You

In an America where only a third of the adult population can correctly identify the three branches of government, I wouldn't want to guess how many know to what period of our history the term *Reconstruction* pertains. Even among those who do associate it with the time and the events of the post–Civil War era, many probably misunderstand its meaning as it was conceived in its time. As the British historian John Keegan explains, "Reconstruction did not mean, as it might to modern ears, the physical rebuilding of the war ravaged states. There was no thought at all, nor would there have been support for, a financial programme to restore the South's economic life. Reconstruction meant the rebuilding of the Union . . . It meant reestablishing the oneness of the nation, and redefining the idea of citizenship, most importantly by extending it to people of all races."

Construed that way, *reconstruction* is an apt word to describe the task before us now. As with Reconstruction in the 1860s and '70s, we are faced with a daunting endeavor. And if we don't get it right now, we'll only have to undertake the Herculean tasks required of us later on, at higher cost. What we must do is clean up the national balance sheet by reorganizing public policies to spark the fastest economic growth possible. As mountainous as that challenge will be, it does not capture the entirety of our historical assignment. We must simultaneously restore—or reconstruct, if you will—a sense of responsible, participatory citizenship among the broadest possible majority of Americans. We need a national government that treats its citizens with respect, and citizens who demand the respect they deserve.

These goals are mutually dependent. We are unlikely to rebuild an

America of economic primacy and upward mobility without rebuilding a stronger sense of national character, identity, pride, and love for one another. We need an America of full citizens who decline to accept shrunken status; who accept and even insist on the duty to provide for themselves, to pay their own way, to make their own decisions, and to live with the consequences of those decisions. It is the assignment of this generation to confound the Skeptics, to demonstrate that the atrophy of the republican virtues is not inevitable or irreversible.

The good news is that, after we tackle the threats facing us, the United States we bequeath to future Americans will be the land of great promise we have been blessed to inhabit. Even in a world of spreading wealth and emerging nation-states, there is none to rival a United States that cleans up its act and puts government back in its proper place. Not China, aging faster than we are, with a huge surplus of men in its population, and soon to grapple with the unavoidable flaws—corruption; social unrest; demands by an educated, more prosperous citizenry for political freedom—that come with command-and-control government by an elite. Not Europe, doomed by demography and paralyzed from decades of bureaucratic sprawl. Not a Middle East still ruled in many places by medieval theocrats and totally dependent on a commodity whose days of dominance are numbered.

There is no reason that the twenty-first cannot be a second American Century, a period in which we benefit from expanded prosperity and freedoms and in which our leadership provides greater liberty and prosperity for others across the globe. Our Reconstruction will be a project worthy of a great people, and it will take a great people to bring it off. In taking the necessary actions, we will renew and revivify the traits prerequisite to self-government, and prove that we still are the kind of people for whom liberty was intended.

Before suggesting a few of the policies that would save and restore our nation, let us briefly explore the principles on which those policies would be based.

First, we must answer the question raised in this book with an unequivocal national decision that government is the people's servant and not the other way around. Sophistry that claims that uniquely enlightened and altruistic governmental officials are the true agents of the public interest must be exposed as defective in practice—look where it's gotten us—and immoral in theory, in its implicit denigration of Americans' capacity to look out for themselves and manage the risks that come with liberty. We must consciously seek to return the public sector to a subservient position of service and support rather than dictatorial dominance over the private affairs of life.

The actions of a properly conceived and restrained federal government must accordingly be aimed in every possible way at the growth of the private economy. We have lost the luxury of being able to saddle our economy with a million Lilliputian restrictions, delays, and mandates. The giant has fallen, and he will not struggle back to his feet if we continue to burden him as we do today. The task here is not merely to stop shooting ourselves in our economic foot, but to adopt a positive mentality that actively searches for ways to liberate job creators and trigger the new private investments that alone can bring us back.

None of this is to suggest a total hands-off attitude. Government must serve as a referee, a definer of limits and an enforcer of rules. But there is an enormous difference between government as boundary setter and government as micromanager. Philip Howard has written powerfully of the advantages of simple, clear rules that leave implementation to the common sense of those being regulated.

Nicole Gélinas, a scholar at the Manhattan Institute, offers in her book, *After the Fall,* one of the most persuasive correctives to prevent a repetition of the recent financial catastrophe. She concludes that "rationally regulating Wall Street doesn't impede capitalism . . . such regulation is a necessary condition for capitalism's growth." Her approach, however, would look nothing like the 2,315-page monstrosity that Congress passed in 2010. A bill written by Gélinas would probably have fit on a few pages at most; she states the principles of such regulation in nine words: "limiting speculative borrowing, circumscribing reckless exposure, and requiring disclosure." To her, government oversight means "setting clear limits within which innovation can flower." That is a succinct statement of general application, not only to financial regulation but to everything government does.

Declaring the superiority of private life, and aligning government around the support rather than the suppression of the private sector, is how we must answer the question "Who's in charge?" It is also essential to overcoming our national debt emergency. The remaining principles of Reconstruction go to the kind of citizens we believe ourselves to be, and in fact must be if we are to keep Mr. Franklin's republic.

We must see our fellow citizens as rational and mature adults, fully capable of making tradeoffs, thinking long term, and favoring the future and their children's interests over their own.

We must trust our fellow citizens to decide for themselves on the basic matters of their lives.

We must assume the best about our fellow citizens, and assume that we can unite in the face of a common enemy, in the interest of a better future, and in the preservation of the American dream.

The years before us will be decisive ones for our nation. Inaction will be disastrously costly, even fatal. The kind of actions we must take will reimpose the rights, risks, and responsibilities of full citizenship on Americans. The politics of achieving those actions will presuppose the prevalence in our people of that same sense of citizenship. Faith that we can do what needs doing starts with the faith that we are still the kind of people capable of doing it.

In 2008, President Obama swept into the presidency on a highly emotional campaign that was grounded much less in any set of programs or ideas than on a vague promise of "hope and change." The campaign's slogan was "Change You Can Believe In," and the election results validated it as a highly effective one.

But on even a moment's reflection, the slogan is a totally empty phrase. Quite likely that accounts for its effectiveness, as every receptive voter could invest it with whatever kind of "change" appealed to him or her. Senator Obama's legislative record, and the shock-and-awe statism of his first months in office, made plain what kind of change he believed in, but there was nothing in the slogan or the feel-good generalities of his campaign to tip off the unsuspecting voter as to what lay ahead.

Still, "Change You Can Believe In" has a nice ring to it, and the sort of cadence that makes for a memorable catchphrase. So let's employ it as a model, but modify it so that it actually carries a substantive meaning, one that sums up both the principles and the program of a second American Reconstruction: "Change That Believes in You."

Saving the Safety Net

America's Reconstruction must start with the reconstruction of our national finances. Failure on this front will moot all our other issues and render trivial all our other arguments. Viewed more positively, triumph over this enemy will simultaneously launch a new era of prosperity and will demonstrate the continuing vitality of our democracy. Its main tenets must be safety net reform, a willingness to touch third rails in politics, unhesitating leadership in rethinking national priorities, and an overarching sense that we must grow the economy as our focused national priority.

We can make a good start by banning the term *entitlement*. As I've said, a free American is not "entitled" to anything except the liberty to make of his life what he can and will. And open-ended programs that run on autopilot and "cost what they cost" are incompatible with national solvency. We should devise a new term, somewhere between *entitlement* and *welfare* to describe our national commitment to see no American destitute, especially in his or her elder years. For now, *safety net reform* will do.

Unreformed, Social Security and Medicare will destroy not only themselves but our national economy. Advocates of reform have nothing to be defensive about in proposing change, as they are the rescuers of otherwise doomed systems. It is the reactionary defenders of the statist quo who are the enemies of Social Security and Medicare. And they are the perpetrators of the worst injustice a society can commit, the exploitation of its young for the benefit of their elders, the sacrifice of the future for the excesses of the present day.

Let me state at the outset that the suggestions that follow are only that. They illustrate one set of changes that would save these programs and the people who depend on them. The desperation of our current circumstances means that we must be open to virtually any alteration that credibly makes the arithmetic work out; if the choice comes to the second or third best option versus inaction and disaster, mark me down for the former.

The best start is to bifurcate these two venerable programs, preserving them as they are for those who now or will sometime soon depend on them, while launching a new affordable version for younger people. Grandfathering the grandparents, keeping the system exactly as it is and they have expected it to be, is only fair and practical as we establish a new, workable compact with those below, say, forty-five or fifty years old.

A deal is a deal, and the compact on which today's seniors and near-elderly have relied must be honored. But it is important to note what a good deal they have gotten, because it is too good to be perpetuated for those coming behind.

Using the official figures of the 2009 Medicare Trustees Report, Andrew Biggs calculated that a typical beneficiary born in 1944 had paid in $65,000 in Medicare taxes and would receive, after retirement premiums, $174,000 in benefits. That 2.7-to-1.0 ratio will reverse for the younger workers, who will pony up that $174,000. When their turn comes, Biggs demonstrates, they can count on "receiving far less in benefits than they will pay in taxes." (Separate research by Eugene Steurle and Stephanie Rennane of the Urban Institute found an even wider gap between benefits received and dollars paid in.)

The fact that, in Biggs's phrase, "The typical senior hasn't come close to paying full freight for his Medicare benefits" signifies not that anything should change for those in or near retirement, but rather that a system this lopsided cannot continue forever and a new version must be crafted if the nation is to do justice to the workers of today and tomorrow.

I call the programs "venerable" to denote not only their important contributions, which are worthy of our veneration, but also to remind us how old they are. In 2010, House Speaker Nancy Pelosi inadvertently strengthened the case for change when she threw a party for Social Security's seventy-fifth "birthday." I wanted to thank her for reminding our fellow citizens, particularly younger Americans, just how very old the old gal (the program, not the Speaker) is.

In a world in which the Fortune 500 turns over every couple of decades, new goods and services appear, thrive, and then are displaced and disappear all within a short time, Social Security and Medicare creak along essentially unchanged, except for the times when a vote-seeking Congress sweetens them further and adds to their unsustainability. There should be nothing surprising or controversial about a Social Security 2.0, redesigned for the fiscal, economic, and demographic realities of an era incredibly distant from the age of Lou Gehrig and Clark Gable.

To me, an obvious place to start is with means testing. Ask any Hoosier, "Why are we sending a pension check to Warren Buffett?" and the answer always starts with a laugh. Especially now that the resources are so clearly inadequate, it is obvious that we should direct the available funds to those most in need, those whom FDR had in mind when he started Social Security.

In truth, there has never been any reason, humanitarian or economic, for this absurdity of giving money to rich people except the nakedly political one. It has always been believed by the statist quo's defenders that to ensure the program's political untouchability, it was necessary to make every single American a recipient, purchasing his undying support.

Set aside for a moment the black hole into which this policy is dragging us. Reflect on the cynicism with which it views the American people. By every measure, we are the most individually generous people on earth. No one gives a larger share of wealth away, no one forms more organizations aimed at helping the less fortunate, than Americans. It sells our fellow citizens short in a particularly harsh way to presume that they would not continue to strongly support a program to protect the less well off among them against hardship in old age.

So by all means let's means test. Concentrate the dollars we can afford on those with the least wealth and the lowest retirement income. Let's hear the no-change lobby answer the Buffett question.

It is absolutely true and necessary that a restructuring of social welfare must involve contributions from all parts of society, starting with the more financially fortunate. Those whose first concern is to make sure that the well-off "do their part" are looking in the wrong place when they argue for higher tax rates. Instead of job-killing tax rates that in the real world never produce the amount of actual revenue projected for them, the place to start is with social welfare benefits that the wealthy do not need. President Obama is fond of thundering, "Warren Buffett doesn't need a tax cut!" No, Mr. President, and he doesn't need a Social Security check, either.

Second, let's get real about the retirement age. Of course, even now Americans are either choosing or being forced to work past the traditional sixty-five or sixty-seven years. Many can relate to Red Skelton's line "I can't retire. I have a federal government to support!" But, in seriousness, it is time for the system to catch up to the facts of life—long life.

I'll spare the reader a regurgitation of figures readily available in a thousand other places, and just point out what's obvious to all: Americans are living longer than they did in 1935, a lot longer. They are reaching their mid-sixties not only in far greater numbers but also in far better health than they did back then. Even now, increasing percentages of people do not wish to cease productive life at that age, and the arbitrary out-to-pasture age of sixty-five, first chosen by Otto von Bismarck well over a century ago, has become utterly obsolete.

And that is today. Just think about the situation twenty and thirty and forty years from now. Barring natural or man-made calamity, today's younger people are going to live to ages never imagined in human history. We live in the safest world ever: accidents, predators, and the elements have never been smaller threats. One by one, deadly diseases are being conquered or managed. Other advances of medical science will increasingly save our lives from the erosion of our own bodies. Soon, centenarians will be more common, and vital seventy-five- and eighty-year-olds will be everywhere. Social Security 2.0 should feature a gradually rising eligibility age that catches up with these changed realities.

There are multiple other avenues we can take to save the grand old lady from herself. We can simply restore FDR's original design and increase future benefits to offset inflation. Most people with whom I discuss this issue think that's what a COLA (cost-of-living adjustment) does. Up until the 1970s, they were right, but then some of those vote buyers Charlie Flagg warned us about went to work. Now benefits go up with wages rather than living costs, so that they outpace inflation almost every year. Going back to a pure inflation adjustment, or doing so for higher-income recipients only, is another fair and sensible way to protect the system.

The old line about Social Security is that it is the "third rail" of our politics; to touch it is to risk incurring a fatal shock. I believe that even if this was once true, it no longer is. It has been delightful to begin reading comments about our fiscal emergency that label Social Security as not a particularly hard problem. *MoneyWatch* editor Eric Schurenberg wrote, "[O]ddly enough, Social Security is fairly easy to fix." President Obama has said, "[W]hat I know is that Social Security is solvable," indicating both that he understands that big change must come and that he shares a sense of confidence that it can happen.

Medicare, a relative youngster at age forty-five, is the harder problem that the president and others have in mind when they talk about Social Security being "easy." Still, there is no alternative but to tackle it. Its unfunded obligations are almost five times larger than Social Security's, more than twice as large as our current national debt. It is by far the worst danger to our fiscal future, and it simply must be changed.

Again, any plan that credibly produces an affordable future deserves a look. (When I say "credibly," I am not thinking of some estimate of political do-ability; the question is whether it actually could work in practice. Enormous tax increases, for instance, flunk the credibility test because they would strangle economic growth, and therefore never produce their theoretical receipts.) But the plan's essence should be with Medicare 2.0 to convert the safety net from a system rigged for overconsumption and open-ended runaway costs to one that focuses its dollars on the neediest seniors, encourages careful consumerist trade-offs, and reasonably limits the taxpayers' exposure.

Everything said about the overall American health care system's bias toward overspending is doubly true of Medicare. It's "free," or at least feels so to the patient. It pays providers on a piecework basis, so the way to make more money is to come up with more procedures and more services. Ineluctably, it places patients and family members in positions in which the only course they can morally take is to demand, at the expense of their fellow citizens, extreme and often plainly futile or temporary actions at the end of a loved one's life.

The degree of waste and outright fraud in Medicare has been widely documented, and no one claims to have quantified all of it. Its inefficiencies—the forty-dollar aspirin tablets, the thousand-dollar ambulance rides—are indefensible. But even if we believed that Medicare was a rational, smooth-running machine, we would have to change it. More than any other factor, it is crushing our national prospect and limiting our younger generations' futures.

The best conceptual way forward is to begin planning for a new future Medicare 2.0, again only for those still a couple of decades from participation, based on Reconstruction principles. Assure every American up to some high-income threshold that a set amount will await them, money they can then use to purchase health insurance suitable for them. The amount can be adjusted not only for income but also for health status, so that the sickest or most infirm participants receive the higher amounts they are likely to be charged for insurance. The taxpayer's—actually, in this case, the working-age population's—bill would be knowable and controllable. This proposal is not novel; in fact, it is tested and proven. It is precisely the approach of the Federal Employees Health Benefit Plan to which members of Congress belong. Medicare Part D, the prescription drug benefit added a few years ago, is structured in the same fashion.

We should couple this new compact with encouragement and perhaps incentives to save money that can augment the Medicare benefit. The choice of insurance would be entrusted to the citizen, in a marketplace where a wide diversity of plans would compete, along with companies offering to help beneficiaries make wise selections and manage their own care to control expenses.

Undoubtedly, most of these policies would keep premiums down by restoring the responsibility for routine and first-dollar expenses to the patient, while providing secure protection against the most expensive costs. We could expect to find the same kind of consumerist behavior that Indiana state employees and Healthy Indiana Plan enrollees have displayed. While moderating today's rocket-sled Medicare cost increases, it would affirm our belief in the personal dignity of Americans, and our confidence in their capacity to make the most basic decisions of their lives.

The most excruciating decisions will be those surrounding the end of life. A stunningly high percentage (40 percent is the common estimate) of Medicare's costs are incurred in the last month of a beneficiary's life.

Much of this, we all have seen, goes for very expensive, "heroic" procedures with only the tiniest chance of success at restoring even minimally normal life functions.

During the Obamacare debate, some of my fellow Republicans, employing the charge of "death panels," pounced triumphantly on the notion that the government might pay for counseling of the patient and family about hospice care or alternatives to attempting heroic measures. As a warning against a different idea, that the government might go further and institute rules determining when and for whom such measures would be paid for, the protest was in order. But, as in the case of supposed "Medicare cuts," I'd have been prouder of my allies if they had honestly confronted this huge problem with a different answer of their own.

Hard as it is to contemplate, the best approach to the unanswerable dilemma of how to decide when not to pay for end-of-life care has to involve the patient and the family in the financial decision. When the question is "Shall we try a hugely expensive and probably futile procedure, and send the bill to someone else?" there really is no trade-off, and therefore no real choice. Of course, try everything. We are all human and would love to live forever, along with our loved ones. But the collision of an infinite want, for immortality, with finite resources—namely, what society has available—in an era of incredibly expensive new technologies, is bankrupting us all and devouring the next generation's prospects.

Ultimately, terrible as these decisions will be, they become all the more terrible if they are made by a faceless and uncaring bureaucracy in a closed room far removed from the actual people involved. If that bureaucracy controls not only its own funding decisions, but also a large segment of the health care industry, it can become especially oppressive if it makes decisions that close off cost-effective options individuals would otherwise have. We need to evolve back to an arrangement in which at least a significant share of these costs fall on the individual patient and his family. They should have the option of consuming much or all of their substance on extreme medical measures, or to preserve it for those left behind. The wealthier the family, the higher the contribution should be.

Of course, we know the kind of demagoguery that will be hurled at this kind of proposal. But these ideas must be advanced with confidence that

Americans will give them a serious listen. It is not just that we believe our fellow citizens to be grown-ups; it is also that there is nothing radical about these approaches. Tens of millions of us have already been through these very changes.

Across the economy in recent decades, countless corporations and governmental units have restructured their retirement programs. At some point, due to obsolete design or changed circumstances, some actuary tiptoed into the office of his supervisor, who then asked to see the CFO, who then took them all before the CEO and maybe the board, with the news that the existing pension or health care plan was going to go bust. And something changed. In Indiana we continue to fund one teachers' retirement plan for those who entered the profession before 1995, and a different plan for those who commenced their careers later. There is nothing at all uncommon about starting over with a new compact for a new cohort, and as long as it leaves undisturbed the arrangements for anyone anywhere close to counting on the programs, it is likely to be seen as a natural and totally fair action—particularly when nothing fundamental changes for years, and nothing changes ever for those who are now or soon will be collecting benefits.

Reform and rescue of Social Security and Medicare are not optional, except for those who could accept the demise and perhaps collapse of the United States as a great nation. There is a host of credible alternatives to the direction just offered, and any one of them deserves a respectful review. This is no time for purism; for example, I just made the case for changes that do not raise taxes further—Medicare taxes have been raised more than once recently, through the device of raising the income ceiling at which they stop being charged—and thereby threaten to defeat their purpose by harming growth. The job of rescue can be done without new taxes. It should be done without new taxes. But it must be done—or we are.

Winston Churchill once said that when the nation's survival was at issue, "[his] conscience became a good girl." As strongly as I agree with the economic wisdom and the moral rightness of keeping taxes on a free people as low as possible, defeating the enemy at the gates comes first. There is no path to national survival that leaves Social Security and Medicare as they are. People who will continue to disagree strenuously about other things will have to unite around some sort of rescue plan. If it comes to the second or third best way, sign me up.

In considering how to restructure the social safety net, it is worth pausing to acknowledge an important issue and those who focus on it. It is beyond argument that the breakdown of the traditional family over recent decades is a huge contributor to virtually every heartbreaking social pathology we face, and to economic difficulties. Crime, drugs, educational failure, and especially poverty are all directly and indisputably linked to lower levels of family formation and higher levels of divorce.

In their book *Grand New Party*, Ross Douthat and Reihan Salam note for us the Brookings Institution research of Isabel Sawhill and Adam Thomas: "Had family structure remained unchanged from 1970 to 1998... the late-1990s poverty rate would have been 13.9 percent rather than 18.3 percent—which over decades represents millions of lives unscarred by poverty and millions of children more likely to become productive, law-abiding citizens."

The increasing marriage gap between well-educated, well-to-do Americans and their less-educated, working-class counterparts is now the biggest driver of income inequality in our country. Sadly, most of those who profess to be offended by this inequality continue to turn a blind eye to its principal cause, apparently because to do so would run counter to their outlook on social mores. They pretend that family structure is not the huge problem it is.

On the other side are many who see the damage and correctly point out that a virtues recovery would help spur an economic one. But these good folks fall prey to a reciprocal error of, in Douthat and Salam's words, "diagnosing the working class's cultural problems and then pretending that those problems are the only ones there are." They remind me of the schoolteachers I meet who argue against education reforms on the basis that the real problem is the parents and the bad home environments to which their students return after class. Their point is valid, but not its conclusion: it cannot be an excuse for acquiescence or inaction in the face of an unacceptable situation.

As governor, I have often said that, if given a magic lamp and just one wish, it would be that every Hoosier child could grow up in an intact house-hold. So many of the most vexing and tragic issues with which we wrestle would automatically and dramatically diminish. I have encouraged mar-riage and responsible parenthood at every opportunity, especially in front of young audiences.

But no one has brought me a bill, or a new government program, that promised to make much of a difference in the number of people who marry before pregnancy, or who stay together, as previous generations said, "for the sake of the kids." Until someone conceives of such a policy, we must do what we can to combat poverty in ways that at least do not foster either immorality or dependency. The negative income tax (which I discuss later) might be one of those ways.

The Rest of the Story

Controlling the long-term hemorrhage of our entitlement programs would send an incredibly powerful, positive signal to the world that the United States will not be committing fiscal suicide, that our credit is good, our dollar still the right choice as the world's reserve currency, and that investments in our country are safe and attractive. Bold action of this sort would also send a great message to ourselves: that we have retaken con-trol of our destiny, that we are in fact a people capable of self-discipline and self-governance.

But, striking as such action would be, it would not complete the finan-cial side of reconstruction. In fact, all this bold seizing of third rails would not do anything to reduce the unprecedented, alarming, unconscionable annual deficits to which our federal government has become addicted. The elections of 2010 brought an encouraging public instruction and an idealistic horde of new congressmen to national office, and the first hope for a reversal of the avalanche of additional, almost entirely useless spending that the last few years have brought.

I have high hopes that the new realism of 2010 will be sustained by the public and expressed in radically smaller budgets by this Congress or by an even more improved version one election from now. But, as I saw close up during my two and a half years of service at the White House Office of

Management and Budget, leaving the job to an even more taxpayer-friendly Congress will be an iffy proposition. Careers there are made by fronting for spending, not by saying no. Campaign contributions flow freely to those who deliver the goods, not so often to those who protect the general good.

Major reductions in federal spending, like those we have effected in Indiana, are likely to cause far less discomfort to the general public than is commonly claimed. Looking back over the 25 percent reductions in most state agency budgets, and an 18 percent reduction in state employees, I see that if there is any pain involved, it isn't felt by the taxpaying or voting public.

Every newspaper story about even the most modest cut in the most marginal federal spending category somewhere includes the word *pain*. This is usually nonsense. We could cease all kinds of federal spending tomorrow and the only real pain would be felt in the real estate markets and retail establishments of metropolitan Washington. If massive government spending prevented pain, we wouldn't have had so much of it the past few years.

But this misses the larger point, which is that today's grossly oversized and overly expensive federal government is itself a major source of pain in America, through the jobs and opportunity it stifles. Left in its present shape, it promises to bring far worse pain than anything we have recently endured.

An obvious starting point is a major downsizing of federal employment. The swollen manning tables of the government agencies should be sharply reduced, with all unfilled jobs cancelled immediately. This should be accompanied by a hiring freeze, which should last for years. Any exceptions begged for on the basis of unique skills should be minimized by being funneled through a hardheaded central office, preferably in the Office of Management and Budget, with the burden of proof entirely on the requesting agency. One side benefit of no hiring is that a higher percentage of the country's young talent would find employment in the productive sector of society, where we really need them.

Reductions in head count should be coupled with a federal pay cut, followed by a long-term pay freeze, kept in place until some reasonable equality with private-sector pay is restored. This is only secondarily a matter of debt reduction; it is even more about reasserting the principle that the private sector comes first and that government exists to serve and not to rule.

The Obamacare mistake should be repealed for both freedom and fiscal reasons. It is now completely clear that, along with its destruction of the private health marketplace, it will add to the deficit and the debt. It has to be exchanged for a consumerist, true insurance model that reengages Americans in the unavoidable trade-off decisions that must be made when wants are infinite and means are finite.

———

No area of the budget can be off-limits, and it is incumbent on a person of my party, traditionally the advocate of national defense, to include military spending among the items for critical inspection. It is undeniably true that the willingness of the United States to build and maintain the dominant military has been a blessing to the world. The United States won the cold war, has helped protect world commerce, and has been a leading force in holding in check any number of would-be adventurous tyrants simply by its mere existence. No great power ever used such preeminence with such restraint or so often on behalf of other peoples. In a noble way, we have liberated lands far from us, and come to the aid of tyrants' victims—all, as Colin Powell once said, without asking for any more land than it took to bury our dead.

But when we are borrowing the entire defense budget two times over and facing debts that could quickly bankrupt us or, through rapidly climbing interest payments, starve those very capabilities that have protected us and others, basic questions are in order: What size and kind of military is absolutely essential to preserve the physical safety of Americans? What, very strictly defined, are the national interests of our country? *Our* country. The answer may or may not encompass the mission to which presidents of both parties have at various times committed us, to attempt to spread universally the human rights we hold dear. As Henry Kissinger has said, "The freedom of every single independent nation had become the national objective, irrespective of those nations' strategic importance to the United States." Instead, quoting Dr. Kissinger from his book *Diplo-*

macy, we should be "careful not to multiply moral commitments while the financial and military resources for the conducts of a global foreign policy are being curtailed." This is equally true whether those resources are being curtailed by deliberate choice (as they were in the Vietnam era, when Congress cut off funding) or circumstances. One other point Kissinger made in *Diplomacy* comes to mind: that our "foreign policy must begin with the definition of what constitutes a vital interest—a change in the international environment so likely to undermine the national security that it must be resisted."

Over the last two centuries, alternative visions of America as freedom's beacon, encouraging freedom's spread by example, versus America as the leader of freedom's crusade, have competed. Very roughly speaking, our first epoch accepted the former role, guarded against the "excessive foreign entanglements" of George Washington's famous warning, and declined to "go abroad in search of monsters to slay," in John Quincy Adams's admonition.

Dr. Kissinger credits Woodrow Wilson (following a brief interlude in which Theodore Roosevelt led the nation into a new global role) with reorienting all foreign policy from his time to ours. Since Wilson, in places as diverse as postwar Europe, Vietnam, the Balkans, and Iraq, the United States has taken on the mission of defending freedom under threat.

We can stipulate to the nobility and correctness of a century of crusading without necessarily agreeing that this policy is right for America's third century. In defense spending, waste is rampant (the Pentagon is the original home of the phrase "It costs what it costs") and excess genetic. At OMB, they say that the Department of Defense motto should be "Wait! There's a harder way!" But protecting Americans for a lot less money cannot happen just by better procurement or a couple fewer weapons systems or, to take a more recent cost driver, less exorbitant lifetime health care benefits. It will have to involve a reassessment of the myriad, worldwide tasks we have assigned our forces. Missions cost money, and we cannot simply demand that our soldiers continue to take on the same amount of work for a lot less of it.

If, after an open-minded, critical analysis of fundamental American interests, the conclusion is that every current mission is truly vital to the safety and prosperity of Americans, so be it. Churchill taught that the first duty of government, requiring no mandate or compromise, is the national security of the people it serves. Still, just as being a crusader nation rather than a beacon of liberty would have been wrong for our nation's first century, it may not fit the realities of our third. It cannot be illegitimate to ask these questions, and the friends of freedom should lead the discussion.

When a pro-solvency Congress and president are elected, they would be well advised to reinstate the power of impoundment, to spend less money than Congress has made available through appropriations. I recognize that the constitutional power of the purse is located in the legislative branch, but no one is suggesting that the executive be allowed to spend without permission, only *not* to spend when the funds are not available.

Stop and think: In what other context in life does an enterprise lock itself into spending money it does not have? To press ahead with a desired expenditure level even though the expected income is not occurring? Does any business operate that way? Any family? Even irresponsible state or local governments eventually exhaust their gimmicks and are forced to reconcile dollars out with dollars in. Only the federal government plunges mindlessly ahead.

In the hands of an administration willing to use it aggressively, some version of impoundment authority would produce billions in savings, immediately. If it was sincerely concerned about the division-of-powers issue, Congress could oversee the process. But one way or another, impoundment ought to be part of an urgent strategy to bring the federal beast back to a size the nation can afford.

Impoundment can be limited—for example, by providing opportunity for a prompt congressional disapproval vote before each reduction took effect. Or, the authority could be granted on an emergency basis; our current debt condition certainly qualifies as one. But the degree of surgery required to bring the federal budget back within even hailing distance of balance, in a fashion swift and decisive enough to stave off the mass desertion of the world's investors, more than justifies the use of this tool. The percentage of spending cuts our administration made in Indiana would translate into some hundreds of billions at the federal level—and, I can say with complete confidence, the federal government is a more, in military parlance, "target-rich environment" than even the one we found back home.

Grow, or Else

For many Americans, 2010 was the year of awareness about our national peril. In the old sixties jargon, they had their "consciousness raised" and many became "radicalized." One of the most telling events in Washington recently was the release of President Obama's budget proposal for the upcoming fiscal year. It forecast, and embraced, staggering deficit and debt levels and announced not only the mathematically impossible position we are headed for, but also the fact that our national leadership was comfortable with it and unprepared to deviate from disaster's path.

Projections of debt at Greek-like levels and record deficits year after year captured most of the headlines and public attention. But perhaps the most important numbers among the budget documents' thousands of pages were those that typically interest only the technocrats among us: namely, the economic assumptions upon which all those projections are constructed. They dictated a conclusion that ought to, indeed must, become the center of national policy in our era of reconstruction: a conclusion that the current administration should reach and act on as urgently as the most determined believer in limited government. Because, by the president's own forecasts, the United States does not have a chance of surviving the years ahead without a vigorous and prolonged economic boom of a kind rarely seen in our past.

It's alarming enough that the government's official forecasts predict bankruptcy and ruin. Just to keep things from being worse, as previously discussed, the government says that the economy will have to grow at an average rate of 3.4 percent, adjusted for inflation. So, bringing down deficits and debt materially will require faster rates of growth in the private economy than we are experiencing now; in fact, because of the overriding impact of the growth rate on tax receipts—a weak economy produces weak revenues no matter how you fool with the tax system—there is no way back to solvency without growing the economy, vigorously and continually.

The lesson is beyond dispute. Every possible step that might foster faster growth in our private sector should be taken, and taken immediately. This is true as a matter not of philosophy but of arithmetic, the president's *own* arithmetic. It should be a matter of national consensus, and unity. One can argue that the more you agree with the president and the adherents to a much bigger federal government, the more desperately you need an explosion of growth to pay for it all, before the whole edifice comes crashing down.

A lively debate of our times centers on the question of whether the United States is an "exceptional" country. It is interesting to me that so many who deny the unique strength of our political institutions seem to believe that our economic system is an exception to the laws of financial gravity, that it can continue to rack up without consequence debt levels that have broken other nations throughout history. We know what doesn't work. Borrowing trillions from foreigners and handing it around, much of it to government employees, in hopes of spurring demand? Been there, tried that. All it got us, as my childhood neighbor Tennessee Ernie Ford used to sing, was "another day older and deeper in debt."

If our Betters would just put their contempt for the private sector aside for a while, perhaps they could agree to a new mix of policies that might give them a chance to pay for all the benevolence they are determined to shower on the rest of us. But that would mean relaxing, or at least suspending, many of the job-strangling clamps they have so enthusiastically placed on the producers of society. It would mean testing, as we did in Indiana, every action and policy against the question "Will this step make it more or less likely that investments, and the jobs they produce, happen more frequently in the United States? More or less likely that investments happen here and not somewhere else in the world?"

Reams of suggestions, from authors far more economically learned than I, are available to those who would construct a maximum-growth menu. I will mention three categories that I believe are essential if we are to jolt our economy onto a higher plane: our tax "system," our regulatory policy, and our energy opportunity.

I placed the word *system* in quotes because, as applied to the Internal Revenue code, it is a complete misnomer. It implies a degree of order and intention that does not exist in the seven-thousand-page mishmash that has grown year by year, one special interest provision at a time. The tax code has been cut back a couple of times, most notably under President Reagan in 1986, but like some fast-growing tropical vine, it regenerated its tentacles more quickly after the pruning. The late William Simon, the great businessman, philanthropist, and treasury secretary, once commented that it would be nice if the nation had "a tax code that looks like somebody designed it on purpose."

We've never needed a purposeful tax code more than we do today, and the purpose for which it should be designed, top to bottom, is economic growth. The good news is we know what an optimal system looks like, and, in any event, we could hardly have a more anti-jobs tax law than we do now. There is nowhere to go but up.

There are few subjects on which economists agree so nearly completely as this one. The fundamentals of a pro-growth tax system are simplicity and low rates. The innumerable special deals in our tax code, each crafted to advantage some narrow microeconomic interest, create unfairness for those not favored by these loopholes, while distorting markets by luring investment into sometimes less productive purposes. They impose an enormous drag on the economy. The IRS has estimated that Americans have spent more than 6.6 billion hours in recent years filling out their tax returns, and in 2002 they spent about $194 billion on complying with the tax code. In analyzing these numbers, the Tax Foundation tells us that as a nation we spend twenty cents in tax compliance for every dollar collected in taxes. Echoing this, a recent study by the Laffer Center estimates that the total direct cost of preparing and filing income taxes is over $430 billion annually. To me, an even greater sadness lies in the massive amount of human talent consumed in this utterly unproductive work; some of the smartest people the nation produces spend entire careers gaming and helping others cope with the Internal Revenue code.

Those who seek, with justification, a means for wealthier Americans to participate fairly in averting fiscal disaster tend to look in the wrong place. Raising tax rates on individuals or businesses may be emotionally satisfying to some people, but if it delivers less revenue and higher unemployment, then the satisfaction isn't worth it and it won't last long. The mutuality they seek will be better found in closing tax preferences, so-called tax expenditures, which can be done without stunting our necessary growth spurt, and in fact could further it by removing distortions that giving special favors to certain investments produce.

Shifting away from economics for a moment, consider the contribution of the tax code to the shrinkage of the citizen. By now, far fewer than half of us are capable of filling out our own tax return. (I confess to this ineptitude; it has been twenty years since I last trusted myself to file on my own.) We should all find it troubling when a large majority of a self-governing people requires the aid of a guild of magicians, a specially ordained priesthood, to perform a basic responsibility of citizenship.

Perhaps worse is the way the tax code has become a vehicle for behavior modification, a morass of incentives for "approved" behavior and occasionally penalties for that which is disapproved. Buy an electric car, or a more expensive house, or "winterize" that home with environmentally friendly modifications, and you are rewarded with lower federal taxes. We can applaud such behavior and the good intentions behind such rules and still regret the way in which they infringe on the sovereignty of the individual to choose for himself.

Back to growth. There is a plethora of variations around the theme, but there is wide concurrence on the essence of a growth-friendly tax code. It involves the elimination of all or almost all current exclusions and deductions, enabling in return a vastly simpler system with lower rates than those of today. It would tax compensation only; income from savings (including interest, dividends, and capital gains) would not be taxed. The system can be made more or less progressive by varying a fixed exemption, so that low-income people pay little or nothing, and by using not one flat rate but maybe two or three.

The business tax counterpart to this approach would use similar principles. The tax base would be revenues minus wages paid to workers and purchases from other businesses. The investment the nation needs for fast growth and jobs would be free of tax. In other words, it provides for the immediate and total expensing of investment. In effect, this is a business consumption tax.

No one knows how profound or immediate the effects of such a reform would be—estimates generally are in the range of a percent or two a year—but no one can doubt that they would be strongly positive. And these estimates do not even try to capture the benefits of liberating a couple hundred billion dollars and the talent that consumes it for more productive economic activity, or the upside of more capital finding its way to job-creating purposes rather than government-directed ones.

Each extra percent of annual economic growth translates into around $3 trillion in additional government revenue over the next decade and reduced expenditure (through lower social welfare spending) each year. For the kind of debt reduction America needs, rousing growth is absolutely, mathematically indispensable, and no amount of it is excessive. If we are to save and restore the promise of America, no other goal rivals it. No other goal can be permitted to interfere with it.

This is said with respect and admiration for the more zealous partisans of social programs, or environmental protection. It is not that their priorities are wrong-headed. What they must comprehend is that their priorities will suffer, and suffer grievously, if we do not promptly move to a growth trajectory that fends off a debt disaster and furnishes the wherewithal to pay for the government they desire.

Please note that a growth-friendly tax system along the lines just mentioned means one that collects more than today's nightmare would produce. Its rates can be set to bring in more or less revenue, at least up to some point where it stops accelerating growth and becomes counterproductive. For instance, a flat rate of 23 percent on both individuals and businesses is estimated to collect about 18.5 percent of gross domestic product in normal times, a bit above the long-term average of about 18 percent. But the rates and the amount they would likely bring in are flexible—and so, I would recommend, should we be in setting them.

Clearly I am an advocate of the lowest taxes consistent with national necessity. The national necessity of our age is to overcome our debt burden before it destroys the America we love. This is no time for theological, think-tank arguments about 18 percent versus 19 percent versus 20 percent of GDP. We can resume those debates after the enemy is thrown back from our gates. If it takes a slightly higher rate to bring together the majorities necessary to pass radical simplification and a pro-growth federal tax structure, count me in.

While We're at It

In addition to serving the imperative that we grow our economy, overhauling our tax system presents an opportunity to disassemble a system of transfer payments and subsidies that creates a culture of dependence on the government. In 1996 we as a nation reformed welfare. But over the past several decades other welfare programs have sprung up that increasingly seem aimed at enticing more Americans into accepting government assistance for health care or home heating oil or any number of other things. Many of these programs were designed with sincere compassionate goals in mind, but their sum total is this: They put a drag on the economy that we can't afford, and pressure on government budgets we can't sustain. These programs also degrade and diminish the dignity of individuals. They need to be reformed.

We can revise these systems while both sharply reducing the size and reach of the federal government and providing a safety net for those who legitimately need it. We can foster a culture of independence and ensure that all members of our society have an opportunity to pull themselves out of destitution.

One mechanism for doing this originated in the fertile mind of Milton Friedman. He called it the negative income tax (NIT), and its workings, like all the best public policies, are simple to understand and implement. Any American or American family with less than a specified level of income would receive cash directly through the tax system. As earnings increased, the amount of the subsidy would drop, but only by a fraction of the increase, so that the citizen would be encouraged to continue to work. If coupled with tax reforms that both simplified the code while also removing other, more complicated and cumbersome welfare programs, the negative income tax could help us restore the right set of incentives to encourage work while also providing for the less fortunate.

Friedman saw the NIT as "a straightforward means of assuring every family a minimum amount, while at the same time avoiding [now dismantling] a massive bureaucracy, preserving a considerable measure of individual responsibility, and retaining an incentive for individuals to work and earn enough to pay taxes instead of receiving a subsidy."[1]

Precisely how the system operated and where the thresholds would be set could be worked out. But, for the purpose of illustration only, imagine a minimum income threshold of $20,000. So, if a family of four had no income, it would receive $20,000 in payments annually through the tax system. However, if that family earned some income, its benefit would be reduced by $0.50 for every dollar it earned. So if that same family earned $1,000, its benefits would be reduced by $500 (half of the $1,000 it earned). It would therefore receive $19,500 in payments from the government to go along with its $1,000 in income.

But that is just one idea. Before any system can be constructed, we would have to take a close and hard look at precisely where the minimum income should be set. We want it high enough so a person or family could maintain a very basic standard of living, while not so high that it bankrupted our governments' budgets.

Central to the NIT concept is the idea that it replace the vast array of social welfare programs we have today. Subsidized health insurance, hopefully in a dramatically different form than today's Medicaid, might remain. But welfare payments, food stamps, housing subsidies, day care support, energy assistance, and the rest of what Friedman called the "ragbag" of welfare systems would all disappear. Collectively, they cost more than what we would need to fund an adequate NIT.

With their termination would go untold thousands of federal, state, and local government bureaucrats, each of whom would be liberated to put their talents to work in more productive private-sector jobs. Gone, too, would be the middlemen, the cottage industries, all the consultants and lawyers who now maintain comfortable lifestyles of their own by sponging off our impossibly complicated government-assistance systems. The balance between public and private realms would take a long step closer to a proper relationship.

Perhaps the greatest benefit of an NIT would be to reduce dependency—not eliminate it, obviously. This would produce a sharp shift away from a system that diminishes the citizenship of those who receive benefits. The demeaning trips to the welfare office, the dictation by others of how government gifts can be used—"this benefit is for food only, this is for housing, this is for your heating bill"—would be dropped in favor of providing the beneficiary with dollars and trusting him to decide on their use. If he misspends them, the responsibility and the consequences are his and his alone.

Such a system would have ancillary benefits. Our current setup of overlapping welfare programs all but tells people to maximize their benefits by gaming the system. This encourages a disrespect for the law and it creates waste within our programs. A clearer system of payments would eliminate a lot of waste and undercut the way of life that has grown up around the multitude of transfer-payment programs. The Indianapolis grandmother, for example, who drew attention to herself by referring to her unmarried teenage daughter as "the breadwinner" of the family for having several children that entitled her to a flow of taxpayer dollars would have a different outlook.

As Friedman put it, "Such a comprehensive reform would do more efficiently and humanely what our present [remember, this was three decades ago] system does so inefficiently and inhumanely. It would provide an assured minimum to all persons in need regardless of the reasons for their need while doing as little harm as possible to their character, their independence, or their incentive to better their own condition."[2] In other words, it would help us focus resources on the poor, while providing incentives for those who receive benefits to provide for themselves. It would therefore reinforce the creation of a culture of prudence and hard work that we need in this country.

When the NIT was suggested by Friedman and others in the past, it drew most of its criticism from the right, where antipathy to the whole idea of public income maintenance was strong. Decades later, it is clear the nation has made the decision that some form of safety net protection is part of the social compact. Utopians can dream of a United States without any sort of welfare protection, but the American public will not countenance it.

Besides, today the opposition to this idea will certainly be concentrated on the left, where the statist quo locks in huge numbers of public employees and their union dues, and gives free rein to the paternalism on which our Benevolent Betters depend for their self-image and often their personal incomes.

We can see evidence of how a negative income tax would work by taking a look at Israel, which has been experimenting with NIT pilot programs. In March 2011, the *Jerusalem Post* reported that the Central Bank of Israel was encouraged by what those experiments had produced: greater employment, independence, and work effort. The bank is recommending that the reforms be implemented nationwide.

In the United States, this venerable idea has enjoyed a resurgence of interest. Scholars ranging from economist/Nobel laureate Gary Becker to Johns Hopkins University's Robert Moffitt have been joined by respected commentators such as Guy Sorman and Charles Murray in advocating versions of the plan. While noting that any income redistribution plan creates distortions in society, Becker has argued that "[I]f society decides that a certain level of redistribution must take place, the NIT is the best, most minimally distorting, solution ever devised." If it made sense in the 1970s, the case is more compelling now, in our fourth or fifth generation of welfare dependent households, as we pay for a welfare establishment far more expensive and paternalistic than what we had decades ago.

By flattening and simplifying the U.S. tax code at both ends—i.e., in the income ranges where people pay taxes and in those ranges below some reasonable minimum level—we can trigger and sustain the long boom that America must have to pay its bills. We can also simultaneously encourage greater responsibility and economic participation by many who have slumped into reliance on the generosity—well, compulsory generosity—of their neighbors. We can grow our economy and grow true citizenship at the same time.

The NIT is far from perfect. Its flaws have been detailed by many thoughtful analysts. Jodie Allen, writing in the *Concise Encyclopedia of Economics*, outlined "a host of problems, both conceptual and economic [that] continue to haunt negative tax advocates to this day." The NIT would likely not provide as generous benefits to some as other programs do. The negative income tax would also create at least some distortions in the incentive to work and in certain labor markets. Every system is subject to some form of abuse, and the NIT is no different. What's more, we would have to be careful in constructing (and maintaining) it to make sure it didn't morph into a new monster that grew too expensive and dependent on just a handful of taxpayers.

These and other criticisms are valid, of course, but as so often in life, the question is "Compared with what?" Today our ragbag of welfare programs is growing ever more expensive. Excluding Medicaid and other health-related spending, federal welfare programs currently spend well over $300 billion annually. That equates to more than $7,000 per person below the official poverty level. At the minimum, if we are going to spend that money, we need a system that is a lot more effective than what we have now.

A huge plus not counted in a pure cash comparison is the incalculable value, and virtue, of disassembling the professional welfare establishment. Lyndon Johnson never succeeded in creating his "Great Society" through massive federal transfers. But today we do have a great (in the sense of huge) society of bureaucrats and middlemen who administer these programs. Its dissolution through an NIT would remove a massive big-government lobby from the political landscape, and that alone makes it attractive.

It would also liberate an astonishing amount of human talent. Think of it this way. Radically simplifying the tax code would allow hundreds of thousands of smart people who now work as tax lawyers or for H&R Block to take jobs in parts of the economy that would enrich our lives, rather than toiling away protecting us from an overly complicated tax system. Likewise, creating a negative income tax would free the talented people who now staff government agencies to take jobs in the private sector, where they might help create the next Google or the next big thing for our economy.

Fundamentally, the reason to consider an NIT, with all its imperfections, is that it would treat its beneficiaries as men and women of dignity. Yes, accepting charity from one's neighbors is a status that a free citizen should strive to avoid. But our incredibly fortunate and affluent and caring society long ago decided to try to prevent the true destitution of any of its members. The NIT would allow us to keep that commitment while also treating all citizens (regardless of income) as persons fully capable of running their own lives. I believe in Americans, and so should our government.

Ruling Out Jobs

There is something almost plaintive about the economic perplexity of the Obama administration. When President Obama took office in 2009, the annual cost of federal regulations was already $1.75 trillion.[3] He and his people appeared not to notice. Later, having piled new mountains of environmental regulation on top of financial regulation on top of health care regulation—just to name the biggest examples—having empowered themselves to write literally hundreds more such rules of unknowable character and cost in the future, having demeaned and disparaged virtually every private industry around, they are baffled as to why joblessness is at record levels and duration. By late 2010 the president began grumpily urging businesses to start hiring people, as though they were being cautious with their shareholders' money just to spite him.

The fact is that, at the very time when the survival of the American experiment requires an all-out commitment to growth, national policy has worked against it in every way possible. As though there were no national economic crisis, federal agencies have acted as if nothing mattered but their chosen mission, as if no new cost they piled onto a staggering economy might be too much to bear. It appears never to enter their minds that the uncertainty stemming from their threats of additional rule making might be a problem all by itself.

Aside possibly from a revamped tax system, no move the nation could make would be more pro-growth, pro-jobs, and pro-solvency than some kind of regulatory relief. We need not retreat one step from the laws already on the books. We can recognize and applaud the results, such as cleaner air and safer workplaces, that they have produced. But no incremental benefit in any regulatory realm can conceivably match the all-important benefits of a much stronger economy, and until further notice, all other objectives, however commendable, should be subordinated to it.

Voices across the spectrum have begun to call for some kind of moderation in the mindless piling of rule upon rule. Senator Mark Warner, Democrat of Virginia, has offered the creative thought of a regulatory "pay-go" law, requiring the elimination of one rule before any new one can be imposed. The unimpeachably independent Robert Samuelson spelled it out plainly: "[National] success or failure ultimately depends on private firms. We ought to encourage their expansion by reducing regulatory burdens and policy uncertainty."[4]

The best and most direct way to do this would be to declare a multiyear moratorium on new rules of any kind. Like impoundment, this could be done on an emergency basis, maybe until the deficit and long-term debt projections fell to some more acceptable level, or until the economy hit and maintained some much higher growth plateau. But it is almost impossible to imagine the country launching into the long boom we need while laboring under the confusing menace of another mountain of rules.

As an alternative, we could commit to a period of self-certification, in which businesses would agree to meet standards of emissions, effluents, reclamation, and so forth, and proceed to build, retool, drill, and employ Americans now, rather than wasting time and money begging for the government's permission. Any employer later found to have fallen short of the standards could be sanctioned heavily. In the meantime, we'd be growing our economy and getting back to work.

Powering Our Economy

The story of human progress is the story of energy, and our species' success in substituting, through our ingenuity, energy from the inanimate world for the energy we can produce through our own exertion. More economic progress by far occurred in the last two centuries than in all of history to that point, and the harnessing of energy from the earth (along with the rise of free democratic systems that allow individuals to match new technologies with that energy) was the single biggest reason.

In the quest for the growth surge our nation so desperately needs, it is encouraging to know that one means of its accomplishment is right at our fingertips, in the gloriously abundant energy on which we are fortunate to sit. We need no cooperation from any foreign power; we need no stunning breakthrough in educational attainment or cultural renewal, as important as those goals are; we need no as-yet-undiscovered miracle of scientific innovation.

All we have to do is start using what we have, with technology that we already possess, to create new direct jobs, indirect jobs, and debt-reducing tax revenue in enormous quantities. In the words of the old song, "There's nothin' to it but to do it"; and if we have heart, a heart for the unemployed, for young Americans facing an uncertain future, for all those generations to whom we hope not to leave an avalanche of debt and a blighted, beaten country, we will do it—"it" meaning exploiting as fully as possible our domestic energy opportunities. By doing so, we will more often pay Americans instead of people, often hostile people, elsewhere for the energy we use.

Although we occupy only 6.5 percent of the world's land mass, the United States is lucky to be home to more of its potential energy than any other country on earth. New techniques for liberating natural gas from shale formations have only extended our lead, based mainly on our massive coal reserves and the still-bountiful oil we have on- and offshore. As the world's number one agricultural producer, we have yet another source of competitive advantage in our ability to generate large quantities of biofuel energy, even while expanding our position as the world's bread basket.

The problem has been that we have systematically denied ourselves the jobs and the dollars that our energy could produce for us. We have locked up incredible quantities of oil and gas in Alaska and the Outer Continental Shelf. We have shut down the expansion of the nuclear power industry, pollution-free and carbon-free for those who obsess about these matters: it is said truthfully that we stopped building nuclear power plants because they were too costly, but it is never mentioned that the huge majority of those costs are self-inflicted. The preposterous time delays that we allow regulation and litigation to insert into the system, and the consequent time value of money forced onto these plants, have been the killing factor, not any problem with the technology itself, which continues to grow everywhere else. France, an avowedly environmental nation, derives 80 percent of its electricity from nuclear, four times our rate.[5] The disaster that befell a decades-old reactor design during the 2011 Japanese tsunami should not deter us from moving forward with the new technologies now available on sites immune to massive tidal waves.

Amazingly, we haven't lost the knack for shooting ourselves in the foot. No sooner were fabulous new amounts of shale gas confirmed in states such as Pennsylvania and New York than antigrowth activists and politicians began conspiring to block access to them, on the flimsiest of environmental claims.

Even ethanol, once a darling of the renewable energy left, has fallen from favor, over contorted calculations of its overall carbon impact and erroneous projections that its wider use would make food unaffordable. On this front, strange fellows have bedded together, as free market purists have joined green extremists in denouncing this source, which today substitutes for billions of dollars' worth of oil we would otherwise buy from the likes of Iran and Venezuela.

The oil dictators, and our economic competitors in China and elsewhere, must rub their eyes in wonder at these boneheaded Americans. How lucky could they be, that the United States insists on shutting down the huge resources beneath its feet in order to gift-wrap billions every month and send it to them?

This must end. The upside for America, in new energy industry jobs and more jobs in energy-intensive industries such as manufacturing, is too large for us to continue a suicidal national policy. I choose that adjective only after reflection; the reason it is not hyperbolic is that the nation we have been cannot survive unless it defeats the Red Menace, it cannot possibly do that unless we go to a maximum-growth footing, and we cannot do that without a commitment to develop American energy, of every kind.

That includes the renewable sources with which most of us have become intrigued and excited in recent years. I join with those who look forward to the rapid growth of wind and solar power, and unlike many of my free market allies, I believe in some degree of subsidy and research to jump-start their arrival as meaningful energy contributors. In the last few years, Indiana has led America in the growth of wind power, with our administration's active encouragement.

Here, too, the basic argument should not be philosophical but mathematical. At the fastest growth rates one can imagine, wind and solar power will still be trivial contributors to our total energy needs for a very long time. And the romantic notion that they will become large sources of "green jobs" in any year soon has been exploded as farcically out of touch with economic reality. (For example, Gabriel Calzada of the Universidad Rey Juan Carlos in Spain recently came out with a study on green jobs in his country with this sobering conclusion: "for every renewable energy job that the State manages to finance, Spain's experience cited by President Obama as a model reveals . . . the U.S. should expect a loss of at least 2.2 jobs on average, or about 9 jobs lost for every 4 created."[6]) We should encourage alternative forms of energy through reasonable means and celebrate each technological breakthrough, but it is willful self-delusion to maintain that these forms of energy are in any sense a "solution" to our economic challenge. It is heartless to condemn millions of less well-off Americans to poverty while leaving our largest source of prosperity, oil and gas, in the ground. To do so is essentially to surrender to our debts and impending economic catastrophe.

Having disagreed with the anti-energy left, allow me to balance accounts by angering the free market right, of which I consider myself a card-carrying member. But I part company when purism rules out, for instance, any encouragement of homegrown biofuels. Businesspeople learn to look at options holistically, in terms of their overall effect on the income statement and balance sheet. To me, an all-in assessment of the national interest argues for continued action to expand the use of made-in-America biofuels alongside that of traditional domestic energy.

Every gallon of fuel we produce domestically allows us to buy that much less fuel from foreign countries that often do not have our national interests at heart. Creating domestic sources of energy is a national security issue as well as an economic one. There is also an economic benefit to creating jobs here in America. Plus, by providing greater demand and therefore price stability in our agricultural markets, biofuels create the best basis yet for ending the costly farm support systems that make up a large part of each year's federal deficit.

Biofuels have been oversubsidized through their adolescence, and I agree that it is time for these subsidies, including the indirect ones of trade barriers, to be phased out. But I respectfully defend the notion of a mandated presence for biofuels in the national energy mix, as part of a total commitment to growing the economy so that we can pay our debt obligations.

The Growth Imperative

The initiatives just mentioned are only the largest illustrations of what must become our transcendent and unifying national objective. We have to ask those who have seen growth as a threat to their cherished goals to search their hearts and think about the harm that antigrowth policies are inflicting on the least fortunate among us. We must help them see the selfishness of indulging ourselves on borrowed money while not only passing the bill to the next Americans but simultaneously denying them the means to work their way out of our debt.

Adopting a "grow or else" mentality will mean viewing every decision we make through that prism. Immigration? We need to accept larger legal limits than today's, because to grow, economies also need to grow their population. We need not only more people, but more young people and more innovative job creators to help shoulder the load. To that end, we need to change the nature of those we allow into this country. Bluntly stated, we need to admit many more immigrants who create the most jobs and economic value, those with brains or money to invest (preferably both!), in lieu of those who merely happen to live next door or who are related to someone who is already here.

Infrastructure? To paraphrase a recent slogan, "Build, baby, build!"[7] A nation out to break growth records will need a backbone far stronger and more modern than the eroded American infrastructure of today. This should be a prime opportunity for bipartisan agreement and unity.

Provided, that is, that all parties recognize and embrace the reality that the private sector has a huge contribution to make. There is an ocean of private capital willing and able to participate in building the transportation, energy, and other facilities we so badly need. Opening every possible project to so-called P3 investment brings not only dollars to augment those the government can squeeze from the economy in taxes, but also cost-saving innovation in design, construction, and financing.

Stretch these new dollars and accelerate the availability of the new public works by throwing out the rulebook. Obtain the speed and cost advantages Indiana has seen by liberating states, localities, and their private partners to build in the fashion and to the specifications they think adequate. Everywhere and always, the questions must become "How can the most jobs occur? What is the fastest way to add them? How can our nation grow and grow and grow until it begins to outrun its debt burdens, and redeems its promise of a chance for even the poorest Americans and a better life for each new generation?"

Taken together, these programs and this new mentality would aim to revive the economic engine on which all other goals, of left or right, rely. And they would operate to revive the sense of dignity and responsible citizenship that gave rise to liberty in our land, and on which its sustenance has always depended. The test of our republic in our age, our "Raison Debt," is not "can we?" but "will we?" And "are we?" Are we still the kind of Americans who brought liberty to this land, and who kept it for longer than history would have forecast?

Somewhere the Skeptics are snickering. They smugly predicted that government by the people would fall prey to the very weaknesses we now display, and would founder on the very consequences we now confront. They believed with the same confidence that the ailments would prove fatal.

America—no, make that *Americans*—must now prove them wrong. I believe fervently that we will.

First, people love their children. Very few of today's adults would want to take to their grave the knowledge that they plundered the young for their own benefit. They never intended to be in this position. It's just that no one ever told them that this was what was happening. In fact, they were actively misled to believe that they were providing for themselves all along.

Now Americans, older and younger alike, are discovering the truth. Even the most self-absorbed of my fellow Baby Boomers can be appealed to on the moral plane on which they have always told themselves they reside: Here at last is a great cause and a potential legacy all our own. At modest personal sacrifice, we can defeat the Red Menace and leave a stronger, freer, safer, greener county behind.

Pessimists point to the large majorities of Americans who say they oppose any changes in the social welfare programs, and there is no denying the point. A Pew Center survey of early 2011 showed a more than two-to-one rejection of any change in either Social Security or Medicare. A slim majority was also opposed to reducing defense spending.[8]

Democrats were against entitlement reform by more than three to one, but so were 61 percent of Independents and 59 percent of Republicans. Even polls of self-identified Tea Party supporters have found strong opposition, so there is no overstating the dimension of the political challenge.

But such data can be read two ways. The same surveys show an enormous shift over recent years in the number of Americans who are alert to the dangers I've outlined in this book, and prepared to support steep cuts in discretionary spending. It is not the fault of these citizens, who have been fed the "noble lie" all their lives, that they do not understand our national arithmetic. It derogates, and in my opinion underestimates, our fellow citizens to presume that their attitude about these questions is impregnable to the raw facts they have not been told.

Much downsizing of government is inevitable anyway. Here in the provinces, budgets will balance sooner or later, one way or another. State and local governments, which account for almost half the total public sector, do not have a Federal Reserve printing press at their disposal. As I forecast in 2009,[9] these governments, having run through every devious and deceitful accounting trick and borrowing scheme they could devise, began in 2010 the process of shedding much of the useless bloat they had accumulated during recent decades. For some, it will take formal or de facto bankruptcy, but the cuts are coming to them, like it or not.

As they do, taxpayers everywhere will discover what Hoosiers found in the last few years: how much government you don't miss when it goes away. They will also welcome the return of fairness, as the number of employees in the public sector come down to head counts and salaries closer to those that obtain in the world of their employers, the taxpayers.

Ironically, some of the European nations that preceded us down the basement stairs to the social welfare state have begun the process of deficit reduction ahead of the United States. The results are more promising than the political experts tell us to expect. Reporting on a scholarly study in late 2010, *The Economist* said, "The idea that imposing austerity is political hara-kiri is widely held." Nonetheless, the article went on, "In only 20 percent of elections in the countries that slashed spending did the government lose power."[10] In other words, cutting spending really wasn't a political killer after all. Indeed, according to *The Economist*, the politicians who sought to balance the budget by increasing taxes rather than cutting spending were three times more likely to be booted from power than those who cut spending. If the Irish, Belgians, Finns, Swedes, and Canadians can muster the necessary maturity, surely there is a chance we Americans can pull it off.

Much of the heavy lifting, such as the establishment of new compacts in the social welfare programs, is radical only in the world of politics. The essential bifurcation of Social Security and Medicare has already been implemented thousands of times across corporate and public-sector America, and experienced by tens of millions of citizens. This approach will reassure those who now or soon will rely on those programs, while offering a deliverable promise of protection to the working generations who presently and with good reason expect nothing to be there for them. Reformers will rightly claim the mantle of the rescuers of these programs; statist quo-ists will be exposed as the programs' enemies not by philosophy but by arithmetic and the common sense of their fellow citizens, who know Ponzi schemes when they see them.

An all-out pro-growth policy will be seen as the most—in fact, the only—compassionate national program for those millions who have begun to fear a diminished economic future. It will be built around the goal not of seeing that people with wealth add more to it, but that people without wealth have a better chance of acquiring some, and doing so through the dignity-enhancing path of personal effort and value added to society. To oppose it with policies of statism will be exposed as a pro-poverty program of society's haves at the expense of its have-nots.

Finally, young America can and will be roused into action. Proponents of reconstruction should seek out and speak to young audiences by every medium and on every occasion possible. Their economic futures, and their ability to practice the individual autonomy that they constantly demonstrate, depend on a major change of course. The changes proposed to them must remind them—or inform them for the first time—of the presumption of individual dignity on which our nation was founded. They must affirm the competence and right of each citizen to make his own decisions and determine the course of his own life.

The appeal should be unifying; this cannot be a war between the generations. It must become a mutual project among those who come from very different places, culturally and attitudinally. A rebuilt economy and a rebirth of personal freedom can be the common cause on which the generations and other segments of society come together.

The reconstruction we envision will not be presented as a way of staving off disaster, although that will be its first objective. The necessary changes must be understood as the catalysts of a new era of unmatched opportunity, a next American Century in which our values spread and the peace is kept because freedom and the land that gave it birth are seen by the whole world as providing the best results in human prosperity and happiness.

National reconstruction is so eminently feasible. We Americans have done so many much harder things before.

In January 2005, in my first inaugural speech, facing troubles admittedly minor in scale and difficulty to those now before our nation, I said, "If we overestimate the task, it means we have underestimated ourselves. When we think of the crises that free peoples before us have rallied to meet, we should gather confidence, and a sense of proportion, about the smaller assignment history has given us in our day. The job ahead may loom large to us, fortunate as we are to live in an age of unprecedented affluence and safety.

"But this isn't Britain at Dunkirk. This isn't a newborn nation at Valley Forge.... When we note what our predecessors overcame in their day, we should be ashamed if we hesitate, sheepish if we pull up short."

Hoosiers proved themselves up to their assignment. We in Indiana are good people, but not extraordinary; if we proved capable of grown-up conversation, of enacting major changes and making unwelcome trade-offs, then so can our fellow citizens everywhere else.

This is particularly so when each change springs from an affirming belief in the worth and the personal dignity and the capacity for full citizenship, of every American. When each reform proposal can be summed up in another paraphrase with the statement "Yes, *you* can!"

In the next decade, we Americans are summoned again to the ramparts. Our historical assignment is less dangerous, and asks far less sacrifice, than those calls our ancestors answered in their time. But the outcome of our success will be in some ways even more historically profound: not merely to defend liberty, but to restore and redefine it; not just to dodge catastrophe but to make possible a future of boundless hope and opportunity; not simply to rescue millions from hardship, but in so doing to reaffirm the dignity and equality of every man and woman God made.

The coming debate is not really about something so mundane as tax policy or health care or energy choices. It is about things more fundamental: who is in charge, the people or those who supposedly serve at their sufferance? What kind of people will we Americans be, free and proud citizens who control our own lives and decide for ourselves or submissive subjects of the Crown who meekly conclude that our Benevolent Betters know best? When we have answered those questions correctly, we will have the enormous satisfaction of being able to say, "Ben, we kept it."

The Skeptics are in for a severe disappointment and a huge surprise. When they sneered at the concept of self-government, they had never seen the American people. To advocate "change that believes in you" is to say that we in this blessed nation all believe in one another, in our common destiny as free citizens, and in an America where all things are possible.

Epilogue

19 NOTES
P. 247

If ever an author earnestly hoped that his own work would become obsolete, it is this one. Believing as I do that America's economic vitality, defining promise of upward mobility, and even the underpinnings of its self-governance are all at desperate risk, it would be a joy to report that a corner had been turned, or a large first step taken, or that glimmers of progress appeared, and that this latest edition of the book was no longer relevant.

Joy will have to wait. The months since first publication have seen at best the marking of precious time, and in most cases a further deterioration of the phenomena that threaten the survival of Ben Franklin's Republic. In early 2012, an annual "dependency index" measuring the extent of Americans' reliance on the largesse of government (i.e., the compulsory charity of their fellow citizens) reported that 67 million Americans depended on the federal government for some form of assistance, an increase of 23 percent since 2009.[1] *247*

Elsewhere, young Americans' understanding of their own history remains abysmal, as confirmed by the recent results of the National *247* Assessment of Educational Progress exam.[2] And across the country, citizens' rights to grow gardens,[3] sell lemonade,[4] Photoshop images,[5] and *248* even eat rare hamburgers[6] have been reduced by new "protective" laws dreamed up by our ever busy, ever benevolent public officials.

Even more menacingly, the economic vigor on which the American Dream, and therefore a stable, hopeful middle class and a healthy, secure democratic process all rely has not returned. Its recovery has been actively thwarted by the most antigrowth, anti–private sector policies in the nation's history. Faced with the abject failure of those policies, their authors have not shifted to a different approach, but rather intensified both their tax and regulatory chokeholds on the economy, and their bullying of those sectors and societal groups who might oppose or impede them.

Like a WWE fighter trying to deliver the knockout punch ("And STAY down!"), the Obama administration continues to pound the staggering economy with one costly regulation after another. Choice examples include Dodd-Frank, EPA's staggeringly costly MACT and CSAPR rules, the altering of NLRB elections procedures, and, of course, Obamacare and its thousands of pages of new rules and regulations.

As we've sadly seen before, the regulators' zeal often has no basis in either science or common sense. While analyzing the economic damage in lost jobs and higher consumer utility rates from EPA's new anti-coal mercury standards, I asked Indiana's environmental scientists to run a little comparison: What is the exposure to mercury from one broken CFL lightbulb (the kind the government is forcing Americans to buy) compared to the exposure from living in a community with a coal-burning power plant?

The answer: breaking one CFL bulb in your home creates a mercury concentration more than 42,000 times as high (not a misprint) as that in the air near a coal-fired plant. Obviously some agenda other than human health is at work in our federal government.

And in a stunningly antigrowth decision, the president blocked the construction of the Keystone Pipeline, which would have brought oil produced in Canada to refineries on the Gulf Coast. In one stroke, he threw away tens of thousands of jobs and a major new source of oil from a friendly country on the most specious of environmental and procedural claims. Amid a torrent of scathing dissection of the administration's defense of its action, *Washington Post* reporter Robert Samuelson's stood out: "An act of national insanity. It isn't often that a president makes a decision that has no redeeming virtues . . . Obama's action was supposed to reflect 'the national interest.' His standard was his political interest . . . The cynicism is breathtaking."

The Obama administration now enjoys the distinction of presiding over the weakest recovery from a severe recession in the nation's history.

This embarrassment is deepened by the fact that until now, the worse the economic decline, the more rapid the climb out. At the same stage in the Reagan recovery of the 1980s, quarterly growth was in excess of 8 percent, more than four times the increase for 2011.

The president "promised" (why do presidents do that when their ability to control the outcome is limited and subject to so many outside variables?) to fix our economy by this year and keep unemployment at 8 percent. The stated unemployment rate as of March 2012 is still at 8.3 percent, but it could be far worse as so many Americans have simply given up looking for work.[10] A better measure, the *employment* rate, fell below 64 percent at the beginning of 2012, the lowest level since the era of the stay-at-home mom.

The beloved actor Clint Eastwood, not previously associated with the "Left Coast" politics of Hollywood, perhaps thoughtlessly accepted a role in a Super Bowl commercial for the U.S. subsidiary of Fiat (dba Chrysler), and read a script that said we'd reached "halftime in America." With so few Americans working, and so many others leaving the labor force in discouragement, we had better hope we're still in the first quarter somewhere. Asked on Super Bowl morning about a modest one-month bump in hiring, I likened it to kicking a field goal while down 30 points.[11]

Such a pathetic economic performance has wreaked its usual damage on our already critical fiscal outlook. Revenues continue to underperform while spending roars ahead at the ballooned levels set in the "stimulus" surge of 2009. Axiomatically, the Red Menace has grown larger, not smaller, and nearer, not less proximate. The deficits for 2013–22, estimated at $8.5 trillion one year ago, are now forecast to be upwards of $10 trillion.

In the least surprising revelation of recent times, the Congressional Budget Office reported that the Obama health insurance system will cost almost twice as much as the administration had led the public to believe, adding nearly $2 trillion to the nation's debt over its first ten years.[12] The anemic 1.7 percent economic growth rate of 2011, less than half that assumed in that year's Obama "budget" (the document so absurd that it lost 97–0 in a Democratic Senate and was never heard of again), all by itself added a trillion and a half dollars of debt to the ten-year outlook.

Faced with erosion this grave, one might expect those in power to consider a shift in policy. Lord Keynes may have allowed the facts to change his mind (see p. 116), but not his acolyte, the president. In September 2011, Obama proposed yet another "stimulus" package containing additional infrastructure spending and aid to states, mixed, of course, with taxes on the wealthy. This might best be labeled "hair of the dog" economics, like the advice of the dissolute friend who urges more drinking as a way to remedy an already-terrible hangover.

That unserious proposal, which the administration knew would never go anywhere, was less dispiriting than its posture as 2012 began. The President delivered a seventy-five-minute State of the Union speech that never even mentioned the national debt, let alone proposed a plan to deal with it. He completely ignored the most dangerous non-military threat we have ever faced, the dominant public reality of our time. One flounders for an analogy large enough. It was as though FDR had given his 1942 State of the Union speech and never mentioned the Japanese.

Just to confirm this was no oversight, the president then released a budget that cheerfully accepted national bankruptcy. It proposed a further string of trillion-dollar-plus deficits and, even with accounting gimmicks and preposterous assumptions, requested $6.7 trillion in additional debt, leading to a projected debt of $25.9 trillion by 2022, well over 100 *348* percent of GDP and beyond all the tipping points economic historians have identified. It made no proposals for saving the safety net or averting the catastrophe unreformed entitlements will bring. It was as though a corporate CEO had published a business plan that proudly announced "All right, everyone, here's how we go broke!" One hopes this "budget" was printed on recyclable material, because it went straight to the landfill without even touching down in Congress. As friendless as last year's, it was defended by no one and quickly dismissed by almost all commentators as a cynical campaign brochure.

The performance to date of the president's potential challengers has not yet risen to the urgency of the moment. Presented during one debate with the intriguing question whether they would consider a deal that would offer $10 of spending cuts for each $1 of tax increases, each of the then eight aspirants said no.[43] Not "Only if entitlement reform and real spending reductions are fully and genuinely in place first." Not "Tell me more about the nature of the tax changes in your 9 percent." Just "No." That was not the response of people who have faced up to the reality of the Red Menace and the need for big change, soon.

Meanwhile, much of the challengers' intramural competition has involved the magnification of minor policy differences and mutual trashing over petty, sometimes personal matters. The mercenaries have run riot with their tired, formulaic attack commercials, often funded not by candidates themselves but by the new phenomenon called SuperPACs. Observance of an eleventh commandment will apparently have to await an agreement on observance of the ninth.

At this writing, hope lingers that the additions to debt and subtractions from freedom posed by the Obamacare legislation may yet be averted or moderated. The nation awaits a Supreme Court ruling that could vitiate the bill at least in part. In the kind of special interest bazaar to which such power grabs always lead, HHS issued hundreds of waivers to companies about to drop employees from health coverage. There was no rhyme or reason to the selection of this lucky group, except for the curious coincidence that most were unionized corporations whose unions were close political allies of the administration.

Any pretense of credibility for the CLASS Act portion of Obamacare dissolved, as it was shut down by its authors as "actuarially unsound." This requirement was mercifully attached to the program as it hurtled toward passage; if the other entitlements had been subject to the same discipline over the years, this book would never have been written. Yet despite its patent fiscal impossibility, the administration has fought repeal of this "zombie entitlement," transparently hoping to cast off these actuarial chains and jolt the monster back to life in some more friendly future Congress.

While the nation waits to learn whether the Supreme Court will permit the federal government, for the first time ever, to order Americans to buy a specific product (health insurance), the zone of citizen freedom continues to shrink. As either a further stick in the eye, or perhaps an act of surpassing political deviousness and shrewdness, on January 20, 2012 the administration suddenly announced that it would mandate all health care plans to provide free contraception and morning-after abortion medications. No exceptions were allowed, not even for those religious institutions that hold fundamental objections of conscience to these treatments.

If this was a calculated political stratagem, it worked brilliantly. Republicans took the bait and allowed the issue to be mischaracterized as simply about contraception, when in fact that argument was incidental to the much larger matter that religious liberties—and basic economic liberties—were being trespassed in an unprecedented and brutal fashion.

The fact that many citizens want to avail themselves of birth control or morning-after abortifacients—and are completely free to do so—does not imply that the federal government should order anyone, let alone everyone, including those with religious objections, to pay for it and provide it to employees for free. Commentary ranging from whimsical to withering demolished the administration's rationale. As one put it, "The essence of [their] argument is that reproductive freedom requires free birth control. By the same logic, religious freedom requires kosher food subsidies, freedom of speech requires taxpayer-funded computers, and the right to keep and bear arms requires government-supplied guns."[14] Another suggested that, given their proven health care value, yoga classes, massages, and fitness club memberships should all be deemed essential benefits, and observed sarcastically that anyone opposing a fictional salad bar mandate must "really want to ban salad and control what we eat."[15]

Meanwhile, what the admirable citizen Erskine Bowles, Democratic cochairman of the presidentially created and presidentially discarded Bowles-Simpson Commission, called "the most predictable crisis in our history" became ever-nearer and more predictable. In late February 2012 came the headlines many had anticipated for some time: "China's Holdings of Treasuries Decline for First Time,"[16] "Beijing Diversifies Away from U.S. Dollar."[17] A typical account read: "Economists have long warned that if China starts to cut back on its purchases of U.S. securities, U.S. interest rates could climb, damaging the American economy and ratcheting up the government's borrowing costs."[18] As though that's where the damage would stop.

About the same time, readers of *The New York Times* contemplated the following account: "Something profound and distressing is happening: the

248

rapid dissolution of a democracy.⑲The writer happened to be reporting from Greece, but she laid out the fate of a nation that spends and borrows its way past the point of no return. "Greece today looks less like a Western European democracy and more like a company in the midst of restructuring, with outside financiers and lawyers advising it on delicate affairs of state. (Note: "Advising" here is a gentle term for "dictating to.")

The report concluded "Greeks do not feel they are unique . . . 'We are a ticking time bomb' a clerk . . . told me last week. If it exploded here, it will happen elsewhere.'" The task and the test of American statecraft in the next decade is to see that "elsewhere" never includes the United States.

Two days before Christmas, my office alerted me that Speaker of the House John Boehner and Senate Republican Leader Mitch McConnell wanted to talk to me. I wasn't savvy enough to guess what they had in mind, or I might have tried to evade the call. They asked me to write and deliver the Republican response to President Obama's State of the Union in January 2012.

This is not an assignment a prudent person would pursue; it falls in the same category as throwing out the first pitch on baseball's opening day. It may sound like fun at first, but once on the mound one realizes that it is all downside; throw a perfect strike and you are forgotten minutes later. Screw up and you are derided for years afterward.

Before accepting, I told the two leaders that if they wanted a strident partisan response, I was probably not their best choice. They quickly said that a positive and constructive tone was exactly what they had in mind. They also made it clear that I could say whatever I thought appropriate to the occasion.

The poor sap who accepts this mission gets no notice or indication of the speech to which he is responding. Had I had any idea that the president would never even mention the debt and its dangers, I would have challenged that omission directly and strenuously.

Nonetheless, the assignment was an honor and a rare opportunity to raise with some meaningful number of our fellow citizens the themes of this book. In less than twelve minutes, I tried to synopsize them in the plain language we Hoosiers favor in the spoken word. In part I said:

No nation, no entity, large or small, public or private, can thrive, or survive intact, with debts as huge as ours . . .

It's absolutely so that everyone should contribute to our national recovery, including of course the most affluent among us. There are smart ways and dumb ways to do this: the dumb way is to raise rates in a broken, grossly complex tax system, choking off growth without bringing in the revenues we need to meet our debts. The better course is to stop sending the wealthy benefits they do not need, and stop providing them so many tax preferences that distort our economy and do little or nothing to foster growth. . . .

[We] say that anyone who will join us in the cause of growth and solvency is our ally, and our friend. We will speak the language of unity. Let us rebuild our finances, and the safety net, and reopen the door to the stairway upward; any other disagreements we may have can wait. . . .

In word and deed, the president and his allies tell us that we just cannot handle ourselves in this complex, perilous world without their benevolent protection. Left to ourselves, we might pick the wrong health insurance, the wrong mortgage, the wrong school for our kids; why, unless they stop us, we might pick the wrong light bulb!

A second view . . . is that we Americans are no longer up to the job of self-government. We can't do the simple math that proves the unaffordability of today's safety net programs, or all the government we now have. We will fall for the con job that says we can just plow ahead and someone else will pick up the tab. We will allow ourselves to be pitted, one against the other, blaming our neighbors for troubles worldwide trends or our own government have caused.

Twenty twelve must be the year we prove the doubters wrong. The year we strike out boldly not merely to avert national bankruptcy but to say to a new generation that America is still the world's premier land of opportunity . . . that Americans are still a people born to liberty.

As a national election looms, one cannot tell if the stakes for our country, the possible solutions to our problems, or the contrasting views of government's proper role and the citizen's rightful autonomy will be well framed. Maybe this will be another election dominated by the merciless mercenaries and their slime-and-smear tactics, by the elevation of secondary or even trivial issues when far greater mortal danger impends.

But even if so, it is always possible that the American people, in their intuitive wisdom, will declare themselves for freedom—their own and their nation's. In full view of the odds and obstacles, I opt for the obstinate optimism that says they will.

But in this prognosis, I cannot improve on the caveat of so very long ago: *Exitus in dubio est.*

Mitch Daniels

March 14, 2012

ACKNOWLEDGMENTS

This book, whatever its worth, would never have happened without the following friends, to whom go these heartfelt thank-yous:

To Joni Evans, Katie Hall, and Bob Barnett, publishing pros who each separately encouraged a rookie to believe he could play in this league.

To Marc Sumerlin and Larry Lindsey, for their daily dose of economic insight, and for helping imagine the meltdown scenario in chapter 2.

To Bill Bennett, the Ol' Professor, for quality control and his contributions to the historical references in chapter 1.

To Glenn Hutchins, Gordon Goldstein, and Andy Stafman at Silver Lake, for the thought provocation and a wealth of useful data and insight.

To Brendan Miniter, for a host of excellent editorial suggestions that brought greater order, clarity, and proportion to the final product.

To Adrian Zackheim, Brooke Carey, Will Weisser, Allison McLean, Christy D'Agostini, and all the crew at Sentinel for their patience, tolerance, and support even when I was at my obstinate worst.

Most of all, to Ryan Cole, Neil Pickett, and Trevor Kight, my invaluable Hoosier sidekicks, for their research assistance and months of helpful reactions and critiques.

NOTES

Introduction

1. Popularly attributed to Balfour, responding to Churchill's *The World Crisis*.
2. Butler University Commencement, remarks by Governor Mitchell E. Daniels, Jr., May 9, 2009, Hinkle Fieldhouse, Indianapolis, Indiana. Full text available here: www.in.gov/portal/news_events/38894.htm.

Chapter 1 | The Skeptics

1. In the pages that follow I use the term *Skeptics* to refer to those who, throughout history, have doubted both the feasibility and long-term sustainability of democratic self-rule. They should not be confused with the ancient Greek Skeptics, or *Skeptikoi*, who questioned the ultimate certainty of man's understanding and knowledge of the world.
2. *Meet the Press*, May 23, 2010. Full transcript available here: www.msnbc.msn.com/id/37279599/ns/meet_the_press/.
3. *Face the Nation*, Nov. 28, 2010. Full transcript available here: www.cbsnews.com/htdocs/pdf/FTN_112810.pdf.

Chapter 2 | The Red Menace

1. Niall Ferguson, "Sun Could Set Suddenly on Superpower as Debt Bites," *Australian*, July, 29, 2010. Article available here: www.theaustralian.com.au/news/opinion/sun-could-set-suddenly-on-superpower-as-debt-bites/story-e6frg6zo-1225898187243.
2. Ibid.
3. David Brooks, "National Greatness Agenda," *New York Times*, November 10, 2010. Article available here: www.nytimes.com/2010/11/12/opinion/12brooks.html.
4. Kenneth Rogoff, "History Will Rue US and Europe Debt Woes," *Financial Times*, April 4, 2011. Article available here: www.ft.com/cms/s/0/1399efba-5eea-11e0-a2d7-00144feab49a.html#axzz1MRKozpcX.
5. Carmen M. Reinhart and Kenneth S. Rogoff, "Growth in a Time of Debt," paper prepared for the *American Economic Review*, December 31, 2009.
6. Mark Steyn, "Dependence Day," *New Criterion*, January 2011. Article available here: www.newcriterion.com/articles.cfm/Dependence-Day-6753.
7. 2011 Annual Report of the Board of Trustees of the Federal Hospital Insurance and

Federal Supplementary Medical Insurance Trust Funds. Report available here: www
.cms.gov/ReportsTrustFunds/downloads/tr2011.pdf.

24
8. These are publicly available numbers. One nonpartisan source, Prudential, compiles
these particular numbers: www3.prudential.com/signature/Social-Security.html.
9. Milton Freidman reported the quote later. He notes it here in an interview with the
Heartland Institute: http://www.heartland.org/article/12013.

27 10. Andrew G. Biggs, "The Market Value of Public-Sector Pension Deficits," American
Enterprise Institute's *Retirement Policy Outlook*, no. 1 (April 2010). Available here:
http://www.aei.org/docLib/2010RPOno1g.pdf.

32 11. Robert D. Kaplan, *Monsoon: The Indian Ocean and the Future of American Power* (New
York: Random House, 2010), p. 36.
12. Ibid., pp. 36, 41, 145.
13. Henry Kissinger, *Diplomacy* (New York: Simon and Schuster, 1994), p. 638.

34 14. David Ignatius, "Washington's Broken Politics Weaken America Abroad," *Washington
Post*, Nov. 14, 2010.

Chapter 3 | The Great Inversion

39 1. Chris Edwards, "Overpaid Federal Workers," The Cato Institute, June 2010, www
.downsizinggovernment.org/overpaid-federal-workers.

40
2. "The Trillion Dollar Gap: Underfunded State Retirement Systems and the Roads to
Reform," study by The Pew Center on the States, February 2010, p. 44. Available here:
downloads.pewcenteronthestates.org/The_Trillion_Dollar_Gap_final.pdf.
3. Karen Tumulty, "State and Local Workers: Gone but Not off the Books," *Washington
Post*, March 9, 2011. Article available here: www.washingtonpost.com/wp-dyn/
content/article/2011/03/08/AR2011030806199.html.

41
4. The details are of this anecdote are drawn from the op-ed "Michigan Forces Business
Owners into Public Sector Unions," by Patrick J. Wright and Michael D. Jahr, *Wall
Street Journal*, December 25, 2009. Article available here: online.wsj.com/article/SB1
0001424052748703478704574612341241120838.html.
5. Brody Mullins and John D. McKinnon, "Campaign's Big Spender: Public-Employees
Union Now Leads All Groups in Independent Election Outlays" *Wall Street Journal*,
October 22, 2010. Article available here: online.wsj.com/article/SB10001424052702
303339504575566481761790288.html.

48
6. Bureau of Labor Statistics, U.S. Department of Labor, http://www.bls.gov/news
.release/pdf/empsit.pdf.
7. Stephen Losey, "Few Employees Denied Step Increases for Poor Performance," *Federal Times*, March 2011. Full article here: www.federaltimes.com/article/20110322/
BENEFITS01/103220301/1001.
8. Ibid.

49
9. Georgetown University's law library has a list of federal department, subcabinet agencies and other federal entities here: www.ll.georgetown.edu/federal/executive/index
.cfm.
10. *U.S. Federal Register* 75 (2010). Available at: www.gpoaccess.gov/fr/index.html.

52 11. John Lanchester, *I.O.U.: Why Everyone Owes Everyone and No One Can Pay* (New York:
Simon and Schuster, 2010), p. 39.

56 12. "Democrats Not Sacrificing Too Much in Reform Effort," *NewsHour*, July 30, 2009.

Transcript available here: www.pbs.org/newshour/bb/north_america/july-dec09/pelosi_07-30.html.

56 13. Arthur C. Brooks, "What Really Buys Happiness?" *City Journal* (Summer 2007). See also Brooks's work on gross national happiness and his book *Who Really Cares: The Surprising Truth about Compassionate Conservatism* (New York: Basic Books, 2006).

59 14. Lanchester, *I.O.U.*, pp. 131, 132.

15. Richard G. Anderson and Charles S. Gascon, "A Closer Look: Assistance Programs in the Wake of the Crisis," Federal Reserve Bank of St. Louis, January 2011. Report available here: www.stlouisfed.org/publications/re/articles/?id=2067.

62 16. "Sebelius Has a List: Political Thuggery from HHS," Review & Outlook, *Wall Street Journal*, September 13, 2010. Article available here: online.wsj.com/article/SB10001424052748703597204575483900330728436.html.

Chapter 4 | The Shrunken Citizen

65 1. "Students at Schools Named for Presidents Don't Know It," *Orlando Sentinel*, February 21, 1995.

2. Matthew Ladner, "Freedom from Responsibility: A Survey of Civic Knowledge Among Arizona High School Students," *Goldwater Institute Policy Brief*, no. 09-04 (June 30, 2009). Full report available here: www.goldwaterinstitute.org/Common/Img/Freedom%20From%20Responsibility.pdf.

67 3. Molly Henneberg, "North Carolina Schools May Cut Chunk Out of U.S. History Lessons" *Fox News*, February 3, 2010. Article available here: www.foxnews.com/us/2010/02/03/north-carolina-schools-cut-chunk-history-lessons/.

68 4. Daniel J. Flynn, "An FBI History of Howard Zinn," *City Journal*, August 19, 2010.

69 5. Charles Krauthammer, "Don't Touch My Junk," *Washington Post*, November 19, 2010.

70 6. "Economic Characteristics of Households in the United States: Third Quarter 2008," U.S. Census Bureau, April 2010.

74 7. David Horowitz and Eli Lehrer, "Political Bias in the Administrations and Faculties of 32 Elite Colleges and Universities," Center for the Study of Popular Culture, August 28, 2003.

8. Michael Medved, *Hollywood vs. America* (New York: Harper, 1993), pp. 220–22.

75 9. "Order in the Court; A Texas Judge Blows the Lid off Trial Lawyers, Inc.'s Secret Asbestos Litigation Scam," Trial Lawyers Inc.: "Asbestos: A Report on the Asbestos Litigation Industry," 2008, by the Manhattan Institute. Full report available here: www.triallawyersinc.com/asbestos/asb04.html.

74 10. The numbers here come from the Internal Revenue Service and were compiled by the National Taxpayers Union. They are available here: www.ntu.org/tax-basics/who-pays-income-taxes.html.

79 11. Andrew G. Atkeson and William E. Simon, Jr., "How to Revive the California Dream," *Wall Street Journal*, January 10, 2011.

80 12. Congressional Budget Office calculates that the United States ran a $3.2 billion surplus in 1969. For a more complete list of historical budget data see www.cbo.gov/budget/data/historical.pdf.

81 13. To my knowledge, the most prominent exception to this general mistake was economist Paul Krugman, who correctly noted the reliance of the surge in revenues on the stock market. I rarely agree with Dr. Krugman, but in this instance he deserves credit for spotting a major phenomenon that almost all the rest of us missed.

14. Martin Crutsigner, "Was the 2001 Slowdown Really a Recession?" Associated Press, published by *USA Today*, July 30, 2004.

Chapter 5 | The Obamacare Steamroller

1. Paul A. Manner, MD, "Practice Defensive Medicine—Not Good for Patients or Physicians," *AAOS Now: Journal of the American Academy of Orthopaedic Surgeons*, January/February 2007.
2. "Defensive Medicine Among High-Risk Specialist Physicians in a Volatile Malpractice Environment," *Journal of the American Medical Association*, June 1, 2005.

Chapter 6 | Taking on the Statist Quo

1. In final negotiations, the legislature voted to put half of any such excess into the Teacher Retirement Fund and refund the rest to taxpayers.

Chapter 10 | Change That Believes in You

1. Milton Friedman and Rose Friedman, *Free to Choose* (Harcourt, 1990), p. 121.
2. Ibid., p. 120.
3. Clyde Wayne Crews, Jr., "Ten Thousand Commandments: An Annual Snapshot of the Federal Regulatory State," 2011 Edition, Competitive Enterprise Institute, 2011, p. 2. Available here: cci.org/sites/default/files/Wayne%20Crews%20-%2010,000%20 Commandments%202011.pdf.
4. Robert Samuelson, "Why Japan Fell . . . and What It Teaches Us," *Newsweek*, November 12, 2010. Available here: www.newsweek.com/2010/11/13/samuelson-why-japan-fell-and-what-it-teaches-us.html.
5. "Nuclear Power, A Changing Landscape" Statement by IAEA director Dr. Mohamed ElBaradei, Ankara, Turkey, 2006. Available here: www.iaea.org/newscenter/statements/2006/ebsp2006n011.html.
6. Gabriel Calzada Alvarez, "Study of the Effects on Employment of Public Aid to Renewable Energy Resources" Universidad Rey Juan Carlos, Spain, March 2009.
7. During the 2008 Republican National Convention, former Maryland lieutenant governor Michael Steele popularized the slogan "Drill, Baby, Drill."
8. "Republicans Are Losing Ground on the Deficit, But Obama's Not Gaining," Pew Research Center for the Public and the Press, March 16 2011. Available here: people -press.org/2011/03/16/republicans-are-losing-ground-on-the-deficit-but-obamas -not-gaining/.
9. "The Coming Reset in State Government," *Wall Street Journal*, September 9, 2009.
10. "Vote for Agony," *The Economist*, December 2, 2010.

Epilogue

1. "Dependency Index Surges 23% Under President Obama," John Merline, *Investors Business Daily*, February 8, 2012.
2. As reported by the *New York Times*, ("U.S. Students Remain Poor at History, Tests Show," Sam Dillon, *New York Times*, June 14, 2011) the majority of young Americans can not correctly identify the importance of Abraham Lincoln or *Brown vs. Board of Education*.

3. "Oak Park Woman Faces 93-Days in Jail for Planting Vegetable Garden," Alexis Wiley, myFOXdetroit.com, July 12, 2011.

4. "Midway Police Shut Down Girls' Lemonade Stand," Maura Kennedy, *The Coastal Source*, WJCL.com, July 13, 2011.

5. "Arizona Bill Takes Aim At Airbrushed Women in Ads," Alia Beard Rau, *The Republic*, February 12, 2012.

6. "North Carolina's Rare Burger Ban Makes Red Meat Illegal," Ben Muessig, *The Huffington Post*, May 17, 2011.

7. Maximum achievable control technology standards and the Cross State Air Pollution Rule, introduced by the Environmental Protection Agency in 2011, force power plants to limit mercury, sulfur dioxide, and nitrogen oxide, and will consequently shutter numerous plants and increase electricity rates.

8. In 2011, the National Labor Relations Board winnowed employers' window of time to prepare for elections and present their case to employees.

9. "Rejecting the Keystone Pipeline Is an Act of National Insanity," Robert Samuelson, *Washington Post*, January 19, 2012.

10. As calculated by Lawrence Lindsey and others, if the labor force was still at the size it was when President Obama took office, the unemployment rate would be around 11 percent.

11. Super Bowl XLVI was played in Indianapolis, and I was "Host Governor."

12. "Updated Estimates for the Insurance Coverage Provisions of the Affordable Care Act," Congressional Budget Office, March 2012.

13. Fox News Republican Presidential Debate, Ames, Iowa, August 11, 2011.

14. "Sandra Fluke's Protection Racket," Jacob Sullum, *Reason*, March 7, 2012.

15. "Coffee Is an Essential Benefit Too," Allysia Finley, *Wall Street Journal*, March 12, 2012.

16. "China's Holdings of Treasuries Decline for First Time," Cordell Eddings and Daniel Kruger, Bloomberg, February 29, 2012.

17. "Beijing Diversifies Away from U.S. Dollar," Tom Orlik and Bob Davis, *Wall Street Journal*, March 2, 2012.

18. Ibid.

19. "The Falling State of Greece," Rachel Donadio, *New York Times*, February 25, 2012.

SUGGESTED READING

Butler, Stuart, Alison Fraser Acosta, and William Beach. "Saving the American Dream: The Heritage Plan to Fix the Debt, Cut Spending, and Restore Prosperity." The Heritage Foundation, 2011.

Ferrara, Peter. *America's Ticking Bankruptcy Bomb*. New York: HarperCollins, 2011.

Mauldin, John and Jonathan Tepper. *Endgame: The End of the Debt Supercycle and How It Changes Everything*. Hoboken, N.J.: Wiley, 2011.

The National Commission on Fiscal Responsibility and Reform. "The Moment of Truth." CreateSpace, 2010.

Reinhart, Carmen and Kenneth Rogoff. *This Time Is Different, Eight Centuries of Financial Folly*. Princeton, N.J.: Princeton University Press, 2009.

Tanous, Peter and Jeff Cox. *Debts, Deficits and the Demise of the American Economy*. Hoboken, N.J.: Wiley, 2011.

Walker, David. *Comeback America. Turning the Country Around and Restoring Fiscal Responsibility*. New York: Random House, 2010.

INDEX